The Semiotics of Passions

The Semiotics of Passions
From States of Affairs to States of Feeling

Algirdas Julien Greimas and
Jacques Fontanille

Translation by Paul Perron and Frank Collins
Foreword by Paul Perron and Paolo Fabbri

University of Minnesota Press, Minneapolis and London

Published by the University of Minnesota Press
2037 University Avenue Southeast, Minneapolis, MN 55414
Printed in the United States of America on acid-free paper

Library of Congress Cataloging-in-Publication Data

Greimas, Algirdas Julien.
[Sémiotiques des passions. English]
The semiotics of passions : from states of affairs to states of feeling / Algirdas Julien Greimas and Jacques Fontanille ; translation by Paul Perron and Frank Collins ; foreword by Paul Perron and Paolo Fabbri.
p. cm.
Includes bibliographical references and index.
ISBN 0-8166-2104-7.
ISBN 0-8166-2105-5 (pbk.)
1. Semiotics. 2. Emotions. 3. Discourse analysis.
I. Fontanille, Jacques. II. Title.
P99.G68713 1993
302.2–dc20 92-17480
CIP

The University of Minnesota is an
equal-opportunity educator and employer.

Contents

Foreword

Paul Perron and Paolo Fabbri

Numerous introductions have been written on Algirdas Julien Greimas's semiotic theory. Some have accentuated its linguistic and philosophical presuppositions and underpinnings, showing how his thought is the product of his times and how, despite its originality, it remains part of the episteme shaping the social sciences over the last fifty years.[1] Others have attempted to bring to the fore its logical and scientific nature.[2] Hence, in our foreword to the last volume of works published in English by A. J. Greimas, *The Social Sciences: A Semiotic View* (1990), we suggested that whereas a dual thrust existed in the general field of semiotics with respect to the application of semiotic theory and its philosophical foundations, the originality of semiotics is that it maintains an articulation between the two extremes defining it, the epistemological level and the level of application. We further stressed that Greimas's semiotic project was characterized both by its speculative and empirical intent and that, for him, methodology constituted the meeting ground for the theory of signs and the human sciences insofar as its function is to establish the missing link between epistemological and textual knowledge.

It could be said of Greimas and the Paris School of Semiotics that an attempt is made both to consider linguistics as a way of thinking philosophically by using a number of philosophical concepts and to think of philosophy in terms of linguistics by integrating a number of linguistic notions. From this point of view it can be seen that the use made of terms such as agent, object, modalization, and aspectualization implies certain philosophical assumptions. Even though for Greimas semiotics happens to be part of the great philosophical tradition, the question that remains to be answered is how to find a pertinent way of speaking about philosophical problems from a semiotic perspective.

It is a truism that Vladimir Propp, who was versed in the tradition of textual analysis and who played a fundamental role in the development of postwar narratology (Doležel, pp. 141–46), emphasized the actional nature of narrative in his studies on the Russian folktale. For him, functions could be reduced basically to actions or spheres of actions, and in his numerous studies he introduced no categories that could help in analyzing passions. Following this tradition, it could be said that linguistics provides us with excellent tools for describing actions but somewhat inadequate ones for describing passions. This became the crucial issue for Greimas and Fontanille as, in the past, working on narrative texts implied primarily elaborating a system of actions.[3] In other words, the first approaches to the analysis of narrative were mainly action oriented.[4]

Linguistics provided Greimas with a limited number of minimal concepts to analyze texts, for example, subject, object, predicate, modality, and aspectuality. Moreover, in many of his writings Greimas has acknowledged a debt to Louis Hjelmslev,whose principle of empiricism he adhered to closely, whereby to satisfy the conditions of "scientificness" a theory must fulfill three hierarchically organized requirements: coherence, exhaustibility, and simplicity. Yet, over the years, the analysis of narrative revealed that in addition to complex cognitive dimensions, texts had complex passional dimensions as well. Hence, what began as a theory of action, attributing to subjects an ability to act and evaluate action, evolved into a theory that considers subjects as acting cognitive beings endowed with character and temperament. Therefore, in order to ensure the coherence of the theory it was necessary to articulate the character and temperament of acting, cognitive, and sentient subjects in terms of minimal concepts borrowed from linguistics. Aspectualities (that allow for the representation of temporalization as processes) and modalities (concerned with defining the manipulating and sanctioning subject) were considered as useful "primitives" in the description of passions.[5] Thus, in order to lay the foundations for a semiotics of passions, in the first theoretical chapter of their study Greimas and Fontanille analyzed the state of the subject (defined as the subject's junctive relation to the object) in terms of modalities: "In other words, the modalization of the state of the subject—and this is what we are referring to when we speak about passions—is conceivable only if it begins by modalizing the object, which, in becoming a 'value,' imposes itself on the subject" (p. 4).

In addition to these linguistic "primitives" narratology also furnished a number of useful concepts to help provide a semiotic interpretation to traditional theories of passions. As Greimas has noted, theories of passions that are part of every major classical philosophical system can be described—for example, in René Descartes, Baruch Spinoza, Wilhelm Leibniz, Friedrich Nietzsche, and Sigmund Freud (1989, p. 546)—as a taxonomy, a paradigmatic operation on lexemes, or in terms of modal syntax that set in place two interdependent actants. The very fact that one of the first definitions in Descartes's theory deals with the relation between active and passive explanations of passions had as a consequence the linking of passions not only to reason but also to actions. Within this framework Greimas's strategy was to work out a semiotics of passions, a pathemic semiotics founded on his own previously elaborated semiotics of action. Yet, to ensure that the theory maintained its coherence by conforming to the principles of hierarchy and interdefinition, it was necessary to establish descriptive procedures that integrated all the prior definitions of the actional dimension into the pathemic one.[6]

The reasons for adapting such descriptive strategies and tools are partially related to the fact that Greimas draws heavily on Edmund Husserl and Maurice Merleau-Ponty's works in phenomenology. For him, the subject's relation to the object is mediated by the body, which is at the same time part of the world and subject. Moreover, the body is also seen as an object situated between other objects and the world, and at the same time the point of view from which the world is experienced. The body is both action on the world and a perceiving, a sensing, of the world. From this perspective, it is evident that Greimas has greatly distanced himself from Ferdinand de Saussure, for whom the sign was a totally disembodied concept. For the latter there was no place for perception, or for the body, nor did there exist a chasm between subject and object. Along these same lines Greimas escapes from another common dualistic philosophical assumption of a separate subject and object, subject and world; the activity and role of the former being to understand that of the latter, and nothing else. However, as we have seen when discussing modalization, passion is paradoxically a phenomenon in which the object, in becoming a value for the subject, imposes itself on the subject. The action of the world on the subject and the action of subject preceding the world as value become crucial in pathemic configurations.

The need to produce a theory whereby the primitives in question can be delineated is intrinsic to this strategy. In addition, it is essential to be able to construct a methodology from this theory so that texts of different types and dimensions, from words to actual narratives, can be described. For example, in one of his prior works Greimas analyzed the lexeme *colère* or anger,[7] and demonstrated the ways in which the definition of anger was a kind of expanding syntagmatic narrative or short story that defined the denomination, anger. It is well known that several approaches are possible in discourse analysis. One can work from a lexicographical perspective, or one can adopt another strategy that consists in treating texts as signs that can be described using a certain type of methodology coherent with a certain type of theory. One can also proceed by espousing a hypotheticodeductive approach, using text descriptions that can enrich the theoretical level. It should be noted that in the latter case the intent is not simply to apply theory to texts by way of methodology but to consider texts as a living experience for reconfiguring theory. This can be considered as the empirical aim of semiotics, which is not just to provide categories, but, as Paul Ricoeur said in a very Husserlian way, to disengage concepts from texts and to reconfigure the texts in the theory itself.[8]

Even a cursory reading of *The Semiotics of Passions* reveals that the volume is organized into two distinct sections. In the first part of the book Greimas and Fontanille attempt to work out an implicit definition between the theoretical and the philosophical levels adopted. The first part focuses mainly on Descartes, Spinoza, Hegel, Husserl, Freud, Charles Mauron, Merleau-Ponty, Ricoeur, Hjelmslev, and René Thom and tries to establish a pertinent level for a semiotic interdefinition of culture. The second part deals more with passional discourse, that of Marcel Proust, for example, and attempts to show the way in which studying passions (e.g., jealousy in Proust) not only leads to a better understanding of literature or of a specific text, but also provides some means of introducing notions gleaned in the analysis of texts to a general description of passions. The question remains, though, of the sort of methodology and tools needed to carry out this mediation between text and theory. Several possibilities, albeit not necessarily of a linguistic nature, come to mind. One can take philosophical tools or concepts and attempt to discover the same underlying philosophy in the text–this is what Gaston Bachelard did on the poetics of space, or Jean-Paul Sartre in his analyses of Faulkner, Baudelaire, Genet, and Flaubert, to name only his most commonly cited studies. Another strategy is to build a theory independently of texts and to use the latter as a means of applying the theory. If this latter solution is adopted, however, one is inevitably confronted with the knotty problem of applying a philosophical approach to the surface level of language when texts themselves are governed by ad hoc rules. Be that as it may, methodology remains an attempt to relate description to theory.

Another series of questions must be addressed: How is it possible to relate theory, and in this case semiotic theory, to philosophy? How is it possible to create a methodology coherent with this kind of theory and philosophy? If the concept of passion is introduced, what must be done to describe a text in addition to what was done when dealing only with actions? Moreover, how can pertinent texts be found and selected that serve to enrich and reconstruct the theory, texts that actually help to disengage the conceptual from the figurative?

Various theoretical approaches can be adopted to describe the universe of passions. A first one could be defined as the semantic domain strategy, for example, derivatives of Aristotle's *Rhetoric*. This technique was rather simple: two or three fundamental primitives were identified (e.g., hate, desire, aversion), which, combined using various approaches, produced longer sequences formed by compounds of the primitives. This type of technique, known as componential analysis, was effective because many passions could be distinguished and described through it. Another instance, from what anachronistically might be called Greek linguistics, had as its assumption that two or three fundamental elements could be taken from a group of lexemes and combined, thereby introducing more complex elements and new lexemes. This is how the Stoics constructed their definition of hope, for example. Hope is first of all a desire. Desire, in turn, is the minimum state of a subject. Hope is then defined as a desire with something added, namely, the future. Thus the concept of time had to be included. Moreover, an object of desire can also be introduced, then a subject desiring the object in question. Furthermore, the modality of uncertainty must be interjected, for if the subject is in a state of certainty, there is no room for hope. Hence, the modality of uncertainty plus time plus desire produces something that can be called hope. More complex passions also can be affixed to desire, for example, revenge. But then how can revenge be described? It is a more elaborate system than hope insofar as it presupposes offense and thus appears as a desire to repair the said offense.

As we have indicated, one of the linguistic strategies of philosophy was to work on compounds by means of the analytical description of systems of lexemes on passions. A second strategy, initiated by Plutarch and Seneca, consisted in describing passions in terms of processes. When Plutarch examined ire he showed the beginning of anger, its development, its end (explosion). The passion of ire was seen as a process that takes place over time (inchoative, durative, terminative) that, for example, can be opposed to revenge (inchoative, durative). In brief, philosophy traditionally put into play two strategic means for describing passions, one being lexicological and the other narrative, a structure of action: offense provokes a desire for revenge, which in turn sets off an action of vengeance.

Greimas and Fontanille attempt to answer two questions: What can a semiotic and linguistic approach contribute to the methodological strategies described above? And, how can one get a better comprehension of the relationship between what we identified as the theoretical level and its philosophical presuppositions? Another series of questions stemming from this work that remains unanswered is related to linguistic and cultural relativity. The examples and texts chosen to help reconfigure the theory are primarily taken from two major literary traditions, English and French. It would be legitimate to ask if passions are culture specific and if different moments in history change their definitions? However, this certainly goes beyond the bounds of this volume, which makes no attempt to address either problem.

In the first part of their work Greimas and Fontanille situate their problematics within a general epistemological framework of any theory that attempts to attain the status of "scientificity." In so doing they point out that there exist two possible attitudes or extremes that enable one to situate various sciences in relation to one another: either the world is considered as discontinuous (this is the position the physical sciences, mathematics, or linguistics take), or the world is considered as continuous (the attitude adopted by the organicist or biological sciences that affirm its tensive nature).

Within this general epistemology, simply put, linguistics traditionally represented discourse as a continuous string that needed to be articulated in order to be understood. The first operation consisted in segmenting the string to uncover its discrete units; the combination and arrangement of these units constituted the elements of a phonetics or a grammar. In its initial stages of development, semiotics took the notion of *doing* as its underlying principle. The *doing* in question, however, received different denominations according to where it was situated on the *generative trajectory.* At the surface discursive level it was thought of in terms of *process,* whereas at the deep level the concept lost its semantic consistency and became an operation designated as a *transformation.* Such a semiotics of action appeared as a transformation of states in which a discrete state was followed by another discrete state. From this standpoint linguistics and semiotics adopted the same strategy in attempting to rationalize their operations.

Just as Saussure set out as his basic principle that in language there were only differences (that is to say, discretions), so too a semiotics of actions appears as part of a rational and cognitive traditional epistemology. Basically we are dealing with a classical theory of knowledge where there is an operating subject on the one hand and the world as object of knowledge on the other. What philosophers called a transcendental subject was here simply called an "operator"; whereas with regard to the world as object of knowledge, the minimal conditions for comprehension were situated at the level of the elementary structures of signification, known as the semiotic square. However, when the transcendental subject or "operator" was considered in terms of the semiotic square, a problem arose insofar as the subject capable of carrying out operations on the square must possess a competence superior to the square itself. Saussure encountered the same problem when establishing the distinction between *langue* and *parole,* which he resolved by introducing the operational concepts of virtual and actual, different modes of existence. If such a solution is applied to the generative trajectory, then the latter can be divided into various levels according to degrees of density of existence that are different modes of existence. It therefore became possible to distinguish between potential, virtual, actualized, and realized existence. What we are dealing with at this level is a sort of presence in absence—*praesentia in absentia.* Thus, the generative trajectory is delimited by *ab quo* and *ab quem* instances that are, in effect, two ontological instances where beings feel, speak, and see. By situating semiotics between these two instances it takes on a phenomenological and not a noumenal mode of existence. Within such a phenomenological space it was possible to establish the gradation, or the phenomenological density of states of affairs that are either potential, virtual, actualized, or realized.

We have noted that Greimas and Fontanille were influenced by Husserl and Merleau-Ponty, who provided them with the philosophical tools to situate the semiotic space at the level of perception and hence to introduce the crucial element of continuity in the relation of subject to world. In perception, three types of properties can be distinguished: *exteroceptive,* stemming from the external world; *interoceptive,* universals conditioning the possibility of perception; and *proprioceptive,* corresponding to the perception of the body by itself. The introduction of these concepts was necessary to explain what happens at the linguistic level between the natural world and natural languages. As far as perception is concerned, the external world is seen as composed of figures, or in Saussurian terms, signifiers of the world. At the moment of perception, exteroceptive semes are transformed into interoceptive semes and integrated into the activity of the mind. Such an operation, whereby figures of the world become figures of thought through the body, enables Greimas and Fontanille to propose the concept of *figurativity.* The mediating role of the body becomes fundamental to understanding how the external world is transformed into a signifying whole and such a proprioceptive component adds a pathemic dimension in which the cognitive forms of the imagination include a passional or *thymic* component. In this way the theory again endeavors to overcome the dualism that characterizes the sentimental and rational aspects of behavior.

Moreover, at another level it can be said that from the point of view of perception the world is constituted by states of affairs that are transformed into states of feeling by the mediation of the body. This shift makes it possible for Greimas and Fontanille to introduce the notion of continuity by means of the body, thereby avoiding the aforementioned duality that comes from the separation of body and soul, world and mind. This same problem of continuity is encountered at the discursive level where aspectualities and tensions extend beyond rationally and cognitively established categories, where the modulations of sentences and emphases placed on words, the idea that certain verbs express things intensely in order to represent them, constitute phenomena that cannot be accounted for by the rational procedures of a semiotics of action. These modulations of discourse demanded that the deep structures of the theory be reexamined in light of the horizon of tensions that occur at the discursive level.

A further area of investigation is related to the epistemology of the semiotic square. We did note that Greimas and Fontanille suggested that the transcendental subject or, in their own words, the subject operator, by producing discrete entities, induced the emergence of the end terms of the semiotic square. However, even though the operator causes the manifestation of signification, the question of its domain of origin persists. This is seen as a sort of shadow, a sort of mist that veils being, that remains unknowable, but whose existence is logically presupposed as the ontic horizon, defined as the set of conditions for the appearance of signification.

In short, what the authors propose to investigate here are the preconditions of signification, a domain where being is veiled, a sort of imaginary theoretical space, to quote Greimas.[9] As can be seen, compared with the state of the semiotic theory represented by the first dictionary[10] in 1979, a new theoretical component has been proposed at the epistemological level, which, in addition to the conditions for the manifestation of signification, now includes the preconditions. *Tensivity* and *phoria* are the two fundamental concepts chosen to simulate a representation of the ontic horizon of the preconditions. Tensivity can be said to translate the notion of universal attraction, whereas phoria directs tension. What led to this reconfiguration of the theory is that when they attempted to define passions or human behaviors as passional, economical, or as social roles, Greimas and Fontanille were faced with an unexplainable phenomenon. They discovered, for example, that the roles of a miser and a thrifty person were semiotically identical, with this difference: only a phenomenon such as *sensitization* could account for the miser's not being thrifty. When passions such as anger and despair were studied, however, the unfolding of passional discourse or normal pathemic discourse was perturbed at a given moment. It was as though a different subject began to speak that could be accounted for only by the intervention of the body at the moment of the integration of the natural world as interiority. Hence, in their theory, as we stated before, tensivity, an attempt to represent the world according to physics, and phoria, corresponding to vitalistic organicist concepts of the biological sciences, come together as phoric tensivity on the ontic horizon. And on this horizon there appears the veil that makes it possible to represent the way in which, from such an energetic and vitalistic minimum, the subject and the world begin to emerge. In short, they are describing a sort of phoric or semic mass that, in rising to the surface, can be articulated into two types of more or less discrete units. There are, on the one hand, modalizations (i.e., the organization of the thymic into modalities) and, on the other, passional modulations, undulations in the unfurling of discourse.

As Greimas himself has indicated,[11] what he and Fontanille attempt to do is to present a more or less coherent foundation to complete the semiotic theory begun over twenty-five years ago. Their work on pathemization, a phenomenon that can be seen as a sort of polarization of energy, can be linked directly to the problem of oneness and multiplicity raised by Hegel, but which also was part of the pre-Socratic tradition. When, in turn, Socrates rationalized the world by attempting to get to its origins, he was forced to posit the world either as oneness that breaks up or as a complex and mixed entity that tends toward oneness. As an extension of this, the problem of intersubjectivity can be posited in these very terms. Does the meeting of two subjects constitute a tension toward conjunction or the broken-up oneness of the world? Such a problem is related to the very conditions under which communication can occur. What is the basis for the minimal cohabitation of *fiducia,* the very center of human conviviality?

Greimas and Fontanille start from an intuition and imagine positions that enable the polarization of the universe. This enables them, on the one hand, to posit a sort of prototype of an actant, linked by Hegel to intentionality and rearticulated by Husserl in the form of the protensivity of the subject, a sort of minimal state of the subject who is not yet a subject but simply a subject striving for something. And on the other hand, they envision a sort of potentiality of the object, which enables them to consider the world as value. What now appears to be the thorniest issue in the theory is the problematics of the object and not of the subject. To understand subjects as being, as meaning, they must be defined by the values they acquire. From this viewpoint the semiotics of passions becomes a semiotics of the values acquired, lost, suspended, and so on, by the subject. In brief, we are now dealing with a subject defined by its protensivity, faced with an object of value that is unformed, a shadow of the value that can be semanticized. In a later phase the shadow of value becomes the valence, which then leads to the question of the value of value. In short, whether it is examining the semiotics of passions or the semiotics of aesthetics, the two main domains of current investigation, Greimassian semiotics has as its fundamental preoccupation the problematics of value.

Throughout this brief presentation we have continually stressed the progressive conceptualization of Greimassian semiotics. We have also sketched the various moves those engaged in this ongoing project have made over the years. In response to the oft-heard criticism of closure, we have attempted to show how this semiotic theory has opened up to other domains, notably phenomenology, which has considerably enriched it. Yet it should be noted that, because of the need to provide a methodological foundation to the theory (each new concept introduced bringing about a redefinition of existing ones), certain theories in their present state are considered to be incompatible. Hence, at this stage of its development the interface with phenomenology could occur only at the expense of the exclusion of the Peircean paradigm of semiotics, which is seen as being focused more on the cognitive than on the passional dimension of semiotics. In a further move, the major theories of discourse analysis were reexamined and an attempt was made to integrate some of their concepts, notably in the domain of aspectualities. Such concepts provided by discourse analysis brought about a reconceptualization of the entire theory. Within this context of hypothetico-deductive procedures, literary texts also played a fundamental role in reconfiguring the theory. Finally, however, we are confronted by a number of problems that still need to be addressed: the relationship between the continuity and or discontinuity of the preconditions, the semionarrative level and the discursive level, which in Thomian terms immediately raises a problem of morphogenesis, the relationship between the modulations of the preconditions, the modalities of the semionarrative level, and the aspectualities of the discursive level. Can, for example, wanting-to be homologated with the inchoative, being-able-to with the durative, having-to with the punctual, and knowing with the terminative? There is also the question of the nature of the relationship between ontology in general and the epistemological level of current theory.

Although semiotics is still considered to be an open and unfinished project striving for scientificity, Greimas and Fontanille have investigated new areas of inquiry by focusing on the passional domain with respect to the cognitive and the actional. Just as the poet at the end of the *Divine Comedy,* who, like a geometer unable to measure a circle for lack of understanding, is nevertheless enlightened by inspiration when he grasps that his own desire and will are commanded by the sentiment that moves the sun and other stars, numerous insights have been shed on the semiotic spheres of passions. Yet again, a number of areas that have been programmatically mapped out remain to be explored in detail.

The editors would like to thank Ms. Linda Lamisong and Mr. Richard van Holst for their help in preparing the manuscript.

Notes

1. See, e.g., Ronald Schleifer, *A. J. Greimas and the Nature of Meaning* (Lincoln: University of Nebraska Press, 1987), or Paolo Fabbri and Paul Perron, Foreword, *The Social Sciences: A Semiotic View* (Minneapolis: University of Minnesota Press, 1990).

2. See Paul Perron, Introduction, A. J. Greimas, *On Meaning: Selected Writings in Semiotic Theory* (Minneapolis: University of Minnesota Press, 1987), as well as Introduction, *Greimassian Semiotics, New Literary History,* 20, no. 3 (Spring 1989).

3. For example, chapters 3 to 6 of Greimas's *On Meaning,* originally published in French between 1968 and 1973, attempt to come to grips with the actional: "The Interaction of Semiotic Constraints"; "Elements of a Narrative Grammar"; "A Problem of Narrative Semiotics: Objects of Value"; and "Actants, Actors, and Figures."

4. See, e.g., the seminal work of the 1960s in Paris, edited by Roland Barthes, *L'analyse structurale du récit,* where he, Tzvetan Todorov, Greimas, Claude Bremond, Christian Metz, and Umberto Eco accentuate the actional dimension of narrative in their analyses. In his introduction, following Aristotle who, setting tragedy (defined by unity of action) in opposition to history (defined by the plurality of actions and the unity of time), already attributed the primacy of logic over chronology (*Poetics,* 1459a), Barthes stresses the need to "dechronologize" narrative and to "relogicize" it (1988, p. 112).

5. See, e.g., A. J. Greimas, "On Meaning," in *Greimassian Semiotics,* pp. 539–50.

6. "Thus to analyze discourse in this way is to construct models which can account for the trajectory of the lives of subjects, of men. Interest was focused on subjects' trajectories, which are indeed realized by means of narrative programs in discourse, or in the subjects' own lived experience" (ibid., p. 546).

7. See, "On Anger: A Lexical Semantic Study," in *On Meaning,* pp. 148–64.

8. See, e.g., "On Narrativity" (1989, pp. 551–62), a discussion between Paul Ricoeur and Greimas, as well as "Greimas's Narrative Grammar" (1989, pp. 581–608). Both texts were originally published in English in *Greimassian Semiotics.*

9. In a seminar given with Teresa Keane on June 7, 1990, at the Twelfth International Summer Institute for Structural and Semiotic Victoria College, University of Toronto.

10. The English translation of this work appeared in 1982 as *Semiotics and Language: An Analytical Dictionary* (Bloomington, Indiana University Press).

11. Seminar with Teresa Keane of June 8, 1990, given during the Twelfth International Summer Institute for Structural and Semiotic Studies at Victoria College, University of Toronto.

Introduction

When a semiotic theory is formulated as a trajectory (i.e., as an encompassing and encompassed hierarchical organization of models), it is necessary to examine this trajectory continually, and consider it as a construct. Apprehended in its "historicity," such a construct then can be reformulated as a "generative trajectory." But in order to produce the next level, the subject of such activity must be competent at the previous one. Under these conditions, a theory claiming to have a scientific status is constantly on the lookout for its own deficiencies and weaknesses, which it tries to overcome and rectify. In this respect, the theoretical construct cannot be worked out simply from a starting point, followed by a series of theorematical deductions. For example, a discovery pinpointed at the surface of a text or an inconsistency noted necessarily has deep repercussions on the theory and causes disruptions that can put into question the general economy of the generative trajectory as a whole. In other words, semiotic practice is deductive as far as the form of its trajectory is concerned, but "inductive" with respect to the exploration of its *ad quem* instance and "hypothetical" as to its *ab quo* epistemological formulations. The construction of the theory, considered as a genetic and generative discourse, attempts to advance going "backward" as it progresses by transforming itself into a coherent, exhaustive, and simple generative discourse respecting the principle of empiricism.

It is therefore not surprising that the best-explored, and perhaps the most efficient, level of the generative trajectory is, in fact, situated in that middle area between its discursive and epistemological components. We are referring above all to the modeling of narrativity and to its actantial organization. The concept of an actant, freed from its psychological frame and defined only by its doing, is the sine qua non condition for developing a semiotics of action.

The World as Discontinuous

Such a semiotics of action, progressively worked out from generalizations, and from the postulated comprehensiveness of the narrative forms considered irrespective of cultural variations, implies questioning the rationality, and in particular the coherence of the concepts on which it is initially based ("upstream"), so that the consequences deductively drawn sanction the ensuing analytic semiotic practice ("downstream").

At a deeper level, the narrative subject's semiotic doing is reduced to the concept of transformation—that is, a sort of abstract punctuality, emptied of meaning and producing a break between two states. Narrative unfolding can hence be considered as a segmentation of states, defined only by their "transformability." The horizon of meaning founding such an interpretation is that of a world considered as discontinuous. At the epistemological level this corresponds to establishing the undefinable concept of "articulation," the first condition for being able to speak of meaning as signification.

Thus, the possibility of narrative syntax, considered as a set of operations affecting discrete units, is based on a rational epistemology that establishes the first articulations of signification (e.g., the semiotic square) as terms that are simply abstract positions manipulated by a summoning subject. When all is said and done, we are dealing with a classical epistemological model that sets into relationship a knowing subject, as operator, and the elementary structures as representations of the knowable world. The subject of theoretical construction can know and categorize only if the horizon of meaning is divided into a series of discrete elements.

Semiotic Existence

Nevertheless, transformation, which can be considered as breaks occurring periodically and hence as constituting discontinuity that can be analyzed, entails other conditions and opens up new queries. This abstract operation, formulated at a more superficial level as the subject's doing, obliges us to think of the preliminary conditions of such activity, in other words, the narrative subject's modal competence that makes realization possible. Two questions crop up. We are, first of all, forced to ask ourselves what the "modal" consists of and, more specifically, whether it is only part of the knowable discontinuous; and, second, we cannot help but inquire about the "mode of existence" of modal competence, the source of all operativity.

Linguistic tradition relying more precisely on the Saussurian distinction between *langue* and *parole* has familiarized us with the opposition between virtual and actual (or actualized and realized). Such distinctions are generally used as instrumental concepts without, to our knowledge, linguists having ever engaged in a fundamental debate over this. Semiotics must, however, get beyond this stage. As long as "phonetically" realized parole was simply opposed to langue considered as a virtual system, one could always situate it extralinguistically, somewhere else. While referring to a "logic of language," to langue as a "social event," or, as the manifestation of the "human mind," it was especially necessary to preserve its status of "autonomous scientific object." As far as the status of the subject of doing is concerned, we need to distinguish two modes of existence in the space of Saussurian parole (i.e., in discourse), or, what amounts almost to the same thing, in life apprehended and staged as discourse. Considered as a prerequisite, as a potentiality of doing, competence exists first of all as a state of the subject that is a form of its "being," a form actualized prior to realization.

In addition, if, at the epistemological level, we examine the conditions in which signification can appear as discrete units (in the semiotic square, for example), the very same problematics arise. We have to ask ourselves, naively and as though we were projecting, what the mode of existence of a subject operator would be prior to its first summons. As epistemological subject, it would also have to experience a virtual instance before being actualized, as knowing subject, through the discretization of signification. The resemblance between the trajectory of the epistemological subject and the one identified for the narrative subject (virtualization, actualization, realization) is not surprising, since the contamination of description by the object described is a well-known phenomenon, at least in the social sciences. It does not matter what labels these successive modes of existence are given, for just as it formerly was for Ferdinand de Saussure when he postulated the autonomy of the scientific object "langue," one of the things at stake in semiotics today appears to be the identification of an autonomous and homogeneous dimension, of *a mode of semiotic existence*. At such a dimension, semiotic forms are found that can be hierarchized by distinguishing different stases: the "potential," the "virtual," the "actual," the "realized," which, by their order and their interdefinition would constitute the necessary conditions of semiosis. What is at stake for semiotics today is to affirm this *praesentia in absentia*, that semiotic *existence* as the object of its own discourse and as the condition of its activity of theoretical construction happens to be, while nevertheless maintaining the necessary distance with respect to ontological commitments. For semiotics, to raise the issue of an "ontic horizon" is to question a set of conditions and preconditions, to sketch an image of meaning both prior to and necessary for its discretization, and not to attempt to lay bare its ontological foundations. It is only in this way that semiotic theory can justify its own activity, without transforming itself into a philosophy, which it can never be.

The recognition of the fundamental homogeneity of the mode of existence of semiotic forms thus enables one to establish a distinctive space where semiotic activity is pursued. At the same time, such a space remains autonomous in relationship to the two ultimate boundaries, the *ab quo* and *ad quem* instances, beyond which the ontic horizon is defined. In other words, the object of semiotics is simultaneously both phenomenal and paradoxically "real." From the point of view of the *ab quo* instance, the semiotic existence of forms is of the order of the "manifested," manifestation being the suspected and inaccessible "being." From the point of view of the *ad quem* instance, semiotic forms are immanent and can appear at the moment of semiosis. From this perspective, semiotic discourse can be considered as the description of immanent structures and the construction of simulacra that are supposed to account for the conditions and preconditions of the manifestation of meaning, and, in a certain way, of "being."

To conceive semiotic theory in terms of a trajectory thus consisted in imagining it as, on the one hand, a pathway crossed by markers but, on the other, as a coagulating seeping of meaning, meaning continuously taking on substance, starting from its original nebulosity and "potential," and continuing with its "virtualization" and "actualization," before finishing with its "realization," passing from epistemological preconditions to discursive manifestations.

Enunciation is the domain of mediation between the epistemological instance of the deep level of theoretization and the instance of discourse. It is at this level, essentially by means of the various forms of shifters (engagement/disengagement) and modalization, that the semiotic universals used in discourse are convoked. Although setting into discourse is the result of this enunciative operation, it is also more than that, as it not only exploits the components of the epistemological dimension in a single direction, but, since it is a historical and cultural practice—that is, a sociolectal one (and to a certain degree an individual-idiolectal one)—it also engenders forms that become fixed, transformed into stereotypes, and directed "upstream," to be in a way integrated into langue. It thus constitutes a stock of generalizable structures (which could perhaps be designated as "primitives," as opposed to "universals"), which function within cultures and individual universes and which enunciation can in turn call on in realized discourses.

Therefore, the instance of enunciation can be considered as a true praxis, a domain of coming and going between the structures called on and those integrated, an instance that dialectically reconciles *generation* (by the convocation of semiotic universals) and *genesis* (by the integration of historical products). Such passional configurations, to name only these, are situated at the crossroads of all these instances, since for them to occur certain, specific conditions and preconditions of an epistemological nature must be met along with certain operations specific to enunciation, as well as cultural "grids" that are already integrated as primitives or are in the process of being integrated within a sociolect or an idiolect.

The "real" and "imaginary" mode of semiotic existence perhaps can be apprehended more easily, through another approach, by suggesting how, starting from natural languages, we can envision its internal homogeneity. It has been noted how features, figures, and objects of the natural world, whose "signifier" they, so to speak, constitute, are transformed through perception, into features, figures, and objects of the "signified" of language, a new signifier, of a phonetic nature, being substituted for the former. It is by means of the perceiving body that the world is transformed into meaning (into language), that the exteroceptive figures are internalized, and that figurativity can be envisaged as the subject's mode of thinking.

The mediation of the body, whose role and activity are to *feel*, is far from innocent, since, during the homogenization of semiotic existence, it adds proprioceptive categories that in a way constitute the thymic "emanation," and sensitizes even—later on we will say "pathemizes"—in parts the universe of cognitive forms that arise. As a hypothesis, we can consider that this process of homogenization by the body, with its thymic and sensory consequences, exists in every semiotic universe, independently of its mode of manifestation, as there is no reason to think that it pertains to natural languages only. The homogenization of the semiotic dimension of existence therefore occurs by suspending the link conjoining the figures of the world with their extrasemiotic "signified" (i.e., among other things, with the "laws of nature" immanent to the world), and by setting them into relationship, as signified, with diverse modes of semiotic articulation and representation. In this case, what is most remarkable is that the figures of the world can "make sense" only through the sensitization imposed on them by the mediation of the body. This is why the epistemological subject of theoretical construction cannot present itself as a pure rational cognitive subject. In fact, during its trajectory that leads to the advent of signification and to its discursive manifestation, it automatically encounters a phase of thymic "sensitization."

The World as Continuous

By postulating the homogeneity of the universe of semiotic forms we can return to concrete problems raised by discursive unfolding, and to the methodological instruments at this level necessary for analysis. We saw that by attributing a formal status to the concepts of actant and transformation, a condition for the establishment of its syntax, the semiotics of action simply shifted the problematics of semantic investments to the notion of state. From the perspective of the acting subject, however, state is either the end term or the starting point of action. There would therefore exist two forms of "state," and the same difficulties arise once again. State is first of all a "state of affairs" of the world that is transformed by the subject, but it is also the "state of feeling" of the competent subject about to act, as well as modal competence itself that at the same time undergoes transformations. With these two conceptions of "state," the dualism subject/world crops up once more. It is only by affirming a homogeneous semiotic existence—made possible by the mediation of the "sensate body"—that we can come to grips with this aporia. Thanks to this transmutation, the world as state of affairs becomes concomitant with the "state of the subject," that is, reintegrated into the uniform interior space of the subject. In other words, the homogenization of the interoceptive and the exteroceptive by means of the proprioceptive establishes *a formal equivalence between the "states of affairs" and the subject's "states of feeling."* One cannot insist too much, here again, on the fact that if the two conceptions of state—state of affairs, transformed or transformable, and state of feeling of the subject, as competence for and after transformation—can be reconciled in a homogeneous *semiotic dimension of existence*, it is at the cost of a somatic and "sensitizing" mediation.

From this perspective, *sensibility* would therefore be found at the level of the establishment and functioning of epistemological discourse, the minimum requirement for the resolution of the aporia in question.

In certain of its developments of interest to semiotics, sentence linguistics has shown that the predicate could be overdetermined—both modified and distorted—in two different ways: by modalization and by aspectualization. Modalization, at least as it was developed in semiotics within the frame of the modalities of competence, could possibly account for the discontinuous articulation of narrativity. However, the introduction of the concept of "modal state" in semiotic theory, and a more careful examination of discourse, produced the image of continuous "undulation," apprehensible as variations of intensity and overlapping processes, which could be considered as its aspectualization. When faced with the discrete segmentation of states, the overlapping processes make the boundaries between the states hazy and often blur the effect of discontinuity. Now this blurring and this undulation cannot be explained—as this would be too easy—by the surface complexity of analyzed discourses, nor can they be presented uncritically as simple "meaning effects." Considerations of the nature of states and more particularly of their instability, combined with a more general look at the state of the world, induce us to investigate the overall conception of the deep epistemological level of the theory. This leads us to ask if, beyond cognitive apprehension that makes signification discrete and "comprehensible," one could not institute a faintly outlined horizon of tensions, which, while remaining on this side of the signification of "being," would nonetheless make it possible to account for the unusual "undulatory" manifestations recognized in discourse.

Ostensibly, the most obvious solution would be to consider these underlying tensions as properties that characterize discourse itself. But it also happens that because of them we can account for narrative categorization and modalization. As a matter of fact, it is on this horizon of unarticulated tensions that the first summonings of the subject operator occur, making the first units of signification appear through discrete operations. In other words, when dealing with the methodological difficulties that crop up in surface discursive analysis, semiotic theory must attempt to record and to resolve them at the deep epistemological level. This critical return of things is characteristic of semiotics considered as a "scientific project." To account for the difficulties that arise from analysis at the level of discourse–induction, then generalization–another mode of hypothetical functioning has to be assumed, going back if need be to first premises in order then to be able to establish hypotheticodeductive procedures. Such an undertaking can be envisaged only within an epistemological frame where coherence is the scientific value par excellence. This is the opposite of what happens in the cognitive sciences based on a "modular" epistemology, which, to the detriment of coherence, accept relatively independent problematics, without incorporating a critical examination of each new theoretical advance that would force us to measure and show its consequences on the entire theoretical construct.

Setting up an operative subject able to produce the first articulations of signification is the first step in establishing a theory of signification as an economy that manages the *conditions* of production and the apprehension of signification. The next step is to imagine and outline the *preconditions* prior to the emergence of the conditions proper. The "being" of the world and the subject are the concern not of semiotics but of ontology; to use another terminology, it is the "manifesting" of a "manifested" that we glimpse. As for semiotics it has to grasp the "seeming" and develop an epistemological discourse that can formulate such preconditions, as a number of explanatory simulacra, in particular with respect to the difficulties and aporias noted in discursive analysis. This hypothetical discourse delineating the "seeming of the being" obviously cannot produce certainty; but, in a way, this is the same type of discourse as found in the epistemology of the sciences of nature, when we speak, for example, of the universe and its origins, of chance and necessity. This undoubtedly characterizes all scientific projects, which, when establishing an epistemological threshold (in the preceding case, the phenomenological imperative), at the same time create an "imaginary" and even mythical theoretical space, somewhat akin to Newtonian angels who act as conductors of universal attraction.

It is self-evident that such an "imaginary of theory"–these few lines traced on the background of the ontic horizon, these faintly outlined concepts–must not be simply arbitrary in nature. Its raison d'être must rest on previously identified epistemological constraints and methodological demands that incite and challenge it. Of course we are dealing with a "seeming of being" that is nonetheless founded on an operative practice striving for efficacy. In our search for materials that enable one imaginarily to reconstitute the deep epistemological level, the two concepts of *tensivity* and *phoria* seem to hold exceptional promise.

Initially, we thought we could master the fully and duly constituted phenomenon of *tensivity*, an inseparable characteristic of all sentence or discursive processual unfolding, by projecting structures of the discontinuous. This was even at the risk of deferring working out an aspectual grammar that would account both for temporal undulations and spatial sinuosities. However, an urgency to complete the theory of modalities by counterbalancing the already operational modalities of doing with an analogous articulation of the modalities of being, combined with ongoing considerations about the nature of the dynamic and disquieting states, made it imperative to tackle the problematics of the passions directly. Nevertheless, a distressing fact immediately became apparent. Not only can the subject of discourse be transformed into an impassioned subject that disrupts its own cognitively and pragmatically programmed statements, but such a discursive subject can also interrupt and shift its own narrative rationality, and follow a passional pathway, or it can even perturb it with discordant pulsations. This is remarkable in itself, not only because it brings to the fore new forms of narrative dysfunctioning, but also because it shows a relative autonomy of the passional sequences of discourse, a kind of autodynamics of tensions that can be perceived through their effects. Moreover, it induces us to situate tensive space on the other side of the enunciating subject, and not only as the regulating principle, after the fact, of aspectual syntax. This being the case, the concept of tensivity can transcend the instance of discursive enunciation proper and can be relegated to the domain of the epistemological imaginary, where it meets up with other already known philosophical or scientific formulations. As such it would seem to be a "tensive simulacrum," one of the founding postulates of the generative trajectory of meaning.

It is not a problem then, when dealing with the conception of the universe, if we link tensivity to the "scientific" signified of the natural world formulated in terms of laws of attraction. For the *human world* tensivity is only one of the fundamental properties of this interior space we recognized and defined as the conjunction of the natural world and the subject, with the aim of constituting the mode specific to semiotic existence.

Although it is a necessary precondition, it is nevertheless not a sufficient one to account for our ontic imaginary and, more particularly, for passional phenomena. First of all, the analysis of some "paper passions" definitely showed what any anthropologist sensitive to cultural relativism cannot disregard—namely, that the idea we have of a "passion" varies from one region to another, from one age to another, and that the articulation of the passional universe, to a certain degree, even defines cultural specificities. This is all the more surprising for semioticians, who have been able to observe that a slice of discourse or a slice of life, while having identical actantial, modal, and aspectual organizations, could accordingly be considered either as a passion or as a simple arrangement of semantic competence (social, economic, etc.). All things being equal, this amounts to recognizing that there exists a pathemic "surplus" and that a sequence of discourse (or of life) becomes passional only because of specific "sensitizing." Independently of tensivity, "sensitivity" is another factor that has to be taken into account.

Instead of considering everyday forms of passional discourse where undulating sensitizing is sometimes difficult to differentiate from tensivity (which is always present in discursive unfolding), if we considered extreme cases, "violent" passions such as anger, despair, dazzlement or terror, we would see sensitivity appear in its inchoative punctuality as a *break* in discourse, as a factor of heterogeneity, a sort of entering into a trance of the subject that carries it off into an unpredictable elsewhere, transforming it, we would like to say, into a subject *other*. This is where passion appears unveiled, as the negation of the rational and the cognitive, and this is where "feeling" prevails over "perception."

It is as though another voice suddenly arose to clamor its own truth, to say things in a different way. Whereas, during perception, the body played the role of the instance of mediation (that is, a domain of transaction between the extero- and interoceptive, instituting a tensive but homogeneous semiotic space), it is raw flesh, "savage" proprioceptivity that appears and claims its rights as global "feeling." It is no longer the natural world that approaches the subject, but the subject who proclaims himself master of the world, its signified, and reorganizes it figuratively in his own way. The so-called natural world, the world of common sense, hence becomes the world for man, a world that can be called *human*. This "enthusiasm," which, according to Diderot, arises, warm, from one's very entrails to be stifled in one's throat, is obviously an extreme case, but it is essential to help us account for, among other things, artistic creation, and also all the other semiotic excesses of anger and despair. Moreover, it explains, *moderato cantabile*, the unfolding of figurativity, the "representational" character of all passional manifestation, where, thanks to its figurative power, the body becomes the center of reference of the entire passional staging. The term *phoria* is used to designate this disturbing doubling on this side of the subject of enunciation.

When, after a series of attempts, we endeavor to construct a model, our semiotic undertaking can follow two distinct paths. We can try to imagine the simplest of all possible states—such as the elementary structure of signification—and progressively complexify the model. But faced with an unclear situation we can attempt to see a little more clearly by breaking it up into extremes. This is how Friedrich Hegel, for example, produced the binary structure from the excessive and tensive polarization of the unitary one. By wanting to make phoria comprehensible within a semiotic framework, it was difficult for us to introduce it as the mellow accompaniment of narrativity on pathemic background music. Only extreme and paradoxical situations can reveal the specificity and irreducibility of the phenomenon, at the risk of later having to reduce the gaps between what is tensive and phoric in the undulation of discourse.

This sort of splitting of the subject into perceiving and feeling subjects, while perhaps a little too "figurative," nevertheless appeared essential to account for the dysfunctionings of discourse, the trances of the subject appropriating and metaphorizing the world, but also the existence of an ephemeral link, intersubjective fiducia, that sustains discursive veridiction. The instance of enunciation that envelops the entire process allows us to transfer the problematics of the deep level to another level, which we can inscribe as a "phoric simulacrum" governing the generative trajectory, within the ontic horizon. It is in this way that without fear of confusion, we encounter various philosophical formulations of "vitalism" and "energism," or Bergsonian "vital force," even so-called scientific interpretations of the conception of the universe, where necessity, a sort of having-to-be extended toward unity, is confronted with "chance," this first break, the epistemological accident that conditions the appearance of meaning. This allows us to circumscribe the theoretical space of semiotics within two preconditions, construct models of them as tensive and phoric simulacra, and conceive the reflection of "being" as *phoric tensivity*.

This does not mean that having reached this point, semiotic theory must link up with one of the aforementioned philosophies. Its justification can be found in the coherence of its own discourse, which is called on to support its practice, to integrate unusual and disturbing observations, to decipher numerous black boxes at all stages of its development. From this point of view, the history of twentieth-century linguistics is instructive. In spite of the organismic or physicalistic ratiocinations of successive generations of linguists opposing one another, linguistics has continued to constitute itself.

In taking into account the passional component of discourse we are led to make resounding adjustments that have an impact on the very depths of semiotic theory. We are then obliged progressively to retrace our way back up toward the surface, and verify the validity of our premises and our methodological instruments.

Chapter 1
The Epistemology of Passions

From Feeling to Knowing

Emanation

In discourse, passions appear as conveyers of specific meaning effects; it is as though an indeterminate emanation, difficult to ascertain, were emitted. The interpretation retained by semiotics is that this specific fragrance emanates from the discursive organization of the modal structures. Shifting from one metaphor to another, we could say that a meaning effect derives from a certain molecular arrangement. Since it is the property of no specific molecule it arises from their overall organization. A first observation is called for: the passional sensitizing of discourse and its narrative modalization take place concurrently. Although autonomous, they can only be understood together and, in part at least, are probably subject to different logics.

Second, to posit meaning effects globally as an "emanation" of semionarrative organizations into discourse is to recognize in a certain way that passions are not the exclusive property of subjects (or of the subject), but properties of all of discourse, and that they emanate from discursive structures, from a certain "semiotic style" that can be projected either onto subjects or onto objects or onto their junction.

If we now examine things from the other end of the generative trajectory, from the perspective of the horizon of meaning constituting a first projection of the world as phoric tensivity, we are led to believe that this phoric mobile mass can emerge progressively at the surface of things by following two distinct paths. Whereas modalization follows a rational organization and produces categorical modal structures, passional modulations occurring as meaning effects seem to originate from another type of structural arrangement. They emanate from pathemic organizations that override the simple combination of modal contents they bring together and, in a way that remains to be determined, elude cognitive categorization. To be able to speak of passions we must therefore attempt to reduce the hiatus between "knowing" and "feeling." Although semiotics initially concentrated on clarifying the role played by molecular modal articulations, it should now focus on the passional fragrances produced by their array.

Life

Feeling is directly experienced as a self-evident mode of existence, prior to any impressions received; whereas, according to some (thanks to the elimination of all rationality), it can be identified with the principle of life itself. To situate passion prior to the emergence of signification, prior to any semiotic articulation, as a pure "feeling," would, in a way, correspond to apprehending the degree zero of the vital, the minimal "seeming" of "being," that constitutes the ontic backdrop. The homogeneity of feeling also, however, gives rise to an equally naive observation as to its polarization: Does the first cry of the newborn infant correspond to the cry of liberating joy or the suffocation of a fish taken out of water, the first apprenticeship of the *Weltschmerz?* Can we continue reiterating uncritically the notion that living beings are structures of attractions and repulsions? Can phoria be thought of prior to the euphoria/dysphoria split?

The aporia we are led to raise is of a dual nature. First of all, we must reach a decision regarding claims of antecedence of either the "sensitive" over the "cognitive," or the inverse. Is the universe governed by a metalogics of "forces" (such as in wave physics, for example), or "positions" (according to bodily interpretations)? These are both undefinable concepts, as Louis Hjelmslev would say. But, at the same time, another equally fundamental question arises that takes up the concerns of pre-Socratic thought: Is the world one, overflowing in its plenitude, a mixed structure ready to burst, or a chaotic mixture tending toward unity? In other words, and in Brøndalian terms, does the elementary structure of "being," or rather the formal simulacrum we can give of it, proceed from a complex term that can be polarized, or from a neutral one, one that is the domain of an irreconcilable binary encounter? Can the cohabitation of these two logics and these two visions be formulated and represented in terms of preconditions?

The Tensive Horizon

Let us return for a moment to the lexical surface, to a more empirical approach to things. We note that certain passions—admiration, for example (at least as far as it can be found in classical French), but also "astonishment" or "stupor"—already suggest the possibility of a not-yet-polarized tensive horizon. There is no lack of textualized passional trajectories that begin with such configurations. For example, in Mme de La Fayette's *Princesse de Clèves*, the Prince of Clèves, even before falling in love with Mlle de Chartres, meets her at a jeweler's and is constantly "astonished" by everything that concerns her; that is to say, he remains in a state of tension and is conditioned to love her (four occurrences in one page). In the same way, in *A la recherche du temps perdu,* Swann's jealousy and love only begin with "the great flurry of agitation" that makes him run around Paris to find Odette de Crécy, an agitation that appears as another modulation of the same nonpolarized tension. Polarization into euphoria/dysphoria, even at the lexical level, can therefore be neutralized, or even considered as not having taken place. In the grammatical sense of the term, neutralization, refers to syncretism that, by rights, is hierarchically superior to binary opposition. One of the paradoxes of semiotics at the epistemological level is that it must attempt to account both for the "nothing," the "void," and for the "all"—of the fullness of phoric tensions. According to a logic of "forces" maximum tension would correspond to (i.e., account for or be explained by) a total absence of articulations. The appearance of "positions," on the contrary, would require a redistribution and a division of "forces"; in other words, the "void of content," characterized by the absence of articulations, can be filled only by the shock of tensive plenitude. The cohabitation of two opposite necessities, respectively attached to "forces" and "positions," allows us to understand that prior to any categorization whatsoever, feeling, torn between two tendencies, can engender only instability.

Yet, as such it can nevertheless be directly manifested, as can be seen from the figures of "stupor" and "astonishment." Regarding this we should note that neutralization as formulated here depends on the intensity of feeling. Particularly intense "classical" admiration is indifferent to the polarization, the positiveness or the negativity, of the object. It would seem that here it is the recognition of value as such that adumbrates the object and makes polarization inoperative. We should note that, in our examples, the admiring subject abandons value as invested in the object, in order better to grasp "the value of value" on this side of it. On the other hand, in its modern sense, admiration, while requiring the positivity of the object, is accompanied by a notable weakening. It is as though passional intensity, a notion that still needs to be defined, neutralized the subject and buried him at a deeper level of the generative trajectory, or again, as though the extension back to the value of the value, from the object of value proper, were accompanied by a more intimate contact with a zone of "energy" where passion would originate. The same holds true regarding "stupor," which undergoes an analogous condensation, congealing the subject into a pure feeling, to such a degree that feeling itself is obliterated: Is "stupidity" not a regression to a state of tensivity prior to life, an extreme point between the living and the nonliving?

The Preconditions (of Signification)

To extend the veil of Isis over the countenance of "being," we previously proposed that the first formulations of its appearance could be defined as simulacra. By linking the universe explainable only in terms of tensive necessity and phoria, introduced by accident, break, the unusual intrusion of the living, we imagined the human world in its *ab quo* state as "phoric tensivity." We are aware that this is a near-trivial representation and that whatever value it has can be determined only by the kinds of consequences it entails – that is, in the progressive modalization of the congruent "thymic mass" that is both tension and phoria, as long as its articulations do not put into question theoretical coherence and conform to the "facts," right up to the surface manifestations.

If original tensivity – tension toward oneness and overflow of excessive plenitude – breaks up, then "positioning," the polarization of what ceases being one at a given moment, occurs at a first crucial moment. Polarization that cumulates energy, however, does not yet correspond to "positioning" and does not imply that poles become discrete, since this can happen only through the cognitive projection of the discontinuous. Under these conditions it is not yet possible to speak about "actantial positions," but only about prototypes of actants, about near subjects and objects, of the subject's *protensivity* (to use a Husserlian turn of phrase), and about the object's potentiality. Before "positing" a tensive subject that confronts values invested in objects (or the world as value), it is necessary to imagine a level of "presentiment," where the subject for the world and the world for the subject are intimately linked. We already encountered a comparable situation when, with modalization in mind we distributed the entire thymic mass on the constituent terms of the elementary utterance. Although the modal mass initially overdetermines the predicate in its junctive function (as is the case, for example, with the alethic modalizations identified in logic), it can separate into distinct parts and invest each of the actantial positions. Although the investment of the subject of doing raises no particular difficulties (cf. the deontic modalities, for example), this does not necessarily hold true regarding the investment of the subject of state. In this case, we note that the subject as being can be affected modally only by the mediation of the investment of the object, and provided it is posited in relation to the subject, its modal mass, in turn, modalizes the latter. In other words, the modalization of the state of the subject – and this is what we are referring to when we speak about passions – is conceivable only if it begins by modalizing the object, which, in becoming a "value," imposes itself on the subject. The situation we need to imagine is comparable, but prior to actantial positioning: a protensive subject, indissolubly linked to a "shadow of value," is outlined against the back drop of "phoric tensivity."

Valencies

The subject's protensivity, which is often too readily identified with intentionality and subsequently is interpreted either as a "metawanting" or as a "metaknowing," at this stage of our investigation does not need further justification. This is not the case for the object prototype that we just designated as a "shadow of value." It is therefore advisable, once again, to reexamine the surface, the discursive manifestation, in order to highlight this simulacrum and justify the relevance of our premises. We have the impression that the most common form this "shadow" takes is a kind of presentiment of value. Hence a reading of Paul Eluard's *Capitale de la douleur* is an excellent illustration of a first articulation projected by protensivity. On closer examination, we note that in this collection of poems, the content of values is not very important; the semiotic subjects obviously are aware of love, nature, work, thought, and life in all its forms. Regardless, however, of the semantic value of the objects yearned for, their value is always of another order: love is acceptable only at its beginning; the gaze, when eyelids open on awakening; the day, at the moment it breaks with darkness; human life, in infancy. It is as though the inchoative aspect predominated over the semantic contents invested in objects and in so doing, as though only incidental intent counted and not the intended object.

Aspectuality here seems to be situated both below and on this side of value proper. It is a kind of "value" of value, and in this sense we could call it a "valency," using the same definition of the term as in chemistry, as designating the number of molecules that make it up. This is what occurs, for example, during exchange, when two distinct semantic values are deemed to be comparable and exchangeable based on their (equi)valence. We can then assume that something constant is exchanged that has very little to do with the objects that are invested differently semantically, and is transferred from one subject to another. In addition, we noted that in discourse, aspectualization constitutes a dimension hierarchically superior to temporalization, but also to spatialization and even to actorialization: in Eluard's poems, love is apprehended on the temporal axis; the "eyelids on awakening" are spatially situated; "human life" is apprehended as the growth of the actor; the whole is regulated by the inchoative aspect. But there is even more in this valorization of inchoativity, and we have to take into account the second definition, of a "psychological" nature of valency, considered as the possibility of attractions and repulsions associated with an object. In this respect, valency would be the presentiment, by the subject, of this shadow of value, which, following phoric scission, enfolds it like in a cocoon before appearing later on in the more articulated form of inchoativity. In short, aspectuality manifests valency in the same way that object figures manifest objects of value.

It is therefore not surprising if the implicit or explicit ethical or aesthetic judgments in this collection of poems are founded on the inchoative aspect of gestures and figures, since, at the discursive level that characterizes it, the latter once again encounters original dissociation, before any polarization and any semantic investment of objects. In Eluard, the valency chosen stems from an "opening" of protensivity; but it could equally, for example, have emanated from its "closure," which would be expressed by the terminative aspect at the level of discourse, and, on occasion, could give rise to an ethics of disenchantment, to an aesthetics of evanescence, making use of figures of decay, fragility, or the obliteration of all things.

In *La chute*, for example, Albert Camus attempted to describe a world without values, from which confidence would be excluded. In fact, his description of the Zuider Zee progresses by dissolving valencies:

> Here is, of course, the most beautiful of negative landscapes! See on your left that pile of grey ashes they call a dune here, the grey dike on your right, the ashen shore at your feet and, before you, the sea that is the color of a weak detergent, the vast sky reflecting the shallow waters. A soft hell, truly . . . Is this not universal obliteration, nothingness that can be apprehended through your eyes? (p. 1510)

An indefinite flatness, blurred distances, an absence of all figurative differences—everything is lost in the stagnating duration of engulfment. This is the end of all valencies, and a fortiori of any articulated value systems that could arise. It is as though, in order to be read in a distinct manner and with some iconic force, the figurative components of the setting into discourse actually presupposed the level at which protensivity comes up against valencies at the moment of actantial scission. On the contrary, with Camus a "soft" protensivity is disseminated and apprehended before its first articulation. This makes it possible to understand, as in a proof by the absurd, why the first articulation of phoria, in dissociating the near subject and the near object, engenders *fiducia*. To return to the soft chaos of nonarticulated tensions, literally, in *La chute*, is no longer to believe in anything, and especially, no longer to believe in belief, since faith in some particular value or other always presupposes a "metabelieving," which is a generalized (nonspecific) belief peculiar to the space of phoria and which, in a way, is the precondition for any particular belief. Thus, Camus's "penitent-judge"—a syncretic actant par excellence—much in the way of cynics of antiquity, practices systematic denigration and sarcastic provocation. It seems clear in this example that the valencies, the entire set of which constitutes what we have just called fiducia, receives its framework from the world of objects, without which they can acquire no value.

It is also necessary to settle quickly the question of the role of the "accident" in Camus's narrative. The Zuider Zee remains impervious to any interpretative activity on the part of the observer, obviously because it presents no apparent differences, no landmarks, but also because above and beyond any articulation, it reveals no figurative "accident" that could be understood as the image of a world in which chance plays no role. Yet, it is an "accident" that shattered everything for the "penitent-judge": it is by a chance encounter that he met the despairing woman whom he did not even try to save after she threw herself into the Seine. Chance can cast down what it helps elevate: the accident that provokes the collapse of a world of values is only the virtual and inverse image of the accident that activates ontic necessity first of all making valency appear, then value.

Instability and Regression

Following the example of Camus, we come to the conclusion that the phoric foundation of all signification is unstable, and what chance does, it can undo. On the one hand, the first activation of meaning does not suffice to engender signification; on the other, the scission caused by the intervention of chance on necessity is menaced by the "pregnanz" of necessity itself. The "dual" tends toward "oneness" at the risk of necessity overcoming the chance of scission. Following another line of thought, in studying "fuzzy" objects and movements of the natural world, mathematicians (in particular Benoît Mandelbrot) perfected fractal theory, which shows, among other things, how the undifferentiated reappears under the influence of chance and recursivity. As a matter of fact, so-called fractal objects are engendered both by chance (stochastic processes) and by recursivity (the indefinite application of stochastic processes to products of preceding operations). Now, if nothing stops or redirects recursivity, then fractalization results in an object that, even though regulated by a principle of internal homothetics, becomes insignificant, irreducibly singular. In the same way, if scission is both "stochastic" and "recursive," it then reproduces conditions of "fusion" and tensive plenitude, or what amounts to the same thing, of maximal dispersion.

Aesthesis. This tension toward unity is what characterizes *aesthesis*, which appears as the opposite movement to the one that determines syncretisms. In a new relationship to the world, the subject experiences value in the first dissociation that actually engenders him. The aesthetic emotion could then be interpreted as the "reexperiencing" of this scission, as nostalgia for undifferentiated "phoric tensivity." This would make it possible to account for the fact that manifestations of aesthesis most often are accompanied by an exchange of syntactic roles. Reimmersed in phoria, the aesthetic subject rediscovers the moment his prototypical configuration could have been constituted, either as object or as subject. This is why in figurative representations we can sometimes see the aesthetic object in the process of becoming the subject of aesthetic activity whose subject of emotion could in turn be an object.

It can be seen, moreover, that in discourse what often happens when a subject has to decide between valencies, and cannot resort to any constituted axiological system, or refuses the very principle of such a system, is that he hence opts for aesthetic discourse. For a subject who does not recognize instituted values, who despises generally acceptable values, evil becomes ugliness, good becomes beauty. Thus the cynic, but also the revolutionary socialist or the anarchist of the previous century, remains sensitive to the aesthetic success of a moral act, or an immoral one, for that matter. In like manner, they also attempt to point out the ugliness of an immoral (or moral) act, by satirical means.

Tension toward oneness, this menace—or hope—of returning to a fusional state, opens up two possibilities that are worthy of note. First of all, the conception of aesthesis as the "reexperiencing" of a limit state and expectation of a return to fusion, based on fiducia, makes it possible to anticipate the existence of an *aesthetic dimension* on the discursive level. The passional dimension, based on phoria as its precondition and its manifestation as objective, would have the aesthetic dimension as its counterpart, which, itself would be based on the possibility—expectation or nostalgia—of a return to phoric protensivity, to the undifferentiated universe posited as the precondition of all signification.

Actantial Instability. Furthermore, the instability of the scission, as well as the interchangeability of the roles of subject and object, noted in the discursive manifestation, leads us to believe that in the interval separating fusional state from dissociated state, the appearance of the "double" can be interpreted both as a prefigurement of intersubjectivity and the subject/object relationship. If we reexamine the way we envisaged the emergence of the protensive subject, we can say that he is solicited by two congruent but near-contradictory forces: on the one hand, protensivity by which the subject is differentiated from the object and which gives him an image of his "ipseity," and on the other, fiducia, the mode of being of the "subject for the world," which, because it defers differentiation, elicits a sort of "alterity." Whether protensivity or fiducia prevails, the split of "oneness" into the "double" results either in a strengthening of the specific positions of the protensive subject and the "shadows of value," or in the appearance of two "intersubjects," whose not-yet-fixed respective positions, because of their lack of precision, are interchangeable.

In the interplay of tensive exchanges that occur within phoria, either intersubjective projections, or roles of the subject and object, appear sometimes as identical doubles, sometimes as different doubles, by means of which, alternatively and congruently, both the subject in itself and intersubjectivity are constructed. This interplay of alternation enables us to understand how, by reuniting with the fusional state, the aesthetic subject maintains a certain image of alterity, and why the discursive manifestation embeds aesthetic emotion in intersubjectivity. All of these protoactantial forms seem to stem from the same instance: phoric tensivity.

When analyzing concrete discourses, especially those that display the trajectory of impassioned subjects, we frequently encounter unstable and interchangeable actantial roles. More surprising, though, the imaginary of the impassioned subject sometimes seems to contain an entire actantial set whose roles can be exchanged and combined. In the indispensable shuttling to and fro between conceptualization of the deep level and discursive manifestation, we are led to posit a reverberation between, on the one hand, protoactantial functioning characteristic of phoric tensivity and, on the other, the actantial functioning of the imaginary of the impassioned subject. Far from appearing as a simple actor fulfilling a number of actantial roles concurrently, the latter emerges as a true discursive subject having "internalized" a number of actantial scenarios by which passion is displayed. More than a simple syncretism, this subject is in fact defined principally by the capacity to call on the entire display of the actantial roles necessary for the discursive manifestation of passion. Such a trait is conceivable—within a semiotic framework, of course—only if, beforehand, provision has been made for the possibility of "oneness" splitting into several "protoactants" within tensive space.

It is easy to see that within phoric tensivity, made up of tensions between "oneness" and the "double," the phoric mass tends to become polarized, because of the ascendancy of chance over necessity, and tensions between the "double" and "oneness" created by necessity regaining ascendancy over chance. A true polarization such as euphoria/dysphoria has not been attained, but rather a simple oscillation between "attraction" and "repulsion"; polarization as such will occur only at the time of categorization. The image of *the stirring of meaning* seems appropriate here. It is as though minimal feeling both confirmed and infirmed the first flexion of phoria; as though it oscillated between fusion, scission, and reunion. At the level of discourse, a passional configuration, "anxiety," makes it possible to identify an expression of this constituent instability, since it is a movement before euphoria and dysphoria, and it suspends, so to speak, polarization. It should be noted here that anxiety prevents any evolution of the tensions of phoria and that, consequently, it prevents the formation of "valencies" and of all definite orientation of protensivity. This is why the subject suffering from anxiety wishes only to master the oscillation that overcomes him. This is also why anxiety most often appears as a resurgence of insignificance at the level of discursive manifestation.

Becoming and the Premises for Modalization

The recognition of the tension that characterizes phoria enables us to envision a first representation of the generation of the modalities, which presumably become, at the level of narrative syntax, the modalizations of doing and being. The difficulty arises because these modalities, such as we know them—wanting, having-to, being-able, and knowing—are dependent on rational categorization, whereas from another perspective, when considering the effects of passional meaning effects, they seem to follow other modes of organization that are more "configurational" than "structural" proper. We would like to show that from the level of the preconditions of signification, the evolution of protensivity sketches, among other things, the tensive prefigurations of the four modalities, and that these prefigurations, including the modal universe, once categorized, hold the memory, so to speak, and have an impact on the passional functioning of the modalities.

Protensivity and Becoming. The scission of the undifferentiated protoactant can be prevented from reverting back to original fusion only if it is endorsed by an "orientation" already present in the proto-space-time on which the ontic horizon is foregrounded. By putting things somewhat into perspective, though, we can consider that of all the tensions that impel phoria, those that most favor scission and those that tend toward fusion can either counterbalance or subjugate one another. When they balance one another they remain in a state of oscillation, and when, on the contrary, tensions favorable to fusion carry the day, necessity takes over and signification cannot occur. We can see that for signification to emerge from phoric tensivity, tensions favoring scission have to prevail. It is only under these conditions that protensivity can occur as orientation. Moreover, this type of orientation is a necessary condition for phoria to prefigure syntax, since only this type of disequilibrium seems to favor the emergence of the "near subject" and the valencies. Pursuing this line of thought, we can call *becoming* the "positive" disequilibrium that favors the scission of the phoric mass.

In order to try and understand how a modicum of syntax can be ascribed to phoria we can refer to the little-used notion in semiotics that has the advantage of resonating the manifestations of continuity observed in the discursive syntax back onto the epistemological level. The current definition of becoming as the "passage of one state to another" or as a "series of changes of states" does not take into account the distinction between being and doing and subsumes states and transformations. Other more philosophical or near-semiotic definitions present becoming as the principle of a continuous change, a pure evolutive direction, at a level of analysis where "human" change is not yet distinguished from "natural" change: it happens, it becomes, we could say. With respect to the two discontinuous entities, being and doing, becoming would be, so to speak, a compound syncretism and a precondition. Between the "near subject" and the "shadow of value," it is not a question of junction or of states and transformations, but of a fiducia tension that is rendered dynamic by oscillations of attraction and repulsion and disequilibrated in favor of scission. If protensivity can be understood as the archaic modal effect of scission in the space of phoria, becoming can be seen as its "positive" version that promulgates the appearance of signification.

Few things in fact separate these notions: "protensivity," "orientation," and "becoming" more or less designate, with different emphases, the same thing. Protensivity is the first modal effect of scission; orientation is its figural attribute; becoming is the result of a disequilibrium of tensions that confirms scission. In addition to the fact that the term "becoming" is intuitively easier to use than "protensivity," it offers a dual advantage. First, as a precondition of the epistemological level, it induces us to refine our analysis of protensivity. It obliges us to think of it both as orientation and evolution, that is to say, as *bearing a historicity*. From this perspective becoming is compatible with hypotheses dealing with anthropological and biological evolution. This does not mean, however, that it will become a "bridgehead" for a possible theoretical invasion, but, more prudently, that it is at this level of theoretical construction, the preconditions of signification, that discussion is possible about such hypotheses. Second, regarding the discursive manifestation, where the term remains somewhat relevant, it designates spatiotemporal unfurling and expansion. However, at the level where aspectualization, considered as the regulator of the discursive continuum, can account for such surface effects, the use of the term appears redundant. On the other hand, at the level of the preconditions through selection of a principle of unilateral orientation and evolution from among all phoric tensions, it creates *an effect of intent* that makes syntax conceivable, especially when one considers that the effect of intent can be fragmented into an *effect of origin* (subject) and an *effect of purpose* (object).

The Modulations of Becoming. To resolve this syncretism we shall follow successively two paths: first, *modulation* and then *discretization*, which engenders modalizations. The former constitutes a prefigurement of discursive aspectualization. The latter, by taking up once more the results of modulation, establishes a link between variations of tension in the space of phoria, on the one hand, and the modal categorization at play at the narrative level, on the other. The approach applied to becoming follows the two main procedures used until now in dealing with continuity: demarcation of tensive variations, which highlights modulations, and segmentation, which foregrounds discrete units. Demarcation, which we shall focus on for the moment, complies to a logic of approximations and progresses by overlappings and breaks in tensions, giving rise to phases of acceleration or deceleration, of origins or ends, of openings or closings, of suspensions or delays. These variations, which are intrinsic properties of becoming, are inscribed in the definition itself. Indeed, tensions that favor scission prevail only globally; for a distant "observer," becoming is simply a "favorable disequilibrium," whereas, in detail, and for an "observer" situated nearby, flashbacks, inverse disequilibria, locally compromise the continuity of evolution. Modulations of becoming can be thought of, so to speak, as a certain way of regulating both the heterogeneity of tensions and the global homogeneity of orientation.

The prototype of wanting, for example, could begin with an "opening," actualizing the intended effect, and at this tensive level would be identified through the acceleration of becoming; moreover, regardless of its position, each new occurrence of wanting would determine a new opening or a new acceleration. The prototype of knowing, however, would close off becoming, since it would actualize an effect of "grasping," the inverse of the intended effect. It would stop the flow of becoming in order to measure its evolution. Generalizing this modulation to the totality of the space of phoria, by stabilizing tensions, opens up, as we shall see, the possibility of a cognitive rationalization of the universe of meaning. As for the prototype of being-able, its role is to "sustain the flux of becoming," to accompany its fluctuations that maintain the disequilibrium favorable to scission. The three modulations – respectively "opening," "closure," and "cursiveness" – prefigure what at the level of discourse will become the aspectual triad "inchoative/durative/terminative." Yet, it should be noted that the aspectual triad, as a discursive form of process, has very little to do with the three modalizations we have just examined. Obviously they have the same foundations, but they are derived through two entirely different processes. As a matter of fact, if, beginning with the three modulations of becoming, we apply categorization, they then follow the generative trajectory, and, in the semionarrative universe, they are converted into modalizations. Inversely, if, starting from the same modulations, they set processes into discourse, at the level of manifestation they appear as "aspects." This presentation offers the advantage both of an economy of means (a single concept and two very general procedures) and a distinction between *conversion*, reserved for the generative trajectory, and *enunciative convocation*, reserved for the setting into discourse. These apply to variations of phoric tensivity as well as to the products of the generative trajectory that characterizes the semionarrative level. Again it should be noted that it presupposes a representation of the general economy of the theory in three "modules" linked by operations: that of the preconditions, that of the semionarrative, and that of discourse. We shall reexamine these later on.

As for the prototype of having-to-do, it appears as a suspension of becoming, insofar as it transforms the latter into another necessity. Instead of the fusion of "oneness," it offers us the coherence of the "whole." For, once the principle of scission has been established, another danger arises: dispersion. If nothing opposes the dispersive forces set in play by the first stirring of meaning, after the insignificance of "oneness" another insignificance settles in, chaos. And we already encountered the effects of such an insignificance of indefinite scission when dealing with the disorderly and sterile agitation that characterizes anxiety. The prototype of having-to-do confronts this danger as a cohesive force, striving to constitute a totality of tensions. In practice, this means adopting with respect to becoming the point of view of the distant observer who, as we saw, smooths over the risks of phoria and neglects variations and phases. In fact, the prototype of having-to-do proceeds by "punctuating" modulation, thereby neutralizing the "opening," "closure," and "cursiveness" effects. Such a hypothesis enables us to account for the very particular functioning of the ensuing modalization.

Modulations, Modalizations, and Aspectualizations. The preeminence of the inchoative in *Capitale de la douleur*, which we interpreted as the manifestation of a valency, takes on all its meaning here. It signals the domination of a prototype of wanting, the "opening" modulation and its intended effect, which in the collection of poems appears explicitly as resistance to necessity. More generally, when exploring the text through its variations or its aspectual choices, we can recognize the dominant forms of tensivity. Insofar as these choices define a certain mode of access to signification for the epistemological subject and access to values for narrative subjects—this is the case with the inchoative in Eluard's text—we can consider that they express what we could call "semiotic styles." The agitation of the worrier, the hesitation of the procrastinator, the aggressive style of the determined individual are all aspectual manifestations of the way in which signification and value occur in various types of discourses, or for any of the subjects so designated. From another point of view, in the absence of direct and indirect manifestations of the modalizations, the examination of the dominant aspectual choices makes it possible for us to posit the existence of various dominant modulations at the deep level, which have been specifically convoked for setting into discourse. This modulation being presumably predominant, we suspect and predict that the modal organization, if it exists at the imminent level, should be affected or oriented. Hence, hesitation, which is based on both an opening and a protractive modulation, enables us to make provision for a complex articulation of wanting (wanting and not wanting), and incites us to seek possible specific traces in the discursive manifestation. In the same way, agitation, as a superficial aspectual form, takes on a specific form of protractive modulation that is secured by the pure oscillation of tensions, the inconclusive equilibrium between fusion and scission. Such an unstable equilibrium can be interpreted as the coexistence of two modulations whose effects cancel each other out—for example, an opening modulation and a closing modulation, or a cursive modulation and a punctualizing modulation. One could therefore advance the hypothesis at the narrative level of a modal conflict either between wanting and knowing, or between being-able and having-to. In either case we would be able to encompass the contours of anxiety and anguish. Moreover, it seems that this discovery procedure is the one used intuitively or with other means of investigation by psychiatrists, when, from the aspectual and superficial form of behavior (cf. agitation), they infer a psychic disposition of a modal and passional nature (cf. anguish or the worrying component of depression). The three instances—modulation, modalization, and aspectualization, respectively distributed on phoric tensivity, the semionarrative level, and the discursive manifestation proper—constitute, so to speak, the theoretical triangle whose heuristic value we are attempting to demonstrate.

To return to phoric tensivity, the number of possible modulations for becoming is at present undefined, and it probably is so by definition. On the one hand, the few forms we have suggested and partially illustrated do not exhaust the cases of possible figures, and, on the other, since we remain in a continuous mode, the logic of approximations and overlappings that occur at this level allows for as many mixed or intermediate types as can be imagined. It is clear that if we have given priority to the opening, closing, cursive, and punctualizing modulations, it is because of the modal categorization that selects them, according to a principle that shall be examined shortly, in order to integrate them into the semionarrative level.

Toward a Knowable World

Summons. The subject, modalized by fiducia at the phoric level whose principal characteristics we have just sketched, and associated with the "shadows of value" by protensivity, is not yet capable of recognizing value. He can experience only its valency, in particular as aesthetic appreciation.

To understand, the subject first of all has to negate. Evidently, "proforms" of objects are already available to the subject, the modulations of becoming already introduced a sort of "breathing"—a rhythm? a tempo?—in protensivity, but nothing has yet been categorized, nothing has discrete contours. Negation is the first operation by which the subject founds himself as *operative subject*, and founds the world as knowable. This would be in a way a sort of disjunction, the first being the disjunction with the continuous modulation of tensions and a world of nonknowable values. This negation can be analyzed in two stages.

The first gesture is a pure act, an act par excellence: a *summons*. The subject operator summons a position, which, starting from the shadow of a value, delimits the zone of a category. This summons is itself a negation, or rather an apprehension, a halt in the fluctuations of tension. In fact, the world as value opened itself up entirely to the feeling of the tensive subject. But to comprehend it, we must stop its continuous march; that is to say, "closure" has to be generalized. This is therefore the source of the first negation: delimit a zone, summon a place—that is to say, negate what is not this place.[1] Hence, in Proust, before hearing Vinteuil's phrase, Swann is an ordinary individual, without ideals, without a project, subsisting intellectually and emotionally on little things, void in an insignificant world. Vinteuil's phrase is the figure of this initial operative subject, for it will indeed summon a place, designate in his mind the zone where, as Proust writes, Odette's name will be inscribed:

> So that in the parts of Swann's soul where the little phrase had wiped out the concerns of material interests, the human considerations that preoccupy everyone, and had left them vacant and blank, he was free to inscribe Odette's name. (*A la recherche du temps perdu*, vol. 1, *Du côté de chez Swann*, p. 233)

The second gesture, which is simply the obverse of the first, is a *contradiction*, a negation in the categorical sense. The summons-negation applied to the shadow of value can set up only non-S_1, the first term of the semiotic square. In fact, the tensive subject that has become the operative subject through this disjunction can make discrete only the shadows of values from which scission has separated him. Absence is the only thing left for him to requisition. In other words, for signification to occur and for tensivity to be stabilized, the only solution for the operative subject is to *categorize the loss of the object*, and that is why negation is the first discrete operation. It is only on this condition that, by the introduction of discontinuity into continuity, behind the shadows of value, the subject will be able to have knowledge of the object. Without contradiction, summons simply determines a pure singularity in the tensive continuum and does not succeed in making signification occur. This is why, after having seemed "singular" and irreducibly individual, Vinteuil's phrase appears as a network of contrasts, internal negations, to be discovered and uncovered, and ends up being the sign of an absence, an absence whose existence Swann never suspected, and which will give meaning to his life.

Summons can be readily justified. All we have to do is to concentrate on what can happen to the tensive subject and his valencies. Once they have been confirmed and sustained as becoming, the actantial scission and the distribution of the tensions on the whole counterbalance one another. In this way a phase of equilibrium is attained where the internal dynamics of phoria comes up against the stabilization of becoming. Two possibilities arise: either fiducia prevails, and with it the tendency to return to fusion, or the protensivity of the subject is converted into act and the subject in question becomes the operative subject. Such an evolution is inscribed in the very definition of becoming, since the maintenance of a "positive" disequilibrium can end up only in accentuating it and therefore, in the final analysis, in stabilizing it. Finally, the confirmation of the scission in a way that founds the cognitive can be seen as a sort of certification of the separation of the world and the subject.

Categorization. The *semiotic square*, or any other model that could take its place on the generative trajectory, establishes a signifying rationality where, as "horizon of being," we expected simple necessity. *A contrario*, aesthetic emotion, for example, cannot easily be broken up into discrete elements. The world is aesthetically marked, or it is not. It can be more or less aestheticized in a continuous mode, but it then no longer falls under the purview of categorical semiotic differences. However, the "soft" protensivity of *La chute* is accompanied with a universal suspension of differences. We are all the same, all guilty; there are no values in the axiological sense of the term, or values in the structural sense.

This engendering of the elementary structures of signification makes it possible for us to understand at the same time their stabilizing role. By their summons-negation, the operative subject provokes a new entity, *category*, which appears like a response to the solicitation for unity emerging from original necessity. But this unity now forms a network of stable relations, where the composition of contradictions, contrarieties, and implications, while breaking up the category into several terms, provides us with a totalizing image that is nonetheless in the state of becoming. The elementary structures of signification end up reconciling a principle of evolution, by means of a syntax of dialectical nature, and a categorical form of totality. Hence, tension between "oneness" and the "multiple" is resolved by the establishment of dialectical and discontinuous relations between the category and its terms.

Furthermore, discretization transforms becoming into a succession of discontinuous disjunctions and conjunctions. The first summons, followed by the constituent operations of the elementary structure, converts the modulations into a succession of "befores" and "afters," phases and thresholds of phases. From this perspective, *states* and *transformations* at this level will be respectively defined as zones isolated by summons in the oriented expansion of becoming and as routes that lead from one state to another. In this case, elementary syntax is not added after the fact to the elementary structures of signification. It emerges as part of the same syncretism. We note especially that if the elementary structure emerges from the summons of the "shadows of value," that is to say of the valencies that stand out on the back drop of fiducia, the elementary syntax of states and transformations emerge from a summons of the phases of protensivity. The same procedure, this "apprehension-halt" that we identified as the first negating and founding act, can also engender both the category and its syntax through a simple variation in scope: a localized apprehension in the first case, and an apprehension of the dynamic global effect in the second.

Surface Narrative Syntax: Tools for a Semiotics of Passions

Having attained the level of narrative syntax proper, we are now better able to define the conceptual tools that can be used directly to analyze passions.

Modal Structures

The breakup into discrete units occurring after and during the modulation of the tensions of becoming can consequently be applied to the results of this modulation. More specifically, it converts modulations obtained through "demarcation" (opening, closure, cursive, punctual) into modal categories.[2]

If we assume that summons must confirm and stabilize scission, withstand ontic necessity, and proceed through *negation*, then the first modalizing operation consists in wanting-to negate having-to. The modal category then unfolds as the semiotic square in Figure 1.

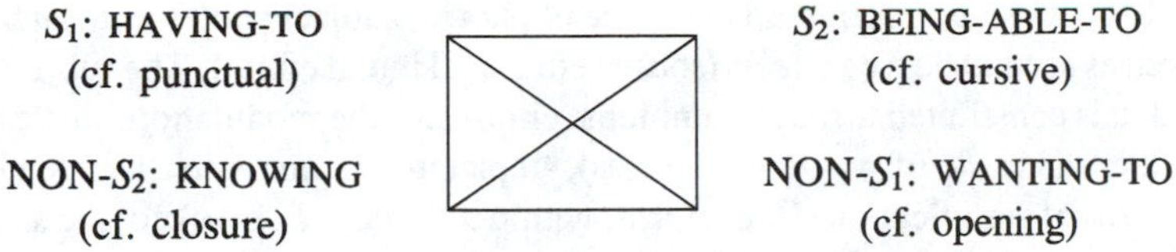

Figure 1

We thus end up with two modal axes: the axis of *exogenous* modalizations, the modalizations of the heteronomous subject (having-to vs. being-able-to); and the axis of *endogenous* modalizations, the modalizations of the autonomous subject (knowing vs. wanting), respectively. Two modal schemata also emerge: *virtualizing* modalizations, or modalizations of the virtualized subject (having vs. wanting) and *actualizing* modalizations, modalizations of the actualized subject (knowing vs. being-able). Two deixes emerge as *stabilizing* modalizations (having vs. knowing) and *mobilizing* modalizations (being-able vs. wanting).

It would be useful, however, to keep in mind the tensive underpinnings of the modal organizations and its modulation of origin. First of all, the very thought of generating the four modalizations from an identical modal category makes sense only if this category has a homogeneous content – what is called a "semantic axis" in structural semantics. Now this content is basically the result of a summons of the thymic mass. In other words, and setting aside details related to the theoretical construction of the epistemological preconditions, we could say that as modalization stems from the thymic mass, it embodies the content of the modal category. Then it would be possible to deduce modal syntax of the passional configurations from the tensive modulations and the homogeneous interpretation can be proposed of all the modalizations.

Subject, Object, and Junction

In the preceding formulations, the different terms and the different relations uncovered within the modal category are essentially related to the subject, and not to the object and to junction. Nonetheless, this does not mean that the object and junction are not affected by modalization. On the contrary, syntactic subjects and objects of junction are not constituted before the modal category is divided into discrete elements. The only real subject at hand is the subject operator (of summons), but the only "object" that can be associated with him is the one assumed through summons, that is, a set of relations within a category – the semiotic square as formal cognitive object. Regarding the rest, we have been dealing only with "near subjects" and "shadows of value." Traditionally, subject and object are considered as undefinable, as end terms of the predicate relations considered as "orientation" or "intent". We should note here that "intent" was already defined as an "effect" resulting from the unilateral and tensive nature of orientation. From this perspective, in the space of phoria, subject and object can be considered as second degree effects (source effect and intent effect). The subject operator that is constituted through summons, eliminates the modulations that can outline the shadows of value (valencies), replacing them with the elementary structures of signification. Henceforth, within the category invoked, the said subject can cover states and transformations discontinuously by treating the different discrete terms (S_1, NON-S_1, S_2, NON-S_2) as different forms of junction (conjunction, nonconjunction, disjunction, nondisjunction). This description conforms to the procedure suggested earlier that makes becoming discrete. But then, the object is basically a syntactic form that appears as different positions open to the subject within the category. Consequently, it will be defined at this level as a set of syntactic categories that appear as simple constraints imposed on the subject's trajectory. The "participatory" character of a syntactic object would be, for example, such a property, since it determines a type of junction.

It is therefore necessary to assume after the first summons that, under the impetus of a prior dynamics, the new subject operator pursues an itinerary without yet knowing the outcome. We can state here that protensivity is *recursive* and that, if the summons remains in force and converts its modulations, it does not affect its dynamic orientation. The two syntactic actants, subject and object, are therefore set in place by means of this recursive dynamic orientation, the former as the operator of the forces of transformation from one position to another, and the latter as the set of properties (the rules of the game, so to speak) specific to each of the positions adopted successively. Henceforth, as a matter of priority, modalization stemming from the modulations of becoming characterizes the "rules of the game" or the "properties" characteristic of each place occupied by the subject, but not the subject himself. As a matter of fact, having freed himself from fluctuations of phoria by the first summons, the subject operator is no longer animated by a "dynamic orientation" maintained at this level. On the other hand, during our analyses of avarice and jealousy, we shall readily demonstrate that the underlying modulations (for example, the "retensive" modulation for the miser) appear as syntactic properties that overdetermine such and such a position of junction (a cumulative conjunction with indestructible objects, or a nondisjunction with objects that are supposed to circulate). The *valencies* are consequently partially converted into properties of syntactic objects.

From Valency to Value

The question that remains to be asked is the one related to the formation of *objects of value*. Indeed, the term "value" is used in two different ways in semiotics:[3] "value" that buttresses a life project, and "value" in the structural sense, as understood by Saussure, for example. It is through reconciling these two meanings that we can coin the concept of the object of value: an object that gives "direction" (an axiological orientation) to a life project and an object that signifies through difference, in opposition to other objects. The emergence of the object of value, in fact, depends on what happens with valencies. A valency is a "shadow" that incites the "presentiment" of a value. The syntactic object is a form, the "contour" of an object comparable to the one the subject projects when perceiving the gestalt, and which co-defines the subject. The object of value is a semantically invested syntactic object. However—and this is the crucial point—the semantic investment depends on a categorization stemming from valency itself. For example, it is clear that Vinteuil's phrase does not in itself propose an object of value. It first of all designates a valency, through summons; from this valency a type of syntactic object then emerges as "valuable for the subject" without our being able to determine exactly its semantic investment:

> Swann found, in the memory of the phrase that he had heard, . . . the presence of one of those invisible realities that he had ceased believing in, and to which, as though the music had exerted a kind of elective influence on the moral drought he suffered from, he once again felt the desire and almost the strength to devote his life. (*A la recherche du temps perdu*, p. 208)

Once these determinations have been established, any content can invest the place so defined, as long as it conforms to valency. For Swann it will be love, and this love will satisfy the conditions imposed by Vinteuil's phrase. If, semantically speaking, the syntactic subject can be defined by the value aspired to, it is because this value obeys the same criteria imposed by the valency—valency, as we saw, controlling the syntactic properties of the positions adopted by the subject. We could say, in a way, that in this case subject and object select one another reciprocally, the subject because he imposes syntactic properties on the object selected protensively, and the object because it semanticizes the subject, valency being the regulating criterion of this encounter.

The semantic investment, acknowledged as conforming to valency, cursively receives the "attractions/repulsions" that characterize phoria and that, now polarized, constitute an axiology.

Actantial Structures

The subject and object actants that emerged at the previous stage, at the narrative level, become "protoactants" that can in turn be projected on the semiotic square and treated as categories. The principle of the categorization of the protoactant is well known and can occupy four major positions (Figure 2.) We can hence engender the actantial models that are fundamental in the establishment of the *polemicocontractual structures*. Their appearance, in a certain way, reiterates the first "stirring of meaning," since the separation between the "near subject" and

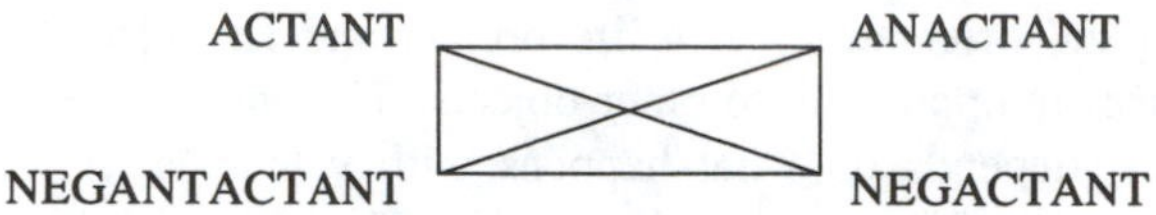

Figure 2

the "shadow of value" that was interpreted as the emergence of fiducia and of protensivity could be attributed equally to the intervention of a form of adversity (we cannot yet speak of the antisubject at this level). The very principle of an indefinite cohabitation between contractual structures and polemic structures is already at play within phoria, since we have located there both cohesive and dispersive tendencies that can be interpreted as either favoring or dissuading the advent of signification. At the level of semionarrative structures, the principle of polemic takes on two different aspects: either the subjects aspire to the same object of value, and, insofar as they share the same system of values, they compete with one another; or, different value systems being invested in their narrative programs, they are in conflict. Moreover, Jean Petitot[4] has suggested that, in emphasizing various strata of the catastrophe of conflict, contrariety between two terms of a category could function either as a polemic relation between subject and antisubject or as difference between two objects.

Two different problems must be identified. The first concerns the appearance, in the generative trajectory, of polemicocontractual relations as such. The fiducia space mentioned earlier could provide us with an adequate point of departure for the contractual communication of objects. A modulation of becoming, affecting fiducia, could adequately explain the appearance of polemic relations, especially if one acknowledges that the aforementioned scission of the "one" can engender either the pair "subject/object" or a pair of "intersubjects," whose interplay of attractions/repulsions prefigures polemicocontractual relations. This hypothesis is interesting from more than one point of view. First of all, it elucidates a phenomenon, related to the transformations of subjects into objects, that is often described but rarely explained. The object becomes subject because it resists, hides from, refuses the subject of the quest, by a sort of projection on the object of the "obstacles" encountered by the subject. The antisubject in a way is ensconced in the figure-object, and more particularly with respect to an impassioned subject. If the conversion object → subject is accompanied by a polemical effect, it seems that this is because it presupposes a reversion to the tensive scission and to the stage of "intersubjects." Next, it enables one to account for one of the aspects of the second problem we raised previously.

This second problem is the one we would like to deal with now—that is, the categorization of protoactants and, subsequently, the categorization of polemicocontractual structures. For the time being, they can be described as shown in Figure 3.

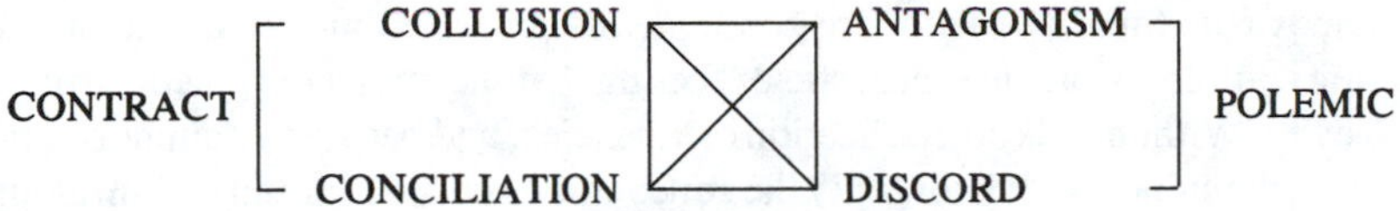

Figure 3

The cohabitation of contractual and polemical structures is constant and sometimes critical in the passional universe. As a matter of fact, many passions will appear as the staking out of a contractual zone in a polemical universe – for example, "emulation," which appears as a contractual parenthesis, and fair play, accompanied with a possible reward, within a domain of rivalry. Inversely, other passions confirm the eruption of polemic in a contractual universe. This is the case with "anger," which gives rise to frustration within a contractual and peaceful horizon. This sort of interplay between the polemical and the contractual (which makes life bearable in a way), between uneventful peace and uncontrollable rift, could be described as the result of aspectualization occurring in discourse. It can be explained, however, only through reexamination of phoric tensivity.

If we assume that the polemicocontractual structures are prefigured during scission and the first stirring of meaning, it can be shown that they follow a logic of approximations and of overlapping. We can easily demonstrate that a passion such as "conservatism" in nineteenth-century novels, in particular with Balzac and Stendhal – but not only in novels – by opposing the flux of political and historical becoming, with resistance (a "deceleration") from this retensive modulation, creates a conflictual zone from which all political and social antagonisms will stem. This vision of things, which indirectly borrows the idea of a complex term from Viggo Brøndal, presupposes within the polemicocontractual structures proper a mixed form governed by variable dominancies. Insofar as variations of dominance invariably occur in a continuous mode, because of the increase of the influence of a term (accompanied by a corresponding decrease in the influence of another), they confirm their adhesion to the tensive modulations of phoria. In light of these observations, the system (categorial) of the polemicocontractual could be rethought in terms of a series of inequalities wherein each position would be seen as a new equilibrium within variations of dominance. The trajectory on the square would therefore be seen as a succession of inversions of dominance between polemic and contractual forms.

The object protoactant reflects the categorization of the systems of value. After the binarization of phoria, the "shadows of value" marked by euphoria and dysphoria are projected onto the semiotic square. In the relation between tensive subject and valencies, it did not make sense to distinguish between "antiobjects" and "nonobjects," insofar as at this level the object had a fuzzy contour. But after categorization, the multivalency of objects appears, making "good" and "bad" objects come to the fore. The latter are consequently polarized independently of the attraction and repulsion characteristic of feeling that the subject projects through protensivity. Without this objectification of valencies, and because of euphoria and dysphoria, the subject will know only the zones valorized for him and by him along the generative trajectory. These will be experienced as attractive or repulsive, but will not accede to the status of an autonomous axiology. Many passional stories are characterized by a trajectory of the misadventures of the object. For example, at the moment the narrator of *A la recherche* is about to marry Albertine, she becomes a "nonobject," a source of boredom and lassitude that he contemplates leaving. Then, after the revelation of her relations with Mlle de Vinteuil and her friend, she becomes an "antiobject" that he can no longer do without. An affliction, we read in the text, is enough to draw her closer to the narrator – better yet, to "meld" him with her. Here thymic categorization appears independently both of junction and of attraction/repulsion. As a matter of fact, although explicitly dysphoric, this antiobject – the friend of lesbians – is attractive and reactivates the subject's protensivity. Love is reborn from this paradox. In other words, the independence acquired by the axiologies permits several levels of modalization, at the risk of the subject being confronted by insoluble dilemmas. In this example, junction continues to be governed by a modalization of the syntactic object bolstered by a "valency" (that is to say, a "there is something here that is worthwhile doing . . . "), whereas axiology modalizes the object of value as dysphoric.

It is as though the generative trajectory of signification was governed by both cumulative and mnemic rules. The generative procedure does not "forget" the properties of one level at the following level, in the same way as the properties from one level do not obliterate those of the previous one. Categorization of the object of value does not prevent the preexisting logics of approximation and overlapping to continue to make their effects felt. Under certain conditions, many categorized objects of value maintain a level of ambiguity. For example, in the discourse of general practitioners about diabetes, "sugar" can appear either as a positive object that is euphoric in a narrative program of nutrition, or as a negative object, an actual poison – the source of diabetes – at a discursive antilevel. But excess and measure are not properties intrinsic to the object, as the positive or negative effect of the object is related to the sensitivity (physiological) of subjects. We are tempted to compare this function with certain magic potions that can both multiply the faculties of the hero ingurgitating them and destroy those who are unworthy or who are not its predestined receivers. Euphoric as such, the object is nevertheless harmful to the subject. Ambivalence here is a characteristic of the complex term, since the two modalizations do not occur at the same level. One affects the object itself, the other the junction with the subject. We can account for it only if we assume that discourse expresses both the results of categorization and objectivation of the systems of value, as well as valencies defining the value of the "world-for-the-subject."

Modal Subjects

In the process of progressive complexification in which we are now engaged, the recursivity of the operations is critical. Each new conversion (summons, discretization, categorization, etc.) is applied to the results of the previous one, thus reducing the underlying categories or entities. Hence, modalizations affect actants, in particular the subject, through the intermediary of the modalizations of the object and of junction. To start with, we shall identify a subject proper to each type of narrative utterance: a subject of state and a subject of doing, according to whether junctions are considered as results or as operations, as "phases" or as "paths." We shall posit the principle and the working hypothesis, namely, that in the general economy of the theory, passions pertain to the "being" of the subject, and not to his "doing." But this does not mean that passions have nothing to do with activity or with the subject of activity, if only because the latter also has a "being," which is his competence. In the final analysis, a subject affected by passion will therefore always be a modalized subject of "being"—that is, a subject considered as a *subject of state*—even if he happens to be engaged in activity. This question has been raised elsewhere, and there we reduced it to the distinction between *states of affairs* and *states of feelings*, and proposed a procedure of homogenization founding passion and founded on the mediation of the feeling-perceiving body.

Passion and Doing. We should be aware, however, that the subject's passion can result from a doing, either by another subject (such as "fury") and that it can lead to an act, to what psychiatrists call "taking action." For example, "enthusiasm" and "despair" program a subject of potential doing on the pathemic dimension, either to create or to destroy. Passion itself, insofar as it appears as second-degree discourse, can in itself be considered as *an act*, in the sense that, for example, we speak of a "speech act." The activity of an impassioned subject is not without similarity to that of a discursive subject, which he can be substituted for, in actual fact. In this case passional discourse as a series of pathemic acts interferes with receptive discourse—life as such, so to speak—and perturbs or inflects it. Moreover, when analyzed, passion appears to be constituted syntactically as a series of activities: manipulations, seductions, tortures, investigations, construction of scenarios, and so on. From this point of view, and at this level of analysis, passional syntax is not unlike pragmatic or cognitive syntax. It takes the form of *narrative programs*, whereby a pathemic operator transforms pathemic states. We do encounter difficulties, however, when we begin to examine interferences between the various dimensions.

The Being of Doing. To come back to modalizations proper, and to subjects of state that can be affected by passion, we shall begin by distinguishing two kinds. Certain subjects are modalized in relation to the modal values invested in objects, according to a procedure that we have already mentioned. Others will be modalized with an activity in mind, at the level of competence. In the past, this distinction was accounted for by the terminological opposition we established between *modal competence* and *modal existence*. It seems evident, for example, that the subject of "envy" is a pure subject of state that becomes a modal subject only through the intermediary of the wanting-to-be conveyed by the object of value, or even, possibly, by the mediation of a rival. In order to understand "envy" it is not necessary to reduce it to competence *stricto sensu*. On the contrary, the description of "emulation" cannot do without a certain representation of doing and of the modalities necessary to carry it out. The imitator is a modal subject only because of the specific program in which his competence is engaged and put into question. Nevertheless it is always possible to translate modalizations of the second type into terms of the first according to the procedure of homogenization we have envisaged. As a matter of fact, "emulation" establishes a *wanting-to-do* "as-well-or-better-than-the-other"; but here this *wanting-to-do* proceeds from a *wanting-to-be* "him-or-as-he-who-does"—that is, an identification with a certain modal state of the other. In other words, the intent of emulation is to reproduce not the other's program but rather the modal "image" projected by the other in carrying out his program, whatever it happens to be. A "state of affairs," the other's competence, is thus converted into a "state of feeling," the modal image proposed for itself by the subject of emulation.

Along with the modalization of the subject by the intermediary of the object or junction, within the confines of a semiotics of passions, we need to envision the modalization of the subject through the intermediary of the program of activity in which he is engaged. Regardless of the first-order subject in question, subject of state, or subject of doing, passion is also concerned with a *second-order subject, the modal subject* that ensues. Whether the modal mass evolves in relation to the successive avatars of junction, or the evolution of the program, the modal subject appears as a series of different modal identities. According to whether the object is modalized as "desirable," "useful," or "necessary," the subject's modal resources will change and he will undergo *a series of transitory modal identities*, which can be represented as follows:

$$S \rightarrow s1,\ s2,\ s3,\ .\ .\ .\ Sn.$$

where "1, 2, 3, . . . *n*" represent successive modal masses. These modal subjects are necessary in establishing the modal transformations we will need to postulate within passional configurations.

Modes of Existence and Existential Simulacra. Furthermore, in narrative semiotics we have identified a series of roles of the subject that characterize various *modes of existence of the narrative actant* during his transformations. In its most common usage, this series is limited to three roles, each of which is founded on a type of junction:

virtualized subject (nonconjoined)
↓
actualized subject (disjoined)
↓
realized subject (conjoined)

Nevertheless, if we take into account the different terms that can be constructed from the category of junction, we note the existence of a fourth position, nondisjunction, which does not appear in the inventory of the modes of existence (see Figure 4).

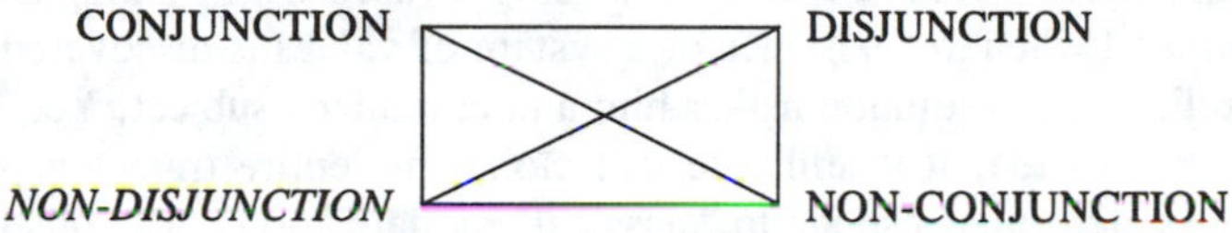

Figure 4

As the modes of existence of the surface syntax subject are defined in relation to the position of that subject within the category of junction, we can consider that "nondisjunction" also defines a position and a mode of existence of the subject that have not been noted until now. We propose to call this role "potentialized subject" insofar as it results from a negation of the actualized subject and where it is presupposed by the realized subject. Two questions arise from this.

The first question, which obliges us to reexamine what we have proposed, concerns the use that can be made of the term and of the notion encompassed within the general economy of the theory. In fact, from the perspective of a semiotic theory considered as a trajectory of the construction of semiotic existence, modes of existence characterize the various stages of this construction and mark off the pathway of the epistemological subject from the deep level to the discursive manifestation. It is within this epistemological framework that the subject of discourse can be said to be "realized," whereas the narrative subject is only "actualized." As far as the subject operator of the elementary structures of signification is concerned, it is "virtualized." Following our previous attempts to establish and conceptualize a level prior to the elementary structures of signification, it is tempting to retain the role of "potentialized subject" for the tensive subject that appears in phoric space. The "near subject" is a potential subject. It can be both converted into a virtualized/actualized subject by a dual negation-summons, and convoked directly during the setting into discourse realizing the discursive impassioned subject. But this affectation is not self-evident. Situated between actualized and realized subjects within the syntax established from the category of junction, the potentialized subject in this case would appear at the beginning of the trajectory, before the virtualized subject. We shall reexamine this difficulty.

The second question deals with the relation between the modal subjects defined earlier. It is clear that the modes of existence of the subject of narrative syntax should not be mixed with the modes of existence to which we have alluded. Nor do they necessarily coincide with those at the syntactic level. We know, for example, that syntax is converted into narrative anthropomorphic syntax at the moment of the acquisition of competence; wanting and having-to determine a "virtualized" subject, whereas knowing and being-able determine an "actualized" subject. For the subject in question to be "realized," performance must come into play. For want of more concrete analyses, it is difficult to see what place could be assigned now to the potentialized subject on this trajectory. For the time being, we could imagine that the subject of quest, before being infused with wanting and having-to, is instituted when the existence of a system of values is discovered, and that such a preliminary institution makes him a potentialized subject. Yet, no matter the solution adopted, it is still true that along this entire trajectory, only two modes of existence correspond to "classical" modalizations. The other two, the "potentialized subject" and the "realized subject," do not seem to fall under the canonical series of the four modalities. We could also note that the institution, linked with the "presentiment of the value," is not foreign to modalization, be it even modalization related to fiducia. In this case we would be dealing with belief. Likewise, performance has no modal effect, since activity can be apprehended at the second degree as the *being of doing*. Intuitively, this would correspond to the difference that exists between an "acting" subject, a first-degree subject of doing, and an "active" subject, the subject of the being of doing, apprehended at the second degree. In other words, the so-called active subject's being is characterized by the realization of performance itself, a characterization that in no way bears on "modal competence" proper.

These brief observations lead us to believe that impassioned subjects cannot be defined solely in terms of the four modalizations generally identified, specifically within the framework of competence with the view toward doing. For example, we will speak about "hyperactivity" to designate a modalized state that owes nothing in particular to wanting, knowing, being-able, having-to, or believing, but that is nonetheless sensitized and called upon as a criterion for identifying a certain state of anxiety.

Independently of the modal masses defined in terms of the modal categories (wanting, being-able, etc.), the impassioned subject can be "modalized" by the modes of existence, which amounts to saying that *junction per se* is a first modalization. Apprehended independently of any passional configuration, the mode of existence simply corresponds to a certain stage in the trajectory of narrative transformations; but, within passional configurations, it becomes modalizing for the subject. As an example, let us briefly examine "humility." Is the "humble" person who considers herself willingly as insufficient necessarily incompetent, stupid, or idiotic? Without getting involved in a religious-ethical discussion, we could point out that humility does not characterize the existence of a state of affairs but rather a mode of existence characteristic of a state of feeling. In other words, whether the humble person happens to be poor or rich, disjoined or conjoined, what is important is the disjunction in which she represents herself and toward which she leans.

To differentiate between the two types of functioning, it would be appropriate, undoubtedly, to designate them in two different ways. The expression "modes of existence" shall designate what it has in semiotics until now, and we shall use the term "existential simulacra" for the subject's projections into a passional imaginary.

Modal Subjects and Existential Simulacra. The relative independence of existential simulacra and of specific modal masses should not dissimulate the fact that such simulacra can be constituted only by means of modal masses. For example, except for passional configurations, an actualized subject is a disjoined subject, and this disjunction can be seen not only from his point of view but throughout the entire enunciated discourse. But in the case of "apprehension" inherent in *wanting-not-to-be*, if the subject can project himself as "actualized" and disjoined, it is not in relation to a state of affairs but *by the intermediary of the modal mass of "wanting."* Likewise, with "avidity," if the subject can be represented as "realized" and conjoined, regardless of his position with respect to the state of affairs, and therefore, regardless of the mode of effective existence that affects him, this all depends on the effect of the modal mass. The examination of modal existential simulacra leads us to set out a fundamental role for modal masses in the constitution of passional imaginaries. By inserting itself between the narrative utterance and its effectuation in discourse, the modal mass opens up an imaginary semiotic space where passional discourse can unfold. From this perspective, the passional "imaginaries," far from stemming from a possible psyche of individual subjects, result from properties of the semionarrative level, generally recognized as the semiotic form of the human imaginary, in the anthropological rather than psychological sense of the term.

This is why the comparison of the two series, *transitory modal identities* and *existential simulacra,* will be one of the procedures of the analysis of passions. In fact, the principal modal mass characterizing a passional subject does not necessarily and directly give rise to all the existential simulacra needed to interpret its trajectory. For example, a "terrorized" subject is characterized by a *wanting-not-to-be*, but its imaginary trajectory is founded on a conjunction (dreaded) with an antiobject, that is, on the dysphoric image of a realized subject, in the imaginary space opened up by the modal mass of wanting, the virtualized state presupposing an actualized state. The latter, in turn, is overdetermined by a prospective believing, a dysphoric expectation modalizing it, and so on. In addition, the superimposition of these two series would have some heuristic value.

Simulacra

The emergence of a "modal imaginary" obliges us to examine the status of the passional dimension of discourse. Indeed, passion *presents* within the host discourse a set of data both tensive and figurative, as is the case, for example, with nostalgia for a situation that was or could have been, or jealousy, for a stereotypical situation, bringing together the object of love and the rival, creating a strong apprehension. In numerous cases, we are obliged to note that passion is indifferent to the mode of effective existence assigned to the subject in the state of affairs. Nostalgia and regret for a moment past can very well overcome a perfectly happy subject.

Modal Simulacra. This is why, within the framework of the semiotics of passions, the establishment of modal subjects must be accompanied by a theory of modal simulacra. This theory can have as point of departure a more general observation, consisting in noting the great instability of actantial roles in passional configurations. In the passion of love, for example, we see the loved object transformed into a subject. This is all the more impressive when the object in question is not an animated being, in the narrative of the fantastic, among others, but also more tritely in fetishistic behavior. Curiosity also tends to transform its object into a subject, even into an antisubject that resists, flees, dissimulates, and so on. There is also no want of misers who treat their "coffers" as subjects, as actual alter egos. In short, in passion the object has a tendency to become the subject-partner of the impassioned subject. Hence the hypothesis that the only generalizable structure to describe passion is an intersubjective structure, or, more precisely, a structure wherein each objectal relation encompasses potential intersubjectivity, a sort of fuzzily contoured interactantiality. We shall attempt to demonstrate, with respect to avarice, which seemingly manifests itself as a passion of objects, as the prototype of solitary passion, that, in fact, it comprehends an intersubjective (de)regulation, and that what could be taken for the properties of objects is, in fact, simply a set of rules that functions within a community of subjects.

The instability of the roles reveals the dissociation between two semiotic universes: that of the host discourse of passion and that of passion itself. An "object" for the former, the coffer, becomes a "subject" for the miser in the latter case. The impassioned subject can be split into an "effective" subject on the one hand (manifested as such in the host discourse) and subject of state "simulated" in the passional configuration, as projected into a second-degree representation. This splitting of the subject into two instances is particularly clear in the case of "obstinacy," where an external observer compares a subject of state effectively disjoined and an impassioned subject whose simulacrum is that of a realized subject, and concludes that the two instances are heterogeneous. It is nonetheless true, however, that for the obstinate person, conjunction remains an important consideration, whereas it seems highly unlikely in the host discourse. In one way or another, the semiotics of passions must account for this imaginary splitting. It is clear that the discursive overlapping mentioned earlier, even if accompanied with operations of engagement and disengagement, is an economical way of presenting things, since it is not simply an enunciative delegation among others, but a very specific splitting.[5]

The notion of modal subjects resulting both from modalizations acquired during the generative trajectory of signification and the modulations of tensivity provides us with a temporary solution. It does appear that the effects of the thymic mass as such, while undergoing a categorical conversion, continue to coexist in discourse with the product of this conversion, and in particular with modalization proper. One of the consequences of this tensive remanence is to provide the subject, who has become the subject-operator, then syntactic subject, subject of the quest and subject of discourse, with the possibility of projecting complex actantial and modal representations, that is to say, once again, to appear as a mixed category.

This possibility occurs in discourse by means of a dual *convocation:* on the one hand, the summons of the semionarrative forms of subjectivity; on the other, of the tensive actantial forms. Hence, this results in what metapsychology would call an effect of "internalization." Starting from an impassioned subject that is apparently unique and homogeneous, this makes it possible to project actual passional "scenarios" with several actantial roles and several interactional modal subjects. Modal subjects, as we have defined them, both determined by the modalizations of the subjects of doing and subjects of state, while nevertheless maintaining their status of being autonomous, become the instruments of passional duality.

Passional Simulacra. Such a conception is not without consequences on the theory of communication and interaction as a whole. Once they have been identified, we can opt for either of two extensions of these "simulacra." In a restricted version (for example, the one that has been alluded to until now), we consider that the simulacrum is a configuration resulting only from the opening up of an imaginary space by the modal masses affecting the subject. The existential simulacra and the "imaginary" changes of the actantial roles—that is, everything that affects the syntactic representation of the utterances of junction—are the principal properties of these simulacra in the restricted sense. In discourse, they appear as effects of localized disengagements by which the impassioned subject establishes scenes of his own "imaginary" in the discursive chain. The comparison of utterances shifted out and utterances shifted in can give rise to judgments of an epistemological and veridictory nature. But then one is basically confined to an interpretation in terms of discursive veridiction.

In a more radical version, one that would have the merit of drawing all the consequences from the features uncovered during our analysis of passions, the status of the interlocutors or of the interactants in communication in general could be put into question. This putting into question already occurs when, in sociolinguistics or in psycholinguistics, one affirms that each speaker constructs his own discourse, even adapts his own vernacular, to the "images" his interlocutor projects, as well as those that he has of himself. To draw all the consequences from the analysis of passions is to posit that all communication is communication (and interaction) between modal and passional simulacra. Each one addresses his own simulacrum to the other's simulacrum, which all the interactants, along with the cultures to which they belong, have contributed to constructing. Such a position simply consolidates the suggestions stated, at the epistemological level, on the way of conceiving intersubjectivity when the tensive subject splits into the "other" and internalizes *the other body* as an "intersubject" on the backdrop of fiducia.

The simulacra of interacting actors are, for the most part, aggregations of figurativized and sensitized modal subjects. Two consequences come to mind. First of all, the functioning characteristic of the passional universe, consisting of imaginary projections of sensitized modal subjects, far from being an ad hoc descriptive mechanism, is basically a particular case of interaction in general. Second, all communication is virtually passional, if only because all one needs is that one of the modal simulacra used in interaction be sensitized, in the culture of at least one of the interlocutors, for the totality of the interaction to be affected. This extended version of the simulacra, which shall now be designated as "passional simulacra," integrates the totality of the subjects' modal devices. In the restricted version, it is the modal mass (external to the simulacrum itself) that opens the imaginary space of the impassioned subject; whereas in the extended version, communication as a whole is founded on the circulation of the simulacra.

Narrative Actants and the Passions

We have scarcely mentioned, except incidentally and indirectly, the anthropomorphic actantial structures that, along with the object of value and the subject of the quest, organize, on the axis of the communication of values, the Sender and the Receiver. These two roles will not be very useful to us here. For even if the Receiver is directly concerned with passions, the establishment of the subject(s) of state suffices most of the time to deal economically with the passional configurations. As for the Sender, his role is considerably diminished by passion.

Whether or not the Sender happens to be at the origin of the program, we note that the passion of the subject is all one needs to develop the said program, so much so that he appears to be autonomous with respect to possible Mandators or Manipulators. This does not mean, however, that the Sender cannot establish passions in the subject. It only means that, much in the same way the monster escapes from Dr. Frankenstein, the impassioned subject eludes the control of his Sender, a passional disposition having been substituted for the Sender's making-to-do.

Such a functioning is easy to understand once the difference between phoric space and value system, or between valency and object of value, has been acknowledged. For the impassioned subject, the object is always governed by valency, and fiducia is enveloped within the first outlines of the object. In other words, it still functions *grosso modo* as a projection of the subject's protensivity. However, within a nonpassional narrative framework, the institution of an object of value within a system of values stems from objectivization, which delineates, so to speak, the place of the Sender. Obviously these two functionings can be combined, but the impassioned subject will always tend to suppress any reference to the Sender. This suppression, which can be simply temporary, is one of the conditions for the autonomous evolution of passional syntax.

Yet, discursive analysis brings to the fore the major classes of passions founded on the typology of narrative actants, and on the various roles they adopt in following the successive stages of the canonical narrative schema. For example, it would be possible to envisage passions of the subject of quest, either at the moment of the contract, as "enthusiasm," or during performance, as "tenacity." There are also passions of sanction, either from the perspective of a Sender, as "esteem" or "contempt," or even "fury," in the sacred meaning of the term, or from the perspective of the Receiver, as "despair." Such a classification is unsatisfactory although, at best, it enables one to situate specific passions within a more general problematics; but, after analysis of concrete discourses, it seems that any actant can take up any one of the passional configurations. For example, a subject of quest can also experience fury or contempt. This would tend to prove that the impassioned subject is grounded in a "protoactant" that has "internalized" all the actantial roles and, consequently, in the throes of passion, can adopt any one of them independently of the effective actantial role attributed to him on the pragmatic or cognitive dimension.

Moreover, what we traditionally call "narrative structures" are the products of two different levels: as syntactic universals narrative actants belong to the semionarrative level, as do their modalizations; the canonical narrative schema, however, is only a generalizable structure, undoubtedly peculiar to certain specific cultural domains, and at the semionarrative level it assumes a fundamental role because of enunciative praxis. As for the passions themselves, the narrative question arises also at two levels. On the one hand, we shall attempt to set up, along with the pragmatic and cognitive dimensions, an autonomous thymic dimension, by seeking to establish a passional functioning proper of the actants and modalizations situated at the semionarrative level; and on the other, we have to ask if a *canonical pathemic schema* can be conceived and constructed, as a generalizable structure. If, at the semionarrative level, we succeed in demonstrating the autonomy of the dimension on which passional transformations unfold, during the analysis of texts we can expect to outline progressively a discursive schema sufficiently general to account for various stages of passion and organize them into "narratives." But before envisioning such generalizations, which require numerous concrete analyses, we should examine first of all the setting into discourse of passional modalizations and arrangements.

Modal Arrangements: From Arrangement to Disposition

The Modal Regulation of Being

Most passional configurations are defined in standard dictionaries as "tendency to," "feeling that leads to," "the inner state of one who is inclined to," followed by the description of the "tendency" or "inclination" in terms of behavior or action. If the tendency or inclination leads to a "doing," we can legitimately suppose that it implies a certain regulation of "being" with a view toward "doing." However, to raise the question of the efficacy of passion in these terms is basically to consider it as competence, modalizations of which would produce ipso facto a passional meaning effect.

Passional Surplus. If we confined ourselves to this, the passional universe would be coextensive to the modal universe, and it would not be necessary to distinguish and, a fortiori, to attempt to fathom the principles of their articulation. Even when passion can be expressed in part as a "competence to do," this neither exhausts nor explains fully the passional effect. For example, "impulsiveness" can be translated as a certain association of *wanting-to-do* and *being-able-to-do*, and then described as a "way of doing." But such a passion ends up with a modal "surplus" that appears on the surface as a variant of the "intensive" and of the "inchoative." What characterizes the impulsive person is rather a way of being while doing, a way of being (i.e., "intensive" + "inchoative") based on the association of *wanting-to-do* + *being-able-to-do*. In this case we encounter the major principle of homogenization referred to previously, insofar as competence to do is treated here as a state. Yet, this modal "surplus" has a role that makes it much more than a simple supplement of meaning. For if we envisage only impulsive "behavior," the dual feature "intensive" + "inchoative" appears as a simple accidental overdetermination of base modal competence. But if, on the other hand, the subject is characterized as being "impulsive," we then consider that this overdetermination *governs and pathemizes modal competence* and ensures its actualization in all circumstances. More precisely, it is as though, in this specific case, modal surplus enabled us to anticipate the concomitant appearance of wanting and being-able, and, in a way, ensured the actualization of the act.

Insofar as the previous observation can be generalized, the passional configuration will be governed by a regulating principle that is partially independent of modalizations proper, and more specifically the modalizations of doing. At least in the preceding example, this principle appears in the form of an aspectualization, and at the level of tensive modulations evokes a specific "semiotic style." This is why it seems necessary in all cases to refer back to an autonomous modal regulation of being, which cannot be deduced directly from performance, and to consider it as a modal arrangement that is characteristic of each passional meaning effect defining it.

The Paradoxes of "Obstinacy." Another example will enable us to illustrate and clarify this position. "Obstinacy," defined as a "disposition to carry on in a single-minded way, without being discouraged by obstacles," offers us the particularity of maintaining the subject *in a state of continuing to do*, even if the success of the enterprise is jeopardized. The "tendency" in question puts the subject in the state of "doing in spite of *X*," including when *X* is an expectation about the impossibility of doing. For this the subject must be endowed with the following modalizations:

a *knowing-not-how-to-be* (the subject knows that he is disjoined from his object);
a *being-able-not-to-be* or a *not-being-able-to-be* (the success of the enterprise is jeopardized);
a *wanting-to-be* (the subject wants nevertheless to be conjoined, and will do everything to this end).

Although the definition itself happens to be oriented by a project of doing, the modal arrangement characteristic of the passion "obstinacy" is constituted by modalizations of being. As a matter of fact, a simple *wanting-to-do* could not explain the indefatigable pursuit of action in this case, since innumerable other examples can be found where, in spite of the presence of a *wanting-to- do* presupposed by doing, the subject abandons his program and gives up when confronted by an obstacle. It is therefore the regulating "modal surplus" specifically characterizing obstinacy that ensures the pursuit of performance in spite of the obstacle. It is also the presence of this surplus that leads us to formulate the passional arrangement in terms of the "modal regulation of being" rather than in terms of "competence with the view toward doing."

This passion is particularly interesting, as it accumulates a couple of paradoxes: a *wanting-to-do* that outlasts a *not-being-able-to-do* and uses it to reinforce itself; and an ongoing doing whereby everything is decided within a certain regulation of being. We must suppose here that the two syntactic segments, the one pertaining to the modal syntax of doing and the other to the modal passional syntax, are both autonomous and linked to one another. This specific articulation appears as an aspectual form—"to continue," "to resist"—that is also the expression of a "semiotic style" that makes becoming remain open-ended. Moreover, it is now clear that the modalizations of being characteristic of the passional configuration are not exactly the modalizations of competence for doing, but instead constitute a "representation," a "virtual image"—that is to say, a simulation. In the passional simulation of obstinacy, the obstinate person "wants to be the person who does," which is not the same as he "wants to do."

Two problems immediately arise that shall be addressed briefly. On the one hand, we are led to wonder how a modal inventory such as the previous one is organized as an "arrangement"; on the other, we must try to define the status of the "disposition" as "potentiality" of behaviors or programs.

One of the corollaries of these two questions again consists in asking if the description of the arrangement, this regulation of being that we postulated as characterizing each passion, satisfactorily deals with disposition and can adequately account for the impassioned subject, or if, possibly, it adds something essential to our understanding of passional behavior. The emphatic presence of aspectual forms and of "semiotic styles" encourages us to examine the question more closely.

Superficially, "dispositions" appear as kinds of discursive programs that can commute with thematic roles. Such an observation does not, however, constitute an answer to the question at hand, insofar as the phenomenon we are attempting to define, between modalizations of being and of doing, once again is, so it seems, specific to the semionarrative level.

Description of the Modal Arrangement

The modalization underlying passions is not organized like a modal structure. On the one hand, competence that leads to doing is progressively constituted. Each modalization affecting doing constitutes a modal predicate (*wanting-to-do*, for example) that can be treated as a modal category and projected onto the semiotic square. In a way, the modal structure is a means of describing the mode of being of modalities, resulting both from the projection of this modality on the elementary structures of signification and from the distinction between being and doing, following a procedure that has already been described. Hence, "desirability," projected on the square, generates variations of *wanting-to-be*.

On the other hand, by definition a modal arrangement is a heterotopic ensemble on which, at the level of modalizations proper, it is impossible to project a categorizing model such as the semiotic square. The arrangement is not a structure but the intersection of several structures with several terms organized according to a principle that has yet to be described. The same holds true for the competence of the pragmatic subject of doing, for, though we may know how to describe each modalization taken separately, we certainly do not know how to describe the subject's trajectory from one modalization to another, that is to say the way in which competence is progressively constituted before leading to doing. The solution proposed by Jean-Claude Coquet,[6] of a modal series governed by presupposition and determination, is a first step in the right direction. However, we still must examine how modalities are transformed one into another within these series. If we consider the case only of the heteronomous subject that happens to be under the mandate of the Sender, the solution is to examine the trajectory proper of the Sender, who, accompanying the subject in the acquisition of competence, plays the role of "attributor" and transmits the necessary modal objects to him. But as soon as we deal with an autonomous subject, even provisionally, the series of modalities can no longer be explained by external intervention, and can result only from an intrinsic dynamics.

More on Obstinacy. To illustrate the difficulty, let us reexamine obstinacy. We can obtain the modal arrangement through the intersection of three modal structures: *knowing-how-to-be, being-able-to-be*, and *wanting-to-be*. But this conjunction of modal categories becomes an arrangement only if two types of relations come into play. First of all, as terms of a structure, the modalizations will enter into relations either of contrariety, contradiction, presupposition, or conformity. Thus, in obstinacy, *wanting-to-be* contradicts *being-able-not-to-be*, or is the contrary of *not-being-able-to-be*, whereas *knowing-not-how-to-be* presupposes *not-being-able-to-be*, or conforms to *being-able-not-to-be*. Then, as a set of terms that can be organized linearly, the arrangement must be organized according to a principle of presupposition. Here, for example, *knowing-how-not-to-be* presupposes *being-able-not-to-be*, and *wanting-to-be* presupposes, paradoxically, the two others. The paradox, in this case, stems from the projection onto the syntagmatic axis (governed by presupposition) of relations of nonconformity. Thus linearized, the arrangement will appear as a modal series:

/being-able-not-to-be. knowing-how-not-to-be. wanting-to-be./

The first difficulty stems from the existence of a "paradoxical presupposition." Such an expression is a true oxymoron in semiotics. In its most general logical sense, a presupposition is a relation that links two propositions, in such a way that the negation or falsification of the presupposer does not cast doubt on the presupposed. In semiotics, this definition by negation is replaced, most specifically for syntactic presuppositions, by the notion of necessity. This is why the fact that an utterance is necessary for its own negation, by contrariety or by contradiction, is, in a way, paradoxical. From the numerous varieties of presuppositions they noted, Umberto Eco and Patricia Violi proposed some that are paradoxical in this sense.[7] For example, for "to forgive" the presupposed founded on *having-to-be* ("S_2 should be punished") is negated by the presupposer ("S_1 not punish S_2"), which includes at least a *not-wanting-to-punish*, or a *not-wanting-to-be-the-one-who-punishes*. For these authors, the transformation is simply correlated with a temporal change ($[t^1 \rightarrow t^0]$). The principle itself of modal transformation—that is to say, the change of modal content (having-to→wanting-to)—and the negation (having-to→*not*-wanting) are not in contradiction with the fact that the presupposed is not put into question. The fact that S_1 does not want to be the one who punishes does not cast doubt on the fact that S_2 must be punished. But, if we consider the question from the point of view of necessity, such necessity is, to say the least, somewhat surprising. How can the fact that S_1 must be punished be necessary for the fact that S_2 does not wish to punish him? Probably because if S_1 were not to be punished, S_2 would not have to want that he not be punished! The "paradoxical presupposition" hence casts light on the overdeterminations between modalities: *wanting-to-pardon* presupposes *having-to-punish* insofar as it is a wanting of *resistance*, a wanting by which the individual subject affirms his autonomy in the face of collective rules.

In the preceding example, obstinacy, and even more so in its moralized version, "stubbornness," the passional meaning effect is doubtless produced by the confrontation between a knowing that is concerned with both an impossibility, on the one hand, and an unwavering wanting on the other. The obstinate person wants, *no matter* what he knows, unless he happens to want *because* he knows. We cannot escape this difficulty by evoking an external observer, who would note the temporary uselessness of the obstinate person's efforts. Such an external observer is present, of course, in the value judgment implied in the term "obstinacy," in French. But the impassioned subject *himself* must know that his object escapes him, otherwise he is no longer obstinate, but rather "unaware" or "inconsistent."

The Internal Contradictions of the Subject. There is another solution that consists in dealing only with modal comparison and considering it as a sufficient explanation. But the comparison with another passional configuration, "despair," clearly shows that the phenomenon in question remains unexplained. If we compare obstinacy and despair, the modal differences are minimal. The despairing subject is modalized by *having-to-be* and *wanting-to-be*, and, moreover, he *cannot-be* and *know-how-not-to-be*. In both cases, the regulating modality is *wanting-to-be*, which can end up either in revolt or depression on the one hand, or in a stubborn doing, on the other. The only notable difference resides in the syntactic organization of the arrangement. Let us assume that the comparison of the modalities can cause incompatibilities to appear in the arrangements. They express the internal contradictions of the subject. There can be two types of internal contradictions. Either the regulating modality is affected by others or it is not. In the first case, the modal arrangement will be *paradoxical:* because of the presence of impossibility in the arrangement, the obstinate person's desire has become a "resisting" desire; in the second case, the modal arrangement will simply be "conflicting." The desperate person's desire is not changed at all by an awareness of impossibility. In the case of despair, the subject's modal cohesion is threatened, to the point of breaking; in the case of obstinacy, the subject's modal cohesion is confirmed.

Despair has a modal organization of a conflictual nature, insofar as *wanting-to-be* on the one hand, and *knowing-not-to-be* and *not-being-able-to-be* on the other cohabit without reciprocally modifying each other. They contradict and oppose each other by bringing about the internal breakup of the subject. Hence, in this case, *wanting-to-be* does not presuppose other modalizations. Despair is truly composed of two incompatible modal universes. Knowing about failure and failure itself are not necessary for the appearance of wanting, and vice versa. Despair is made up in a way of two independent modal identities, failure and frustration on the one hand, confidence and expectation on the other. The break is a result of their independence and their incompatibility. Only the procedure of modal comparison can account for the passional meaning effect linked to this type of modal organization.

On the other hand, the *wanting-to-be* of the obstinate person presupposes syntactically its knowing: he is not only both stubborn and lucid, *he is stubborn because he is lucid.* This is why we are dealing here with a paradoxical modal arrangement, where modal confrontation, occurring between two modalizations of a same series, does not suffice to explain the passional meaning effect. In fact, instead of ending up in a breakup of the arrangements, contradiction or contrariety accentuates the cohesive force, which, independently of the various modal roles played by the subject, preserves for him the same orientation and makes him persevere in his being.

In either case, the modal subjects find themselves in conflict; but as far as despair is concerned, conflict is insoluble, and can end only in the annihilation of being, that is to say, in the very least, in a solution of continuity in the subject's being. Whereas with obstinacy, conflict is resolved by the victory of the volitional subject, which presupposes a modification and reciprocal adaptation of the modalities in question. In short, in spite of conflict, it is as though for the obstinate person, knowledge of the obstacle gave rise to wanting, as though the two presupposed modalizations produced or sustained the presupposing modalization. It should be noted that the meaning effect "resistance," present in obstinacy, is aspectual in nature and that it evokes a "semiotic style" favoring the unfolding of becoming, which is not the case with despair. This would tend to prove that passional meaning effects cannot be explained satisfactorily at a single semionarrative level. Modal arrangements belong to the semionarrative level; they are the "products" of the semiotic schema, but passions that live off them are constituted within the discursive level.

From Organization to Disposition

We have now reached the core of the problem, since we have to know under what condition(s) modal arrangements can produce passional meaning effects. In examining passional "disposition," we abandon the semionarrative domain, strictly speaking, for the discursive one. At that level we can invoke the results both of the tensive modulations and of the categorizing generative trajectory, that is, both the entities resulting from the preconditions of signification, and the entities of a discontinuous nature emanating from the semionarrative proper. This is how processes appear at the level of the discursive structures, both modulated on a continuous mode (because of aspectual variations proper) and segmented on a discontinuous one (because of the concatenation of stages, tests, and sequences). On several occasions we have invoked the representation of the general economy of the theory in terms of three modules that can be represented as shown in Figure 5:

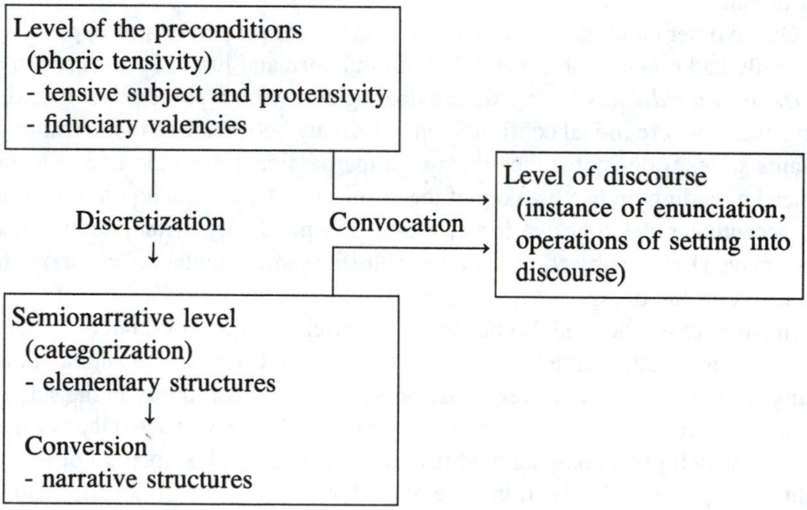

Figure 5

What concerns us immediately—that is, relations between organizations and dispositions—can be represented by the schema in Figure 6.

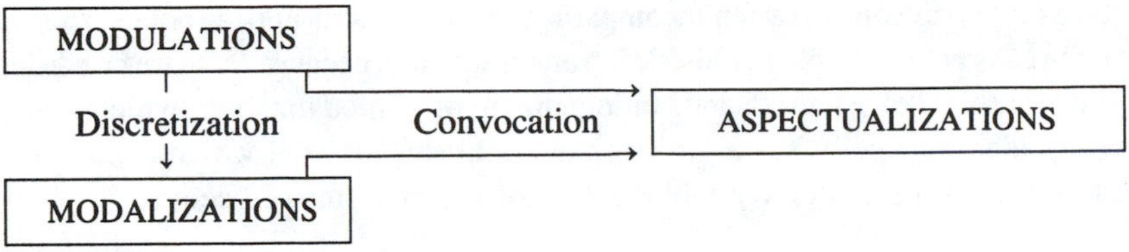

Figure 6

We could wonder why the representation adopted is triangular, and not linear. The reason is simple: a linear representation presupposes that the operations ensuring the passage from one level to another are minimally homogeneous. It seems more and more clear, however, that conversions proper are defined as increase and coagulation of meaning. They function as such in all levels where categorization and discretization alone prevail, that is to say, within what we call the "semionarrative." On the other hand, the passage to the discursive level, essentially as a result of its characteristic of shuttling to and fro (which we previously identified and shall continue to explore further on), can no longer be treated as conversion, but must be treated as summons. Ideally (from a theoretical perspective) we would like discourse to invent nothing new, but only to "convoke" by specific operations of setting into discourse what the two other instances have generated. Were this to be so, discourse would still "invent," if only for the primitives it refers back to "language" as stereotypes developed through usage. Likewise, the evolution of tensions at the level of the preconditions, as well as the passage from preconditions to the elementary structures of signification, cannot be considered as "augmentations and coagulation" of meaning, since the development of tensions is not yet part of signification and also because the first gesture of categorization and discretization is an epistemological operation that is certainly a conversion, but a different one from all the others that follow.

Disposition as "Semiotic Style." From this perspective, the modal arrangements, at the semionarrative level, converge with the continuous modulations of becoming that we postulated at the level of preconditions. In this case, *modal arrangements would become dispositions by means of their aspectualization*. As a matter of fact, the internal dynamics that characterizes passional dispositions also seems to give rise to a series of overlappings and approximations, and progresses by successive shiftings and stops and starts, all the while continuing to respond to a principle of tensive orientation that makes a superficial form of the subject's "becoming" homogeneous. We did note, for example, that if knowledge of failure or of the obstacle could incite or strengthen the resolve of the obstinate person, this could only be because of a "resistant" and "durative" semiotic style ("continuing in spite of *X*") that, by a sort of overlapping of *not-being-able* and *wanting*, results in a modification of the former in terms of the latter. In other words, if the transformations between incompatible modalizations appear not as true internal breaks but as simple paradoxical transitions, it is because they are conditioned and controlled by a tensive and homogenizing protomodalization, which we intuitively identified before as a "governing modal surplus" and which is nothing but the result of the discursive mobilization of modulations of becoming.

Disposition as Discursive Programming. When all is said and done this property of passional dispositions explains many things. To begin with, the existence of a governing principle emanating from protensivity enables us to define "dispositions" as "discursive programmings," and to explain that, at the level of discourse, they can appear as potentialities of doing or as a series of organized states (most commonly referred to as "attitudes"). In this respect, the impassioned subject functions like certain backup programs for memories in computers. On the one hand, the files are compactly stored, unreadable and unusable as such, and on the other, there exist commands that retrieve them and make them accessible to the user. The modal arrangements would be like this "compressed" and inaccessible version; the protensive and governing principle would be the restore command code; and the disposition would be the readable, accessible, and consequently operational result of the entire procedure.

Disposition as Aspectualization. Furthermore, the aspectual syntax governing the establishment of the dispositions is more superficially expressed in the form of temporal aspectualization, which is one of the most obvious and most immediately identifiable features of the passional universe, especially in the dictionary definitions given of different feelings or passions. "Spite" is a "lasting resentment," "patience" is "a capacity to endure," "hope" is "waiting confidently for something"; a "quick-tempered" person is said to "get angry easily." It seems to us that we have to know whether aspectual forms simply overdetermine modal structures after the fact, or whether they are an intrinsic component of these structures. In some of the cases we have alluded to, we can say without hesitation that aspectualization is an overdetermination. For example, "anger" for a "quick-tempered" person is an inchoative and intense variant of anger in general. Others, on the contrary, seem to include an intrinsic aspectuality. Because hope consists in waiting in confidence, it is based on *having-to-be* and *believing-to-be*, that can be interpreted almost temporally. In its aspectualized version proposed earlier, the *having-to-be* could be based on the modulation of becoming, which as we have seen, operates by punctualizing suspension. *Having-to-be* founds expectation insofar as it ensures the identity of every moment of becoming. Duration is simply a delay; the different instances composing it no longer have any potentiality for change, for these "micropotentialities" have become neutralized by modulation.

This brief examination shows within the modal arrangement that has become a disposition an aspectuality specific to the passional effect. Possibly temporalized during the setting into discourse, this aspectuality can be apprehended from two complementary points of view. First of all, with respect to the generative trajectory as a whole, and to the conditions and preconditions of signification, as we already suggested, aspectualization projected on the modal arrangement is the result of the convocation of the modulations of becoming. Aspectualization as "form" can appear only after having given form either to time, space, or the actor. In brief, this is the primary form of discourse, its rhythm, its dynamics, and, as such, it embodies the tensions that are foregrounded on the ontic horizon in discourse. Once becoming has been constructed and defined in the theoretical space of minimal feeling its embodiment in discourse can transform modal series into passional dispositions, insofar as at the same time it implies that narrative and cognitive rationality pure are suspended. From the perspective of the discursive subject, the resurgence of minimal feeling appears as a *reengagement onto the tensive subject*.

Second, with regard to the modal arrangement itself, aspectualization transforms a discontinuous sequence into a homogeneous process, into "discursive programming." Nevertheless, just as the classical narrative process is based not only on a series of narrative states, but also on transformations between states, the passional process cannot be based only on the modal series, which as commonly utilized, are basically series of modal states. We are therefore led to believe that, prior to their being called up as disposition in discourse, modal arrangements are organized into a complete syntax that includes modal states and transformations. We will call this "intermodal syntax," to differentiate it from the syntax that brings about changes in "positions" in modalizations within an isotopic modal system.

As a working hypothesis, it is now possible to envisage, alongside the series of conversions that occur from the fundamental syntax to narrative figurativity, a series of stages that in the trajectory of the epistemological subject would be more specifically germane to the theory of passions: at the level of phoric tensivity, *feeling and becoming*; at the semionarrative level, *modal arrangements and intermodal syntax*, which make them dynamic; at the discursive level, *dispositions and aspectualization* (most often but not always temporalized), which govern them. As far as enunciation is concerned it functions by reshifting onto the tensive subject, and thus defines the scope of passional simulations in discourse.

Intermodal Syntax

It seems that intermodal syntax involves a postulate whose consequences are difficult to evaluate. According to this postulate there is a syntax not based on the elementary syntax derived from the constitutional model. There remains a question to be answered that we can no longer avoid. How can we theoretically ensure the transformation of one modality into another, which, beside the fact that it is necessarily heterotopic, can also be its contrary or contradictory? The conditions of the answer to this question have been described in detail, but the answer itself has yet to be formulated.

In a semiotics that would include only the discontinuous and the categorical, for a knowing to be transformed into a wanting, for example, one would have to suppose both a common category /M/, and distinctive features to be transformed $/m^a/$ and $/m^b/$; category /m/ would guarantee the homogeneity of the transformation $/m^a \rightarrow m^b/$. This amounts to introducing an isotopic constraint where, because of discretization, one would normally postulate modal heterotopy. The existence of categories common to the modalities solves nothing, since this simply transfers the difficulties to the "distinctive modal features." The fact of the matter is that we already have a "modal base," phoric tensivity, which has often been examined, delimited, and described, and which through recursivity perpetuates the modulations of becoming in the generative trajectory. Starting from this modal base, we note, for example, that knowing can be transformed into being-able only if the modulation of "closure" that sustains the former is neutralized (after "stopping" or "stopping stopping" as Claude Zilberberg[8] would say), where becoming can be substituted for wanting only at the cost of suspending becoming, and therefore of canceling the "opening" modulation that characterizes wanting. The tensive base of intermodal syntax could therefore be the modulation of a becoming that progressively gains (or loses) its autonomy in relation to necessity. This is why successive modal positions appear as different forms of "submission," of "dislocation," of "procrastination" with regard to necessity, which systematically demands its rights. Thus, wanting, knowing, being-able always refer to different "semiotic styles," to different ways of grasping phoric scission. The existence of such "semiotic styles," which was previously suggested when we were dealing with becoming, is apparent in the intermodal transformations of passions. With obstinacy, for example, *being-not-able-to-be* or *not-being-able-not-to-be* depends on a "cursive" semiotic style, in which the modal subject stops the flow of events. It is then that another style, the style of *wanting*, steps in, through which the modal subject again displays the event as becoming. The common modal base serves as the basis of intermodal syntax regardless of the name we give it and, epistemologically speaking, originates in the resistance to fusion in the tug-of-war of cohesive and dispersive forces, which allow the tensive subject to escape ontic necessity.

Since, theoretically speaking, there are no articulations to speak of, it is difficult to attribute to phoric tensivity the ability to produce in and of itself distinct identifiable "semiotic styles," no matter what precautions we take in formulating them. What kind of status would those "semiotic styles" have that seem to be determiners of intermodal syntax? The analysis of obstinacy, with its *wanting* overlapping and retroacting onto *not-being-able-to*, as we have seen, produces a specific passional meaning effect, gives us a clue to a possible answer. We note, in fact, that the impulsive person's *wanting*, for example, insofar as it is *followed* by the immediate appearance of a *being-able* that seems naturally to stem from it, does not produce the same meaning effect as the obstinate person's *wanting*, which *follows* a *not-being-able* that paradoxically seems to feed and invigorate it. At the level of discourse, these various meaning effects appear as distinct aspectualizations. By presupposition and at the level of the tensive continuum, these same meaning effects also correspond to different ways of modulating becoming.

We would like to suggest the following hypothesis that contains five propositions:

1. Modal arrangements are mobilized into discourse and undergo aspectualization. This aspectualization results from the said mobilization of the tensive modulations, and transforms them into passional dispositions.
2. As a result of sociolectal or idiolectal usage, these dispositions are frozen and stereotyped before becoming part of connotative passional taxonomies.
3. Once they become stereotyped, they are relegated to the semionarrative level and can then be mobilized as such.
4. Among all stereotyped modal sequences, intermodal syntax is the frozen form, itself stereotyped by usage, of the aspect referred to in proposition 2, and thus of certain tensive modulations. The meaning effects produced by the insertion of a given modality in a frozen organization hence result in the codification by usage of the dispositions of the discursive level.
5. By combining the stereotyped organizations into discourse, codification of dispositions and, consequently, frozen forms of the tensive modulation are also mobilized. From this perspective, "semiotic styles" result from stereotyped tensive modulations, set and frozen by usage along with the modal dispositions selected for passional taxonomies. Just as passions cannot be thought of independently of the enunciative praxis that fashions them, "semiotic styles" ("ambiances" as Per Aag Brandt[9] would say) only appear in the tensive modulations through usage.

The Methodology of Passions

Terminology

Whatever degree of conviction the previous suggestions and propositions can inspire, a rapid survey of the theoretical body we have just examined highlights several ideas that nevertheless remain indispensable to a semiotics of passions.

Thus it would seem worthwhile here to make a brief terminological assessment of the tools necessary to describe the passional universe.

Phoric tensivity designates the set of preconditions of signification, among which we have identified *protensivity*, on the one hand, which defines a *tensive subject* or "near subject" and which, under the effects of tension that encourage scission, generates *becoming*, and on the other, *fiducia* on which "shadows of value" are delineated that are destined to produce *valencies*.

Leaving the continuous world of preconditions proper, we then encountered, on the *semionarrative* level, discretization of the modulations of becoming, which generates *modalizations*. We found that there are two kinds of modalizations: in the restricted sense they encompass only what traditionally are called *modalities*; in the broad sense, they also encompass *existential simulacra*, that is, junctions projected by the subject into the imaginary space opened up by the modalities. Apprehended at the level of surface narrative structures, modalizations affecting the pragmatic and cognitive dimensions, under certain conditions, can act as *modal arrangements*, sorts of simulacra in which the *modal subjects* acquire provisional identities throughout the syntactic unfolding of the arrangements. The specificity of this syntactic functioning, and especially what we call *intermodal syntax*, ensures the independence of the *thymic dimension*, a third dimension (in the deductive order of thymic construction) of surface narrative syntax. Variations of "euphoria" and "dysphoria" are part of the three dimensions, but they function more specifically on the thymic dimension as *thymic objects*, and appear among other things as figures of "suffering" or "pleasure," results of thymic transformations.

Insight can be gained from a comparison of the theoretical evolution of this dimension with that of the cognitive dimension. The latter was first identified to be a constitutive part of the pragmatic dimension, especially at the moment of the contract or sanction. As soon as we noted that gaps of knowledge, ups and downs in the circulation of information, as well as many modal variations belonging to the cognitive, could function without reference and without necessarily being linked to transformations of the pragmatic dimension, the theoretical evolution in question then acquired its own autonomy. First understood as a syntactic path cutting straight across the group of cognitive effects produced by pragmatic narrative syntax, the cognitive dimension then became a narrative dimension proper. In the same way, the thymic domain was progressively thought of as encompassing two other dimensions, as a product of the "passional" effects of the modal series that accompany the pragmatic and cognitive programs, as well as the alternation of euphoria and dysphoria that ensues from objects of value being inscribed in axiologies. Second, it also seems that the modal restrictions and the results of euphoria/dysphoria produced by the pragmatic and cognitive dimensions cannot in themselves explain passional meaning effects. This is why, in order to account for passional trajectories that no longer owe anything to pragmatic or cognitive narrative syntax, we instituted the thymic dimension as a separate dimension of surface narrative syntax.

As we have already suggested, the relation between the level of preconditions, which is specific to the continuous, and the semionarrative level, which falls under the discontinuous, cannot be a simple relation of conversion. If we actually consider the two possible kinds of conversion – "horizontal" conversion, or "transformation," and "vertical" conversion – we note that they only take place between discontinuous entities. The same holds true for Emile Benveniste's concept of "integration," according to which we can only "integrate" discrete units on a given level with discrete units of the following level. It seems that *discretization*, with its subcomponents *summons* and *categorization*, is more appropriate in this case.

When we move on to the discursive structures, on the contrary, we make use of *convocation,* defined as a group of procedures that is supposed to reveal in discourse entities appearing at the epistemological or semionarrative levels. These entities are continuous as far as phoric tensivity is concerned and discontinuous as far as the semionarrative is concerned. To give an example, the convocation of the modulations of becoming in discourse appears as *aspectualization* and the convocation of thymic dimension takes the form of a *pathemic dimension* of discourse, which includes the set of manifest properties of the passional universe. In the same way, *pathemes* are defined as the set of discursive conditions necessary for the manifestation of a passional meaning effect. In this regard, we can distinguish *process pathemes* and *pathemic roles*, depending on whether we are trying to grasp passional syntagma or provisional identities of the discursive subject in these syntagmas. If we take "susceptibility" as an example, it is clear that the process patheme displays the whole of the sequence, including the reception, interpretation of the wound of pride, and then the reaction and behavior that stem from this. In addition, the pathemic role, which can be identified by the recurrence of one process of this kind for the same subject, can characterize the subject just as readily at the stage of the interpretation of the wound of pride as at, say, the stage of behavior of a "vexed" person. Furthermore, if we can distinguish a generalizable form of process pathemes based on the concrete analysis of discourse, this form will be called the *canonical pathemic schema*.

Yet, the idea of "pathemic role" overlaps the idea of *disposition* in that they both characterize a "discursive programming" of the impassioned subject. As a matter of fact, if the same discursive property of the impassioned subject can have two different names, it is because of a difference in procedure. If we reconstruct the properties of the impassioned subject by presupposition, on the basis of a functional repetition and by cognitive calculations based on the results of a process – that is, on discontinuous entities – we identify and designate it as a pathemic role. If, however, we try to understand these same properties as a way of feeling, as a programming that stems from an aspectual form, we are led to apply a logic of motivation to them, and so we treat them as a disposition. In short, disposition includes an aspectual component because the procedure we use to construct it remains true to the tensive base of the passional universe, whereas the thematic role does not include an aspectual element because it is the result of a procedure of cognitive reconstruction of the classes of passional behaviors.

Connotative Passional Taxonomies

The terminological assessment in a way constitutes the contribution of epistemological reflections to methodology. But, no matter what theory we adopt, starting from passional meaning effects, the construction of passional universes comes up against a major difficulty that cannot be solved by epistemology or terminology. In this particular case, we are dealing with the screen that analysts, whether they happen to be semioticians, philosophers, or lexicologists, are confronted with in the form of cultural variations at the heart of passional meaning effects. It is easy to understand that if from a theoretical point of view the analysis of passions cannot be undertaken without enunciative praxis and setting into discourse, from a methodological point of view, it will encounter passional idiolects and sociolects.

Enunciative Praxis and Primitives. Linguistics distinguishes between *language*, as a universal human fact and which as such can include "linguistic universals," and *langues*, systems that are specific to cultural areas and that complete and reinterpret universals. Both *language* and *langues* fall within the province of the virtual or the actualized, and are realized in discourse. In general semiotic terms and not in linguistic terms per se, the semionarrative level, organized as a generative trajectory, should include, on the one hand, universal entities characteristic of signification understood as a universal human fact, and on the other hand, entities that can be generalized within a given culture and that are characteristic of signification as a cultural fact. These two kinds of semiotic entities, which continue to belong to the semionarrative level and are spread evenly over the generative trajectory, both fall under the virtual and the actualized. Cultures, understood as systems of selections, shifts, and complements applied to the universals of signification, would be to these universals what *langues* are to *language*. We know, for example, that if both the basic structures of signification and the system of natural elements underlying the most widespread figurative axiologies can appear in this theory as universals, the same does not hold for figurative axiologies proper, where the four elements are distributed in a variable and specific way, depending on which authors and cultures we are dealing with.

A very simple way to tackle these cultural entities and to distinguish them from universals is to treat them as "connotative taxonomies." As a matter of fact, we are sometimes very tempted to consider "selections," "shifts," and other "complements," whose universals are affected by individual or collective cultures, as separate operations produced simply by the initiative of the subject of enunciation, and to make a direct assessment in terms of the operations of enunciation. It so happens that, if only because they include "langue," the set of these particularities forms a system that, once it has been set up, acquires in its own right a mode of existence independent of enunciation. These operations are realizable – either virtualized or actualized – and not realized.

It is up to the praxis of enunciation to bring about this change in status. In fact, cultural specificities are integrated through usage onto the semionarrative level. Social discourse is formed not only by convoking universals, but also by discourse turning in on itself, thereby producing ready-made and stereotyped configurations. The stereotypes thus produced are sent back to the semionarrative level as *primitives* that are just as organized and systematic as universals. Enunciative praxis is this movement back and forth between the discursive and other levels that enables us to form cultures semiotically. Very often, but not always, the "primitives" thus produced appear as taxonomies that underlie the configurations convoked in discourse and function in a way as connotations, distinct from the denotations that result from the convocation of universals. In this sense, the praxis of enunciation reconciles generative and genetic processes and associates in discourse the products of an atemporal formulation of signification as well as those of history.

Passions offer us remarkably fertile ground for such connotative taxonomies and the analyst will immediately recognize that this is a domain that especially lends itself to the study of the cultural, social, or individual "grids" that are projected onto the universals. Actually, since the modal "arrangement" is the end-term entity of the generative trajectory of passions, its expression in discourse produces "dispositions" in accordance with the procedure of convocation. But convocation is, in principle, conceivable for all logically possible modal combinations. In fact, this is not true, and we observe that each culture only selects some of them that will appear as passional meaning effects or lexeme passions. By definition, the disposition, rooted in both intermodal syntax and protensivity, is more or less predictable. It certainly plays a part in predicting the behavior of the subject, but it always includes an element of indeterminacy and "invention." On the other hand, the "pathemic role" that is constructed by presupposition on the basis of iteration is extremely predictable and tends to appear in discourse as a stereotype. In a way it is the "usage" of a certain modal arrangement as a disposition in a given area of culture and discourse that makes it a stereotype, and retroactively a *passional primitive*. It is only then that, in the culture under consideration, only the modal arrangements that have undergone this treatment will become the objects of a discursive convocation within passional configurations. If it were simply a question of modal structures or categories, the cultural "grids" would have limited influence. But, insofar as we are dealing with "arrangements" (that is, intersections between structures and potential combinations between categories), passions can only appear as such in discourse if an instance directs and actualizes these potential combinations, and this instance is enunciative praxis, which produces passional taxonomies that bring together primitives produced by usage.

Types and Levels of Taxonomies. Language itself proceeds by classification, insofar as it conceptualizes the natural world. As for cultures, they are distinguished as ethnotaxonomies characterizing a whole area or period, and as sociotaxonomies specifying different taxonomical layers of a given area or period. Depending on which criterion we use these can be sociocultural, socioeconomic, or sociogeographic: passions from the North or the Midi, passions from Corsica (Prosper Mérimée) or Normandy (Guy de Maupassant), passions of the aristocracy, the middle class, or the lower class. From another point of view, certain taxonomies can appear to be intrinsic to a given culture, whereas others, while still remaining constitutive of a culture, will appear to be constructed, because they belong to a more general system. Theories of passions thus appear within ideological or philosophical systems, and even within systems that have a scientific bent, such as biology, and even . . . semiotics. Finally, the difference between sociolects and idiolects will be just as relevant in the case of passions. We could say, for example, that René Descartes's theory of passions is based on an immanent, sociolectal taxonomy, on the one hand, insofar as it is based on a sociocultural tradition and insofar as it is influenced by aristocratic ideology. It is also based on a constructed idiolectal taxonomy because it is part of a philosophical system.

One example comes to mind that gives a concrete illustration of the relative nature of connotative taxonomies. "Ambition," "envy," and "emulation" share the same passional configuration, but in a way that varies according to cultures and periods. These variations especially depend on socioeconomic divisions: emulation remains circumscribed within each social class or group, ambition and envy go beyond these boundaries. Furthermore, ambition and emulation are "upward bound," whereas envy seems to presuppose a more egalitarian principle. This is what will seem to be ambition in a divided society that has a great number of social levels with clearly defined boundaries, and what will be seen as emulation in a society that has only a few social levels and weak divisions. Moreover, if on top of this the social norm aims to keep people firmly in their original class, emulation will find itself reduced to ambition, and ambition itself will be brought down to envy. In their work *L'enfer des choses*, in the light of the theories of René Girard, Jean-Pierre Dupuy and Paul Dumouchel have shown that intersubjective and social relations are organized in this case by a strategy whose main goal is to channel mimetic desire. If, as we have indirectly suggested by the notion of "intersubject," we admit that a phenomenon such as mimetic desire appears even before the existence of objects of value, we are led to observe that the selection made by connotative taxonomies occurs from the preconditions of signification onward, and that, while they are not yet axiological systems (which would be incompatible with the status of the preconditions), they already accommodate norms, regulating principles that define the way the collective subject functions. It would seem here that the subject of communal enunciation inscribes within the tensive continuum its own mechanisms of internal regulation as primitives. The suggestions we have made regarding "semiotic styles" tend in the same direction.

There are several theories that, on the level of what we would call basic structures, propose to organize passional systems or affectivity in general according to the major types of axiologies that have been recognized as dominants in the study of discourse. The abstract axiology of life/death, which psychoanalysis has used rather unevenly, by opposing either life drives and death drives (Sigmund Freud) or "good objects" and "bad objects" that consume and attract at the same time (Melanie Klein) but also the figurative axiology of water/air/earth/fire, at the basis of the theory of humors and more especially of the passional taxonomies of the Middle Ages.

On the semionarrative level, as far as modalizations are concerned, connotative taxonomies operate on a grand scale, since they authorize or forbid each of the logically possible modal arrangements to be revealed as passions. Thus, an entire set of behaviors that come under honor is excluded from the passional domain in the seventeenth and eighteenth centuries, and to a degree, in the nineteenth as well, whereas they would appear as "susceptibility," "irritability," "easily offended character," or violent rage today. As long as these behaviors are part of social norms, encoded as thematic roles in the competence of subjects, we remain within the framework of a collective agreement and ordinary modal competence. As soon as this codification and the accompanying norm fall into disuse the same behaviors no longer refer to an isotopic modal structure, such as the structure of *having-to-be* or *having-to-do*, but to a complex modal arrangement that is not regulated by any contract, with its own syntactic independence, and that, in the new culture in which it appears, can be interpreted only as a passional "disposition." In the same way, the posture of preparing for a challenge and the posture of respect for someone else's social position, described by Pierre Bourdieu for the Kabyles, are strictly functional and regulated as *being-able-do* and *knowing-to-be*, but they are commonly recategorized, by others than the sociologist, as pathemes of "disdain," "arrogance," "pride," and the like.[10]

Passional Nomenclature. Language suggests its own conceptualization of the passional universe, and we find a first formulation of this in a specific lexical field, the field of "passional nomenclature," which shows the main outlines of a taxonomy that is coextensive with a whole culture. We will of course turn our attention to French nomenclature.

The dictionary definitions of passions include a series of taxonomical designations that form as it were the main areas of affective life. In French, we have distinguished the following types: "passion," "sentiment," "feeling," "inclination," "penchant," "emotion," "mood," (humoral) "disposition," "attitude," "temperament," "character," complemented by adjectival phrases like "inclined to," "likely to," "susceptible to."[11]

Before even the division of the passional universe by lexemes that designate passional meaning effects, there seems to be another, more abstract cultural grid that reveals an immanent theory of passions within the very foundations of cultures. Because this classification is a primary ethnocultural organization of the passional universe and because it is an implicit theorization of this same universe, it deserves to be examined for its own sake, so that we may bring to the fore the main parameters it uses. Actually, psychological and philosophical theories of passions take up without examining it the nomenclature of the language they use and try, on this very relative basis, to rejustify them within their own system. As far as this is concerned, we can easily prove that in spite of the attempted definitional rejustification, the basis of the system remains relative to a given culture.

We will remember that *sentiment* is given as a complex affective state, stable and durable, linked to representations.

As for *emotion*, it is a generally intense affective reaction, appearing through different disorders, especially of a neurostagnate nature. The psychologist Théodule Ribot insists that it is momentary in nature.

Inclination, which refers directly to "propensity" and to "disposition," is defined as a desire, as a constant wanting characteristic of the individual. Whoever is "inclined to" is "led by a natural and permanent penchant."

Penchant, which has the circular definition of "natural tendency" and "inclination," in fact presupposes recognition by an external observer of a specialization of the subject's affective life, in relation either to objects or modalizations. This specialization is sometimes evaluated in a pejorative way, but this is not the case for "inclination."

Moreover, the one who is *likely to* is the one who can feel, offer, receive a feeling, an impression, one who, in short, has a latent capacity that can sometimes be utilized.

Temperament is defined originally as "stabilization of a mixture," which helps us to understand the use of this term in the domain of affectivity, based on the Hippocratic definition of humors. Today the term designates a group of innate characteristics, a psychophysiological complex that determines behavior.

Character is also a set, but a much more homogeneous one than temperament. It groups together customary ways of feeling and reacting, ways likely to distinguish an individual from his or her fellow creatures. Here the whole is no longer defined by the stabilization of the component elements but rather by the dominant ones.

Finally, *mood* (humoral), which characterizes the individual, is fleeting. It defines a moment of the affective existence of that individual.

The variables used in this classification are the following:

Aspectualization, which constantly arises, concerns either affective movement itself, which can be permanent (inclination, temperament, character, likeliness to), long-lasting (feeling), or fleeting (mood, emotion) or the resulting passional manifestations, behaviors, and actions. These can be continuous (temperament, character, inclination), episodic (likeliness to, mood), or separate (feeling, emotion). We can see immediately that even with such a narrow typological base, (French) nomenclature covers only some of the possibilities. For example, what would we call a long-lasting affective movement that occurs only episodically? An "episodic feeling"?

Dominant modalization also varies according to types. Feeling involves *knowing*, emotion, by its results and expressions, affects *being-able*; inclination and penchant are rather concerned with *wanting*. With temperament and character, all modalizations seem to be involved, but in the form of interaction. When such interaction occurs it corresponds to the modal subjects defined earlier. These occurrences end up either in individual and explicatory stability dominated by *being-able* (temperament) or in distinctive dominances that result in individualizing, or they are ultimately expressed as variants of *wanting* (character).

All these passional categories appear more or less as varieties of competence in the broad sense of the term. Still, they offer some very different images of competence. In definitions of character and temperament, competence, as "the being of the subject," is recognized by an outside observer, who is capable of identifying the modal degree characterizing this competence. In definitions of inclination and penchant, it is presupposed and reconstructed by an observer able to predict behaviors and attitudes. On the other hand, in the definition of emotion, it is considered as weakened, and even suspended.

Passional nomenclature in French is basically built on three variables among which aspectuality plays the dominant role. The resulting connotative taxonomy is shown in Figure 7.

In spite of this effort to clarify and systematize, passional nomenclature remains a vague body whose underlying variables we can identify but whose terms we cannot precisely define. It appears to be an incomplete and poorly defined lexematic covering of a classificatory macrosystem. As a system it lacks hierarchization, and it is practically impossible to decide which one of aspectualization, modalization, and "compententialization" is the presupposer and which is the presupposed. On the other hand, this system cannot be generalized since it is the product of a cultural selection from among all possible figures. As a matter of fact, cultural selection occurs twice, first in taking only three axes of variation from among all possible choices—and we should recognize that they are all the

	Sentiment	Emotion	Humour	Likeliness	Inclination	Temperament	Character
Disposition							
permanent				*	*	*	*
durable	*		*?				
temporary		*	*?				
Manifestation							
continuous			*		*?	*	*
episodic				*	*?		
isolated	*	*					
Modalization							
knowing	*						
being-able		*		*		*	
wanting					*		*
mixed			*			*	*
Competence	?		?				
acknowledged						*	*
supposed				*	*		
negated		*					

Figure 7

same at the heart of our theoretical problematics – and second in keeping only some of the varieties from among all the imaginable choices. Nomenclature is, in a sense, a first draft, an intuitive product of history, of a theory of passions developed within a culture. Since this theory is one of the elements of the linguistic system itself (that is, one of the products of the praxis of enunciation), it induces us to take a closer look in order to try to understand, both how language, as a system that is relative to a particular culture, goes about producing passional meaning effects based on modal universals, and what the properties of these "intuitive theories of passions," which connotative taxonomies generally are, happen to be.

The Sociolectal Passional Universe

To begin with, we can distinguish the passional universe of a whole culture partially expressed in the vocabulary of the dominant language of that culture, from the sociolectal microcosms that characterize social discourses. These discourses sometimes offer us a reinterpretation, or a recategorization, of this or that passion that can be surprising.

Didactic Humiliation. This is true, for example, of didactic discourse, at least as it is practiced and codified in its most common form. It is based on negating the knowledge of the "student" and asserting the knowledge of the "teacher." All pedagogical strategy that consists in valorizing the knowledge of the student is in this respect only a trick that precisely allows for compensation of the "parasitic" passional results of the negation of the original knowledge. This negation is necessary both for successful transmission and building of knowledge, and for the constitution of the collective actant, since whatever group is being formed, it is brought together based on an evaluation that can be either arbitrary, such as age, or motivated, such as an entrance examination, but which always measures what the student knows and does not know, which comes down to defining what he or she still has to learn. Furthermore, under pretense of measuring acquisition, there is a proliferation of "diagnostic" or "prognostic" evaluations, but it is always the extent of things unknown that is kept in the actual didactic strategy, as well as the resulting relative heterogeneity of the group being formed, with the future aim of organizing teaching programs to treat both the deficit and the heterogeneity.

Now, this negation of competence brings with it, at least in its modal principle, "humiliation," that is, a pathemic manipulation that aims at establishing in the student a certain stereotyped modal segment in which *awareness* (knowledge) of incompetence must lead to an *acceptance* (wanting) of the proposed learning. *Knowing-not-to-be* is transformed into *not-wanting-not-to-be*. For example, Freud, in his preface to the *Introduction to Psychoanalysis*, uses this pathemic role persistently. Addressing his students, he clearly asserts that, in order to come and listen to him, they must first admit that they know nothing, that they are just as ignorant as those who have never studied medicine. He does not hesitate to make it clear that those who still think they know something should not attend the second meeting. Finally, he suggests to those students who agree to come back under these conditions, and only those students, that they can listen to him.

Here is a sociolectal microcosm in which a passion that is normally considered harmful and negative is used "positively" in a form that is the object of such agreement that in general neither teachers (except for Freud, it seems, among others) nor students recognize it as such. In other words, within this passional taxonomy, it is not listed as "humiliation." But the fact that there is, on the edges of this sociolectal microcosm, overlapping onto other social, cultural, or ideological discourses or onto individual nonintegrated universes, is enough for the meaning effect "humiliation" to reappear and conflicts over the interpretation of the modal arrangement to arise. Numerous pedagogical debates result from this.

Nevertheless, such a form of discourse is undoubtedly relative to a cultural zone limited in time and space. What would become of this form in ancient India for example, where, as Georges Dumézil observes, the master "swallows up" and "vomits out" his disciple, and vice versa?

The Theory of Passions and the Theory of Value. Looking now at the passional universes that organize whole cultures, even beyond language, we see that connotative taxonomies have a much greater effect than the distribution of modal arrangements and their passional interpretation. We note, for example, that during the individualistic revolution of the eighteenth century the *theory of passions* is replaced by a *theory of value* and by the dynamics of *interest*. Paradigmatic variations of history consist here in replacing a focus on the subject by a focus on the object, and at the same time in modifying the balance and relationship between *wanting-to* and *having-to*.

Within philosophical systems, but also, more generally, within the *episteme*, political economy is taking the place of theories of passions, which are waning, and theories of needs are displacing theories of desires. This is mainly expressed by a change in the modalization of objects of value. From being desirable, they now become necessary or indispensable. In theories of passions, the pragmatic dimension *affects* the body, and the body in turn *affects* the soul by arousing *wanting* for example. In theories of needs, the pragmatic dimension *determines* the body, and the body *determines* the mind by means of reflexive knowledge, which for subjects consists in becoming aware of their interests.

The difference between the two theories is apparently minimal. It could be summed up in the opposition between "affecting" and "determining"—the body affects or determines the mind. In theories of passions, the thymic and the cognitive are articulated not by the pragmatic as such but by its dysfunctions. In Spinoza, for example, these dysfunctions produce only "inadequate ideas," which themselves are reinterpreted as passions. In theories of needs, however, the cognitive and the thymic are articulated by the pragmatic as such and as a whole. Thus, in this regard, theories of passions would seem to be theories of narrative dysfunction, capable of grasping the passional "remains" of narrativity. On the other hand, theories of needs presuppose and exploit a totally determined narrativity that absorbs passional effect by totally exhausting modal values in the search for descriptive values. As a result we are witnessing, along with the rapid development of theories of needs and political economy, a vast ideological (and epistemological) enterprise that aims to reduce this "modal surplus" nourishing the passions and to make sure that the whole body of modal effects remains directly or indirectly dependent on the pragmatic or cognitive dimensions.

Semiotics of passions must take a stand on this point. It is no longer just a matter of deciding between wants and needs, between passions and interests—which remains a subject of debate between two cultures; it is a matter of defining the epistemological minimum needed to ensure the independence of the thymic dimension. The epistemological minimum that is needed seems to lie in the fact that modal arrangements can be something other than simply conditions for performance. It is clear that if behind every connotative taxonomy of passions an implicit or explicit theory is at work, cultural changes are likely to reorient the way in which we intellectually represent passions. It is a truism to remind ourselves that every scientific project comes within the framework of a culture and an *episteme*, and that as a result, the semiotics of passions cannot escape such determining factors. To develop a semiotics of passions means to opt for a representation of the narrative dimension of discourse that is not reduced to a sort of logic of action and to a concept of the subject as entirely determined by his doing and by the conditions necessary for its realization.

The Idiolectal Passional Universe

The passional universe of a writer helps in the constituting of the "global text" of his work. Charles Mauron's research, by attempting to uncover the "personal myth" of a work, offers an example of the building of idiolectal passional universes. The personal myth, which is presented as a configuration that associates passional themes and figures, can be interpreted as the permanence of one or more modal arrangements whose recurring figurative expressions are scattered in the narrative or dramatic situations as well as in the rhetorical figures. Moreover, the analysis of the texts by Guy de Maupassant, Georges Bernanos, or Louis Aragon has shown how figurative axiologies (water, air, earth, fire) linked to abstract axiologies (life, death) and polarized by euphoria/dysphoria, constitute the idiolectal forms likely to be displayed on the thymic dimension of narrative.

The "specificity" of the passional idiolect will be more particularly expressed by (1) the overarticulation of certain passions, as we observe in Charles Baudelaire for *spleen*; (2) the isotopic or functional dominance of certain modulations, as Jean-Claude Coquet has shown concerning Paul Claudel's *La ville*; (3) axiological orientations, valorization, and devalorization of certain passions, such as generosity in Pierre Corneille; (4) the recategorization of passions borrowed from sociolectal universes and which, in the idiolect, no longer correspond to their definition "in language." This set of factors causes a slight general shift in the distribution and function of passions and adds to the outline of an idiolectal passional taxonomy.

Optimistic Despair. *La semaine sainte* by Louis Aragon gives us a remarkable example of passional recategorization. We observed that in the novel, despair was a valorized, positive passion at the origin of much symbolic activity, on the condition, however, that it was a question of historical and political despair. The paralyzed lover who commits suicide has only a boring kind of despair and has no right to claim the honors of history. However, the soldiers of the royal house, thrown into despair by the desertion of the king and princes, which the soldiers interpreted as a betrayal, are "positive" despairing subjects. As a matter of fact, their despair, which changes into revolt, as well as the discourse that gives it expression, afterward reveals that they were not as useless as they seemed, that they were loyal; and in the turmoil that throws them into states of distress and apprehension, they reassert the values on which their enlistment was based. In a way, it is the entire competence and the axiological engaging of the subject that are thus reactualized by despair.

We are not dealing here, however, with a simple change of polarization or with the isotopic dominance of a modality. If we compare Aragon's version of despair to Søren Kierkegaard's, for example, we note that in Kierkegaard the specificity of despair stems from a modal dominance, whereas in Aragon it springs from a veritable recategorization. In fact, in the *Treatise on Despair*, despair is a form and a product of the conscience that has as its motivating force a conflict between the self and itself or, in Kierkegaard's own words, "the internal conflict of a situation whose report relates to itself" (I, 2). The despair of the man who invented existential anguish is therefore specified by the isotopic and functional dominance of a reflexive *knowing-to-be*. This dominance is functional because it governs the modal series of despair itself, and isotopic because it intervenes in the "illness"—the term is Kierkegaard's—and in the healing, because it is, when all is said and done, something that belongs to human beings. In Aragon, on the contrary, despair is recategorized insofar as it no longer appears as a passion of the frustrated receiver but as a passion of assuming values, by means of the fiducia contract of belief. In the respective condition of Bernard's beliefs, in the desperate lover, and in the "sons of the family," the politically desperate ones provide us with a significant clue. Indeed, shortly before Bernard commits suicide, he repeats over and over again that "everything is a lie" and actually does behave as if everything were equally insignificant. On the other hand, the sons of the family carefully differentiate the breaking of the fiducia contract caused by the king and the princes from the fiduciary agreement that links them to monarchist values: they no longer believe in their Sender, but they believe all the more firmly in the value system that made them enter his service. When despair is simply an acknowledgment of an enlistment and the reasons for doing so, it does not affect the semiotic subject nearly as much as when it stems from a general breakdown of values. Even though these two passions have the same name and are governed by the same modal syntax, they are very different; the one goes so far as to affect even valency and the tensive subject, the other affects only the identity of the Sender.

Pessimistic Wanting. We can see that recategorization concerns the entire configuration: the hierarchy of modalizations, their expression, the resulting action, but especially the repercussions on deep structures. Another example comes to mind in which modalization itself is recategorized, the example of love and desire in Maupassant. Under Arthur Schopenhauer, Maupassant learned that *wanting* was the source of human unhappiness, as much when it produced an unsatisfied desire, which produced boredom and dislike, as by the effect of frustration, the source of suffering. *Wanting*, in Maupassant, is most often associated with meaninglessness, absurdity, incoherence. In the sociolect, the same modalization induces a search and gives meaning to life's projects, because it allows us to accept values. In the idiolect, on the contrary, it disorganizes human action and arouses only bestial, brutal, or pernicious passions. Recategorization here takes another route than in Aragon, since it is modalization itself, insofar as it originates passions, that is recategorized, and all the passions that include it in their arrangements are themselves affected by it. If we refer to the modulations of becoming, then we see that the "opening" producing desire is nothing more than a wild fluctuation or impetuous outburst. In short, dispersive forces have a destructive backlash. We could say that Maupassant's idiolect has selected a semiotic style that specifies the modality of *wanting*.

In a more general way, if recategorization can be superficially taken for a simple change of thematic isotopy (the taking on of values instead of frustration, absurdity and bestiality instead of the "meaning of life"), on a deeper level it is based on a modification of the modal arrangement and, possibly, on new tensive modulations. We are no doubt touching here on "originality" more than on the "specificity" of an idiolect. Pathemic forms are reorganized in such a way that the entire passional universe undergoes consistent deformation. Moreover, in the case of both Aragon and Maupassant, recategorization is only partially of their own doing. Aragon applies a more general system of thought to despair that he is not the only one to share, whereas Maupassant borrows a lot from Schopenhauer, but in this he belongs to a generation of writers who have come under the same influence. On the one hand, a constructed sociotaxonomy, the ideology of a current of thought, is changed into an immanent idiolectal taxonomy; on the other, a constructed idiolectal taxonomy, a philosophical system, is changed into an immanent sociotaxonomy. These transformations give us a glimpse of a possible method for studying the relationship between text, cotext, and context. Once we have located the constants and parameters on which the connotative taxonomies work, and distinguished the different kinds and levels on which they operate, it would be possible to envision the "genetic" study of the text from this angle, by means of changes that occur among the different kinds of taxonomies.

Philosophy and the Semiotics of Passions

A variety of connotative taxonomies exist that deserve to be examined separately because they offer a systematic quality and an explicit nature that make them close kin of the semiotic process: the taxonomies proposed by the philosophers. Treatises on passions have the peculiarity of hesitating between classifying passions selected from a given culture and an inferred taxonomy that is permanently cut off from any particular culture. It is not a matter of accounting for this or that philosophical system but of quickly showing how they cannot escape such an alternative and how taxonomical doing functions.

Cartesian Taxonomy. In *The Passions of the Soul*, Descartes proceeds exclusively by classification. He begins by enumerating passions by progressive deduction, continues by studying six supposedly "primitive" passions, and ends with "specific" passions. The enumeration as well as the description of passions consists of putting variables into place, of displaying variations, and then providing a description of manifestations understood as symptoms and finally considering the physiological causes. Definitions play on a certain number of parameters that in a way have after the fact come to justify the representation of the passions Descartes inherited from his predecessors and borrowed from his contemporaries. Some of these parameters are the actants in question, modalization, axiologization, and temporal aspectualization. It is in this way that "repentance" is based on a syncretism of the subject of doing, the observer and the impassioned subject. The fact that *wanting* and *being-able-to-do* are implied in passions affecting "the ability to act," such as "indecision," "boredom," and "dislike," would mean that we are dealing ultimately with "durative" passions. Moreover, moralization is all-pervasive and most often superfluous with respect to the axiological polarization of objects, thus ending up superimposing a new taxonomy onto the old one. The principle is thus one of a vast combinatory that claims to be exhaustive with respect to the six primitive passions and only exploratory as far as the others, which are said to be of an "indefinite" number, are concerned. As we have seen, the combinatory is based on a small number of categories that are more or less those that a semiotics of passions having a taxonomic goal would have to manipulate.[12]

Furthermore, the combinatory does not conform to a single taxonomy but to two taxonomies that intermingle. The first is an immanent ethnotaxonomy insofar as Descartes afterward reorganizes the passional universe of a culture, more or less faithfully expressed through language. The second is a constructed idiolectal taxonomy, if only because of the insistent presence of the Cartesian physiological mechanism, but also because of moral judgments that accompany and determine each definition. These taxonomies sometimes operate in a very contradictory fashion and then the hesitations of designation reveal the philosopher's indecision. For example, Descartes, in accordance with his own system, treats esteem and scorn as if they were passions, whereas they were considered only as "opinions" in the seventeenth century. Similarly, bringing out positions that lack designations in natural language, he arbitrarily assigns them a borrowed term. Thus he gives the name "elation" to "a joy linked to a past sorrow" in order to match "regret," which is a "sadness linked to a past joy." But on the other hand, to designate the passion of the one who states that a positive object belongs to one who deserves it, he gives up trying to find a specific name and borrows the closest generic noun, "joy." Whereby we see that the arbitrary nature of designation, which indicates the preeminence of the constructed idiolectal taxonomy, sometimes gives precedence to the concern for justifying the lexicalized distribution belonging to a culture.

Yet, anyone who would want to use such a semiotic perspective would soon encounter an insurmountable obstacle. The combinatory apparently has no limits, but it also has no univocal guiding principle. The taxonomic procedure is skewed from the start by the fact that any taxonomy of passions is relative to a given culture. This does not detract from its philosophical value, but it prevents semioticians from taking advantage of it. In fact, the semiotic method consists, among other things, in predicting and not listing the combinatory, and to predict the possible positions of the combinatory, it is necessary to know its general principle; moreover, to predict occurrences of passions in discourse, it is necessary to know its syntax. With philosophers, for the most part, passional changes no longer belong to the passional domain. In Descartes, for example, they fall under physiology and physical mechanics, and passions as such seem to be purely static.

Algorithms and Syntax in Spinoza. If we now turn to Spinoza, we encounter in his *Ethics* some elements of passional syntax. In this case the theory of passions appears as a series of connected propositions. For example, hatred is "a sadness accompanied by the idea of an external cause." The reader is thus referred to sadness, a passion "through which the mind passes to a lesser perfection," and the following explanation is given for this last procedure.

> The idea of that which increases or decreases, helps or hinders the body's ability to act, increases or decreases, helps or hinders the mind's ability to think. (*L'éthique*, Proposition XI, p. 159)

According to Spinoza, therefore, passion arises from a certain articulation of the pragmatic dimension and more especially of the somatic domain, along with the cognitive dimension. Competence of the pragmatic subject is a spectacle for the cognitive subject, and this spectacle organized as a "passion" then affects the competence of the cognitive subject himself.

This kind of function is based on the most universal principle of passions there is, the principle whereby we postulate the unity of the human subject, the interdependence of the various instances that make him up. Moreover, even the mechanism that engenders passions and results in deductive algorithms that construct them, has its origin in the process that, in our opinion, homogenizes the exteroceptive and the interoceptive through the mediation of the proprioceptive, a process that creates actual semiotic existence. This is why what affects the mind can affect the body, and why the affecting of the body can become a passional spectacle for the mind.

Nevertheless, the idiolectal and restrictive nature of this theory of passions shows through here in at least two ways. First of all, it is obvious that the passional expression of the cognitive on the pragmatic is here considered to be *dis-*

turbing, because the modification of the mental faculties clearly stems from so-called inadequate ideas. Now, inadequate ideas are by definition ideas that come to the mind through the influence of the body's affections and that, because of this very fact, can only be "disfigured and muddled," addressing themselves to the "passive" part of the mind. This philosophical arrangement presupposes the duality of soul and body, represented here as two cognitive spaces between which a modal barrier disrupts (mutilates and diminishes) the circulation of knowledge. Besides the generally negative moralization behind such a concept, it is impossible to imagine the pathemic dimension being autonomous, since the theory of passions is limited to the treatment of the effects of a cognitive dimension disrupted by the pragmatic dimension.

Furthermore, only the modality of *being-able* seems to be involved. The "body's power to act" (*being-able-to-do*), and "the mind's ability to think" (*being-able-to-know*) are actually the only things affected here. In fact, this can also mean that only *being-able* and its variations produce passions, or else that the other modalizations, by their undue interference with it, produce secondary effects. Whatever the case may be, this modality appears to govern the entire system. Moreover, insofar as its effects are then treated as a spectacle, for an understanding that produces only inadequate ideas, the modality of *knowing* then operates as a filter and interpreter of all the passions. Thus the alethic modalities that are dependent on the epistemic modalities make up the framework of Spinoza's theory of passions. "Fear," therefore, is "the idea of a thing in the future or the past of which the result [alethic modalization] seems to some extent doubtful [epistemic modalization]."

We must add a syntax intrinsic to the passional function itself to this syntax of the definition process. Part of the originality of Spinoza's theory of passions lies in the fact that certain passions can change into other passions. For example, "satisfaction" is joy caused by something that occurs *against all hope;* similarly, "disappointment" is sadness caused by something that happens *against all hope*. Such definitions imply a veritable modal sequence in which, for example, doubt changes into certainty. Satisfaction presupposes the syntactic absence of hope; perhaps even fear and disappointment presuppose the syntactic presence of hope. What Spinoza calls "hope" we would call "expectation," but there is no doubt that the impassioned subject is here made up of a series of modal subjects partially independent from one another and that certain passions are produced by a modal transformation. Now passional syntax is itself a factor that imposes no limits on the theory. Even if there are many combinations suggested by a taxonomy, there are still in principle a finite number of them. But insofar as there is no limit to the number of transformations in each sequence, in principle there exists an infinite number of passional syntagmas. Now the *Ethics* never give us the impression of being so limitless. The reason for this is that the connotative taxonomy wins out over syntax, and because it has failed to ensure the independence of the syntactic principle that the philosopher sometimes takes advantage of, it can give us only an idiolectal theory.

In fact, the apparent exhaustiveness of the combinatory is limited both by the premises retained that take into account only passions emanating from the body that alter the smooth functioning of the mind, and by the principle of deductive algorithms that govern the idiolect. This makes Spinoza as much a part of his own time as of the philosophical tradition. Before this, as we have already noted, the choice of a modal isotopy limits the system. Afterward, it is the choice of a certain number of combinations out of all the different possibilities that does so. Our philosopher emphasizes in passing that there are passions that are nameless, thereby indicating the autonomy of his construction with regard to the cultural divisions expressed through language. But it is nevertheless true that among all the possible combinations and modal sequences, only those allowed by the deductive path retained are taken into account. The clearest proof of this is that even though modal syntax has limitless potentiality, it does not manage to go beyond the taxonomy and remains loyal to the combinatory deductive process. We are not challenging the admirable coherence of the *Ethics*, or the relevance of the definitions it offers. On the contrary, in this example where the combinatory principle is pushed to the limit, we can understand why, especially in passional matters, a taxonomic and purely deductive method can justify only a posteriori the divisions imposed by each culture and superimpose on them the a priori of an idiolectal system.

This rapid overview of two philosophical theories cannot account for the philosophical treatment of passions, and it is also not our aim to attempt to do this here. Yet, these theories throw light on the connotative effects of certain methodological choices. Insofar as they are *taxonomical*, they are organized in binary oppositions and because of this cannot easily avoid a discontinuous and categorical mode of thought that, in our eyes, seems to be very ill equipped to deal with the passional universe *as it appears in discourse*. Insofar as they are *deductive* and subordinate to a particular philosophical system, they produce idiolectal taxonomies; insofar as they generally follow a *leximatic* principle, which leads to the systematic association of a justified designation to each definition, they confirm immanent sociolectal taxonomies.

These different characteristics deserve, of course, to be qualified and to be put back in the context of the history of philosophy. It would seem, for example, that after a long period of time where there was an abundance of treatises on taxonomy, the theory of needs and interest put a stop to the production of such treatises. While passional taxonomies were disappearing a concept of passion was developing that would not assert itself until the time of romanticism. Passion as such, given back to feeling, passion as a life principle that could not be divided and left no holds open to taxonomy. In a way the great upheaval set off by Nietzsche and Freud confirms this development by a basic anthropological gesture that places passion at the origin of culture and all things human, as the moving force of collective and individual history. It is evident that any philosophical theory of passions is not a taxonomic and deductive one, but this alternative seems hard to avoid. Either the entire philosophical system rests on a passional principle that seems almost to be one of its unknowables, or it is a taxonomy governed by this philosophical system that produces theories of passions.

Our concern is precisely to promote a semiotics of passions that both ensures an autonomous pathemic dimension within the theory of signification and does not become confused with semiotic theory as a whole while remaining independent of cultural variations expressed by connotative taxonomies. The epistemological and methodological importance we have attached to passional syntax seems to be able to keep us between a rock (taxonomy) and a hard place (passion as the basis of all signification). This is the epistemological minimum we need. We cannot for all that avoid the fact that when we begin analysis, the passions cannot be known except through usage that creates them and integrates them into the semionarrative primitive. Semiotically speaking, we know (almost) nothing about the passions, or at least, for all the reasons we have given up to this point, we must *pretend* we know (almost) nothing. To continue down the path of theoretical construction starting from the basics means, in the long run, that we take the chance of producing a connotative taxonomy among others, because it is now clear that, in this case, no one can escape from shifts and choices emanating from culture. Yet, what usage has produced should now be taken seriously and used in a critical way. This is why we will now begin to examine the passions in actual discourse: the discourse of the dictionary, moralistic and literary discourse, among others, that will allow us to gain detailed insight into the way sociolects and idiolects function. The lexicographical and literary corpora constitute a point of departure for possible generalizations and for raising new questions that will be integrated progressively into the first theoretical hypotheses.

Between two choices, one that consists of "tinkering around" within a natural language to build a passional system that would split language asunder and send it flying in all directions, and the other, which consists of building, in total independence, outside of all natural language, an arbitrary system that would always be problematical when it came to using it, we opt for a critical path, in which the virtualities of language will be recognized and the cultural selections theorized—where, in short, it should be possible to evaluate their import.

Chapter 2
On Avarice

Since passions owe their discursive existence to usage, be it collective or individual, we cannot confine our study of them simply to the generalities or semantic and syntactic "noemes" that constitute them. Natural language is in this respect a demonstration of what the history of a given culture has retained by way of passions among all the modal combinations that are possible. Thus, it is by consulting the dictionary, seen here as discourse on usage as found in a given culture, that we will begin to gather our initial information concerning the way in which passions function in that culture. The study of passional lexemes requires first that we define them, not simply name them, and this must be followed by a syntactic formulation of the definition itself. All in all this means transforming pathemic roles, whose "name lexemes" attest to their existence within a given usage, into *process pathemes*, and of bringing into the open, thanks to a conjugation of analysis and catalysis, their underlying modal organizations as well as the operations that predispose them to participate in passional configurations. This procedure, which has frequently been applied, grows out of our having observed the properties of condensation and expansion of discourse, observations that authorize us, starting with just one lexeme, to lay out the whole of a syntactic organization.

This does not mean, however, that the syntactic model of each passion is naturally contained in some way within its linguistic occurrence. Lexicalization is a secondary phenomenon to semantic structure. It affects the products of usage; that is, it affects the selections and arrangements that we observe in discourse and for which enunciative praxis is responsible. That is why the setting up of the model can come only after a pragmatic analysis of the definitions, which serves only to protect us from our own idiolectal penchants and indeed serves to compensate for our ignorance. In the course of this pragmatic analysis we should have been able to separate generalizable syntactic constituents from those that are not generalizable. The method we have chosen, one that at the same time gives us a deductive basis and explores discourses and the usages those discourses manifest in order to establish syntactic models, clearly shows that our objective is always to use induction to compensate for the shortcomings of deduction. In a process that presents globally as being hypotheticodeductive, hypotheses do not necessarily follow from axiomatizing speculation. The role of induction in all this is frequently a dominant one.

An examination of the lexeme "avarice" and its semanticism will allow us to illustrate and clarify our approach.

The Lexicosemantic Configuration

Performance: Acquiring and Keeping

The *Petit Robert* we consulted presents avarice in terms of three definitional segments: (1) an excessive attachment to money, (2) a passion for acquiring and accumulating, and (3) a passion for hanging on to wealth. The first of these segments presupposes that one already knows the definition of "attachment" and of "excess." Attachment, in turn, is defined as a "sentiment that joins us to people and things for which we have an affection." For instance:

Sentiment	reference to a passional nomenclature
that joins us	mode of conjunction
to people and things for which we have an affection	objects of value of the type "desirable," determined by a "*wanting-to-be*."

NB: "Desirable" is just an approximation by which we hope to account for "affection" and "attachment." We can intuitively recognize in them an aspectual effect, repetition, or duration, and a fiduciary component, namely, confidence in the value of the object. We will come back to this.

As for excess, here it represents an intensity of sentiment that is accompanied by a pejorative moral judgment. Passion is thus measured according to a scale on which the moral system marks out *thresholds* of appreciation: attachment to money can be more or less intense. However, if it goes beyond a certain moral threshold it becomes avarice. Yet the threshold does not represent a border separating a nonpassion and a passion. Rather, it separates two different passional forms that the dictionary, in its nomenclature, would call respectively a "sentiment" and a "passion." Furthermore, this scale of intensity and this moral threshold appear on the surface as a way of normalizing passion and thus also presuppose an aspectualization of the process designated by "have an affection for." Thus, the fact that the ethical judgment consists in projecting the aforementioned thresholds does not necessarily mean that the property so judged (here "excess") is of the same nature: the normative threshold is just the surface means by which the ethical system can manifest the property it is evaluating. Nonetheless, since the utterance of this normative threshold is the only directly observable index of the immanent presence of the property being evaluated, we are supported in our tactical decision to begin our examination by taking advantage of all that is offered by the products of usage. Here moral judgment is an example.

To sum up, the syntactic translation of the definition given by the dictionary presents as follows: an utterance of conjunction is overdetermined by a modalization, followed by an aspectualization. Both are overdetermined by a judgment as to degree of intensity, this arrangement being classed within our passional nomenclature.

The second definitional segment, "passion for acquiring and accumulating" wealth, directly operates a classification within the nomenclature. The term "passion," explained in terms of "intense inclination vis-à-vis an object that one wants, to which one is attached with all one's impulses," appears as a condensed version of the expression "excessive attachment." "To accumulate" is a doing that is carried out to the advantage of some beneficiary: a wanting-to-be, that of the beneficiary in relation to the object, has as a condition here a wanting-to-do, that of the "accumulating" subject. Furthermore, we have a recurring process in which the value of the object includes a quantitative factor.

In sum, "intensity," which we have already seen in the first segment, appears there twice: first as an aspectualization of the process, in the form of recurrence, and second in terms of a quantitative evaluation of the object, thus revealing an aspectualization of the object. Echoing our examination of the first segment, this observation shows that the intensity of the sentiment in question, far from being the last word on excess, brings into question the very nature of intensity itself. If the aspectualization of the process and that of the object are concomitant, we would be able to interpret passional intensity as being the manifestation of modulation of a continuous phenomenon, one that can be distributed, when it is enacted within discourse, on both process and object. It thus becomes integral to the defining of the passion of the subject.

The third segment proposed by the dictionary, "a passion for holding on to wealth," modifies only the nature of the doing. "To hold on to" is a narrative program of nondisjunction, which is different from accumulating, a program of conjunction. We should remember that Théodule Ribot, distinguishing between "static" and "dynamic" passions, classed avarice with the "static" passions. We see that, in fact, avarice includes both a dynamic form (of conjunction) and an apparently static form (of nondisjunction). These two forms can be situated on the semiotic square that demonstrates junction (Figure 8).

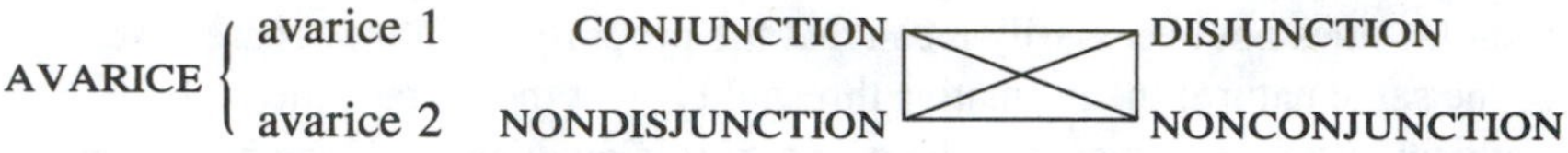

Figure 8

On the other hand, the difference between the two forms of avarice can be interpreted in terms of points of view. That is, they can be seen as a strictly discursive difference. Indeed, if we suppose that avarice is one and only one passion, despite its discursive variations, the opposition between "accumulate" and "hold on to" can be understood as being the opposition between avarice as it is brought into play before conjunction takes place, and avarice as it is enacted after conjunction. Aspectualization then differs according to whether one is dealing with the perfective process of conjunction or the imperfective process of nondisjunction: it is iterative (i.e., discontinuously durative) in the one case, and becomes continuative (i.e., continuously durative) in the other. "Perfective" here means no more than "aiming to accomplish conjunction," and "imperfective" means simply that conjunction has already taken place. This twofold establishment of a perspective from which to consider a single and specific passional process encourages us, when constructing our model, to look for a single syntactic principle that will allow us to account for avarice.

Passional Competence. The three definitional segments of avarice lead us to make this comment. First, if the narrative program of accumulation and holding on to seems to be regulated by a passion, that passion can be considered in terms of a competence. It is thus seen as the equivalent of a "wanting"–wanting-to-be or wanting-to-do–and we thus find ourselves, as far as the narrative schema is concerned, in that phase where a contract is set out between the Subject and the Sender. But, in fact, the miser can accumulate and hold on to wealth without there being any contract and without there being any Sender. One is even tempted to say that accumulating and holding on to wealth are "avaricious" only to the extent that they violate the contract and ignore the Sender and to the extent also that passion functions here as a reflexive substitute for manipulation, persuasion, and the contract. However, the opposite is just as possible. Such is the case, for example, when avarice is seen as characteristic of a whole social group, or hatred is shown by a whole group for its hereditary enemy. The presence or absence of a Sender is therefore not a relevant criterion for our understanding of avarice.

It seems, however, that quite independently of the Sender, we can recognize characteristics that allow us to identify two forms of competence, of which one is specifically passional. First, the competence that is proper to passion implies a programming of the subject that is independent of the programs themselves and that is endowed with specific aspectual forms, and all this to the extent that we might wonder whether or not we are dealing with a case of aspectualization of a behavior that attests to a competence. This competence – its repetition, its duration, its intensity – finds in competence its passional aura. Even better, it is as if passional competence depends on its aspectualization for its effectiveness. The passion of the miser can be enacted and recognized only by virtue of the iterative nature of conjunction and also by virtue of the continuative nature of nondisjunction.

There is yet another distinctive feature: passional competence can be interpreted in terms of a reflexive simulacrum. As opposed to "normal" competence, which we can grasp only by starting with performance and then reconstructing, passional competence is not dependent on performance. Quite the contrary, it is that very competence that regulates performance. On the one hand it always exceeds the doing that seems to flow from it – in effect, even if the miser feels satisfaction in accumulating wealth, he does not therefore stop accumulating more wealth – and on the other, it takes the form of a *goal image* for the subject, so that the object becomes a goal for its own sake, thus neutralizing the value system that is in effect. One might then say that what the miser is after is less the wealth that he accumulates and more the goal image that has been raised up as a potential simulacrum and in connection with which the miser can "fantasize" about being surrounded by wealth.

Because of its aspectual form – repetitive, durative, intensive – passional competence raises a more general problem, that of the acquisition of competences. How can the repetition of a doing, for example, result in a "being," which is a competence that is inscribed in the being of the subject? The question can be extended to cover the whole problem of the acquisition of roles in general. The acquisition of a competence that is transformed into a role through the aspectualization of a doing presupposes a knowing that is progressively acquired, a knowing that has to do with the interaction between a base program and usage programs and that, by virtue of that very fact, can only be discursive – is perforce situated at a more superficial level than the programs themselves. In the case of passion this knowing is a "figurative knowing," or rather a "figurative believing" whose content is the goal image, the ideal simulacrum we have postulated, whereas "normal" competence does not require any such reconstruction.

Passional competence constitutes a kind of "modal imaginary" of the subject, since, according to the definition we have proposed for passional simulacra, the goal image is composed of modalizations that characterize the being of the subject, modalizations that are part of that simulacrum because there has been a cognitive and fiduciary transfer (a disengagement). As a simulacrum, the goal image would constitute the "seeming" of the being of the subject, an appearing that is internal and reflexive, which would regulate, at least in part and in the form of discursive programming, the final behavior of the subject. In this sense, the notion of goal image would allow us to reconcile the logic of prediction with the logic of presupposition. The goal image is the means by which the subject anticipates the realization of a program and its eventual, resulting state. This allows him, through presupposition, to establish his competence. The combination of a *prediction* based on fiducia with a *presupposition* that is based on syntactic necessity leads to the effect of "motivation." The miser dreams of being surrounded by wealth; through presupposition he reconstructs an accumulation/holding on to program that then appears, within the passional configuration, as a motivation oriented by a goal image. The articulation of the "modal imaginary" on the narrative syntax can be understood only if one takes into account its back-and-forth movements on the axis of seeming.

A Community Modulation. Furthermore, avarice can be conceived of only if wealth is considered as constituting objects that circulate within society. Accumulation and holding on to can be deemed excessive only in terms of some norm that regulates exchanges between the subjects of a given community. Holding on to wealth, for example, and in particular the pejorative view of it, can be understood only if one presupposes a general predisposition toward distribution. Likewise, accumulation appears on examination as a superimposition between two processes: acquiring new objects and at the same time holding on to those that have already been acquired. Avarice is thus not the passion of one who possesses or seeks to possess, but is rather *the passion of one who represents an obstacle against the circulation and redistribution of goods in a given community*. All of that is, of course, a matter of custom or practice, one by which the enunciative praxis of a given community takes a given syntactic phenomenon produced at the semionarrative level and transforms it into a passion.

This means that if avarice seen as a passion can now be defined only indirectly in terms of junction, but in essence in terms of variations in the circulation of values, its defining criterion is no longer, at this community level, of the order of categorial discontinuity. Rather it is of the order of tensive continuity. Holding on to wealth now appears as a kind of modulation of social becoming, and it is no longer surprising, given that the essence of the passional effect has to do with aspectual forms, that its being put into discourse requires movement through a temporal distribution of the processes involved: acquiring, then holding on to, and continuing to acquire while all along holding on to wealth. We will come back to this characteristic at greater length and here simply state that, beyond discursive variables having to do with perspective, this phenomenon seems to coincide with a single definition of the passion of avarice.

Parasynonyms

Greed. To be "greedy" is to have an "immoderate desire," "to desire immoderately," whether it be a desire for food, goods, or even knowledge. "Gluttonous," "voracious," "guilty of cupidity," "rapacious," "curious" even – these seem to be the main correlatives of greed. The first thing that is obvious is that two main types of objects are implicated. The first are of a pragmatic order; that is, they are consumable, or they can hoarded. The others are of a cognitive order. Together they give us a criterion for classing these correlatives: food for "gluttonous" and "voracious" eater; goods for "guilty of cupidity" and "rapacious"; knowledge for "curious." Among all these objects, only hoardable goods and inconsumable goods (goods, wealth, money) are appropriate for the category of a "greed" that might be seen as a synonym for "avarice." The others characterize another sememe of "greed," one that has nothing to do with avarice: greed in terms of an excessive desire for food cannot be called avarice any more than can a greed for knowledge.

"Hoardable" and "inconsumable" characterize only the syntactic properties of objects and not their semantic content. More precisely, we are dealing with modalizations that are projected on junction, and which grow out of the syntactic form of objects. "Hoardable" could then be defined as "being able to be conjoined, in large numbers, with only one subject." "Inconsumable" can be explained as "not subject to being destroyed through conjunction with a subject" – that is, to be clear, "being able to be conjoined with an *n*th subject after having been conjoined with an $(n-1)$th subject." Such modalizations, as we can see, explicitly have to do with junction and with a *quantitative* component that we find also in notions of "participation" and "exclusion" (we will come back to this). Be that as it may, what is specific to avarice is, according to this point of view, based not on the semantic content of objects but rather on their syntactic properties. Because the semantic content of objects of value is not implicated in all this, we can no longer think that the assigned semantic value of an object, a phenomenon that is of the order of axiological orientation, can have any kind of power of attraction for the miser. What creates a miser is not money, land, or goods but rather the modalized form of junction and the *syntactic form of the object of value*.

Such an analysis, however, continues to ignore other meanings for our terms, in particular metaphorical ones – but we know to what extent stereotyped expressions reveal what might be called "signifieds of power" – when one is said to be a "miser" with compliments or "greedy" for compliments, or a "miser" with expressions of endearment or "greedy" to receive such expressions. One can also be called a "miser" with words, and so on. Why would our languages put a reluctance to dispense compliments and to express tenderness on the same level with the desire to accumulate and hold on to wealth if the underlying passional principle were not the same? It indeed seems that compliments, words, and endearments, just like hoardable goods and inconsumable goods, can be considered here in terms of objects in circulation, caught up in a general system of exchange, be that system societywide or between individuals. In both cases, avarice is recognized in the fact that circulation is interrupted and redistribution is blocked. This is why greed for knowledge cannot be called avarice, since a curious person does not deprive anyone of anything and in no way interrupts the general exchange of knowledge. On the other hand, keeping knowledge to oneself is something that, even if our language does not call it avarice, is very akin to it. On the other hand, gluttony and voraciousness have nothing to do with avarice because food cannot be put back into circulation once it has been put into conjunction with any given subject. At least that is true in any culture that does not accord any particular symbolic value to bodily excreta.[1]

It appears that in this case the syntactic properties of the object cease to be relevant in and of themselves: their hoardable and inconsumable nature is taken into account only because it allows for redistribution and circulation. But that hoardable and inconsumable feature is not specific to avarice if we remember that other figures such as words, knowledge, tenderness, and compliments, which are not hoardable, can be the object of the will to hold on to and thereby enter into avarice's configuration. On the other hand, the property that seems specific to objects that figure in avarice seems to be this ability to be part of general exchange patterns, to enter into circulation, but also to be held on to, accumulated. The object no longer has any semantic investment, or semionarrative syntactic form. It is no more than an effect of modulations effected on circulation within society. Since, on the other hand, it seems that the quantitative interpretation of phenomena is a matter for the community itself, seen as a protoactantial collectivity, the analysis of avarice has to be moved to the level of the tensive preconditions of signification.

Miserliness and Stinginess. Miserliness is a "sordid avarice." The miser is "base" in his miserliness and "shameful" in his self-interest. He is guilty of "ignoble meanness." Pejorative judgments dominate this configuration. They are brought to bear in terms of specifications that belong to different ethical parameters (shameful, base, mean, ignoble). Passional excess here is linked with moral judgment making, which we find defined in the discourse of the dictionary. It is the point of view of the social observer, guarantor of the community's norms, that is impassioned here, thus doubly intensifying the passional meaning effect of our lexeme.

Stinginess is a "mean avarice." The recurrence of "meanness" in the configuration leads us to make a redefinitional detour, since the definition of a term that is part of yet another definition can only serve to increase and refine our knowledge of the subject. A mean person is one who "is attached to the petty, to the mediocre," who "lacks generosity," who "displays avarice, parsimony." The lack of generosity refers us simply to the refusal to redistribute, to keep the object of value in circulation. On the other hand, parsimony leads us to "petty things" (e.g., saving the ends of burned candles) and brings to the fore another side of the moral code. In effect, we cannot reproach a stingy person for keeping out of circulation objects whose value we have already denied. The excess of "*wanting-to-be*" has meaning here only because it is a basic contradiction, given the object's lack of value. Nevertheless miserliness and stinginess, mean avarices, are two forms of avarice. However, the denial of any value for the object in question is a problem for us here. The first observation to be made concerns the extent of the importance of this denial. We refuse to accord any value to the object even though manifestly it has some value for the impassioned subject. In other words, miserliness and stinginess are based on a mistaken evaluation of value. There is disagreement between the individual subject and the social subject as to the assignment of value.

The notion of goal image and of simulacrum might be of use in clarifying this disagreement: a "passion," for the outside observer involved in our case, is something that involves an illusory goal image (appearing and not being), which results from the failure to see or comprehend on the part of the subject, and in particular from his misunderstanding of the processes of assigning value. Situated within the configuration of avarice, the miser and stingy person accumulate and hold on to objects of value that are not part of the general exchange system, thus introducing false objects into the exchange system of legitimate objects of value (for example, Maître Hauchecorne's string, in Maupassant's *La ficelle*). The general principle of circulation within a community is thus doubly disrupted: first simply by being interrupted and second by the introduction into the exchange system of "nonvalues" for which there are absolutely no receivers in the community in question. *The exchange patterns are therefore derailed.*

There is yet another useful refinement we can add: "sordid" can mean "having a base interest." To be self-interested is both "to have an interest in . . ." and, especially, to admit one's interest *openly*, by quite simply displaying it. The lesser the stakes, the more openly self-interested one will appear. It is against this open admission that we generally see negative judgments. We see that the miser, by holding on to and accumulating – that is, by raising obstacles to the free exchange of goods – actualizes a proform of value and designates where it will be inserted into the system. So we have a discursive manifestation of the assignment of value, of that "shadow of value" that is present within phoric tensivity. Furthermore, by admitting to being "interested," the miser explicitly sets himself up as a syncretic actor bringing together the impassioned subject, the subject of the doing and the beneficiary/subject. The result is that the outside observer, who pejoratively judges this behavior, is blocked from setting himself up as receiver. The social observer who assigns such a configuration a passional status always works, then, in terms of a subjectivizing perspective. Given the general rules governing the free circulation of goods, whose application he can control and monitor by setting himself up as a potential receiver of those objects, he notes in the case of stinginess that, for two reasons – holding on to wealth and the assignment of value – the role of receiver is blocked for him. Given that fact, he passes judgment on the other's passion and manifests this judgment in his discourse by identifying "intensity," "excess," or "insufficiency."

Saving and Being Economical. This moral judgment is softened in the case of the act of saving or being economical, even to the point of disappearing, except when, in fact, it becomes its opposite, namely, a positive judgment. Indeed, saving and being economical are not true "passions" according to the dictionary. One is simply the action of "handling well, using an object with moderation." The other characterizes the person who "spends moderately, who knows how to avoid needless expenditures." Moral judgment here valorizes "moderation" by contrasting it with the excess implied by the previously cited terms. To the extent that the gradated scale of economical behavior has a threshold, here it has not been crossed. Our examination of avarice and of stinginess has taught us, however, to distrust the apparent simplicity of this view of excess and moderation, of these "argumentative scales" that in effect encompass community tensions. We must also note that the dictionary, in its nomenclature, uses an apparently antinomic generic term, that of "action": being economical and saving appear as instances of doing. This does not mean that the saving or the economical person has no competence. Both have the ability to know what they are doing when they spend money, know how to consume only as much as they need. As to the modal aspects of this competence, we can say that knowing regulates wanting, whereas in the preceding cases the opposite was true.

But that is not the main point. The competence of the economical person, and of the saver, is like the story of happy people: there is nothing to say about it; it is strictly presupposed by performance; it in no way goes beyond the realization of the economizing program. This knowing does not bring about the "modal excess" we have already identified as being the usual index of a passional meaning effect. Given that fact, a definition based on doing is the only one that will suffice.

Nonetheless, as an economic role, "saving person" and "economical person" belong to the class of *thematic roles*: the repetition of a like doing installs a fixed competence in the being of the subject, a knowing-how-to-do that moral judgment making recognizes as a social stereotype. The underlying modal setup is thus classed as a product of usage, of how things are done, but that does not mean that it is then considered to be a "passional disposition." One might note here that repetition affects the whole of the program and that it in no way constitutes a specific aspectualization of the modal setup itself. This last is thus lacking in the internal dynamics of intermodal syntax, and without it, it cannot be registered as frame of mind.

On the other hand, when we have "the avoidance of any unnecessary spending," we are dealing with a nondisjunction program and when we have "spending in moderation," we have a disjunction program. But these two options in no way exclude each other: one has to spend without spending too much and one must hold off on spending yet spend a little, of course. Saving and economizing are thus founded on an equilibrium between these two contradictories, on an alternative that can always be chosen between disjunction and nondisjunction. The decision here is regulated by the modality of *having-to-be*, in the sense of what it is one's duty to be, and we see this in the figure of attachment. This gives us the astonishing synonymy between saving and avarice, two instances of *having-to-be*, being what it is one's duty to be, that produce two such different effects as usefulness (or utility) and attachment! But we can easily see that these two instances of *having-to-be* are differentiated by their syntactic properties. First, attachment becomes a *wanting-to-be,* which is all we see directly manifested, and it is that transformation that characterizes the dynamics of passional dispositions or frames of mind. Nonetheless, modalization is different in these two cases. The *having-to-be* of utility or usefulness modalizes the object of value that has been semantically invested, and it modalizes *only* that object. At the surface level this appears as an "advantage." On the contrary, the *having-to-be* of attachment modalizes the junction itself and designates the locus of an object that can fail to be so invested but that, when it is indeed invested, will project that investment on the subject. Now the subject, having become "attached" to something, is defined entirely, semantically and syntactically, by the modalized junction (whence the effect of alienation between subject and object).

It remains for us to try to understand why, within the cultural context of our configuration, saving and economizing are not "sensitized," are not recognized as passions. They also are modal setups that can each function as a competence; they are integrated into the semionarrative level by custom and practice, but they are not granted the internal syntactic dynamics that would make passions of them. To go any further, we have to come back to the matter of the equilibrium between disjunction and nondisjunction: under the cover of moderation, the economizing person is still someone who spends and who, therefore, poses no threat to the circulation of goods within the community. He neither accelerates nor slows down exchange; he keeps up with it, at his own pace. The roles of the "economizing person" and "saver" manifest nothing more than an adaptation, vis-à-vis the individual rate of participation of a given subject, of the general rate of participation in exchange that we can discern as underlying our configuration. A detour that will take into consideration some antonyms is now necessary before we go any further in this direction.

From the point of view of our method, the analysis of the definitional segments of avarice and of its parasynonyms—which have to do with lexical semantics—revealed a set of moral judgments going back to social axiologies that are superimposed on the pathemic but that reveal certain essential features of that pathemic. In particular, they place passion, including individual passion, within *a vast intersubjective field* regulated by norms that are imposed on the circulation of values. Furthermore, our analysis identifies programs and thematic roles that are presented as highly predictable and stereotyped forms of behavior. To define the pathemic level, to ensure the autonomy of the pathemic dimension, requires us first to extract it from those overdeterminations that, while allowing passions to be manifested and, indeed, allowing some of their most basic aspects to flourish, in part mask the manner in which passions function. Overarching moralizing often wipes out passional mechanisms, and thematization has the result of freezing the manifestation of passions into stereotyped "blocks" that are more easily identified in a given culture. We have noted, for example, that "excess" and "insufficiency," which in definitions and in linguistic analyses are usually seen as criteria for identifying passion, must be considered with discretion, since all they do is transpose the axiologies and codes that are intertwined with passional functioning itself.

Antonyms

Dissipation. Dissipation is the "action of dissipating by spending too prodigally." To dissipate is to "spend foolishly." Here we confirm that "excess," given as a criterion of passion through the use of the adverb "foolishly," is the result of a pejorative moralization. Of course one might say that excess, which is a defining characteristic of passion, is the object of the pejorative judgment, but our preceding analyses show that the opposite is true: this pejorative judgment projects excess onto the passional arrangement, and thus we must look elsewhere for the criterion for the passional. The definition, taking its starting point in action, transforms dissipation into a thematic role that one can grasp, as in the case of saving, if one begins with performance. At the same time, however, it plays passion's card. This so-called passion thus poses a problem because it results from the coming together of a saving thematic role and a pathemic role, the whole thing then being pejoratively moralized. Here we can measure the degree of similarity between the thematic and the pathemic role. All we have to do is vary our emphasis on the one or the other in our definition. Furthermore, here we can note—something we saw in neither the case of avarice nor the case of economizing—that the two kinds of roles are compatible and in no way exclude each other. Since they both are the result of enunciative practice, they require us to conceive of two procedures that are at the same time compatible and independent. One integrates roles that have been fixed by repetition after first having inscribed them within a thematic isotopy; the other integrates roles on the basis of the relative syntactic autonomy of the modal arrangement underlying them, after first having inscribed them within a passional taxonomy.

On the square of junction, dissipation occupies the disjunction pole, but it has a property that we must raise here. In effect, "to dissipate" is also to "blot out by dispersion"; it amounts to erasing something valuable or great without leaving a trace of it. The semic kernel, independently of the specific configuration of avarice, is thus one of the destruction of an object. The dissipator spends, indeed, but no one can benefit from the goods so destroyed. The image of dispersion, if one sees it as a quantitative operation, is quite clear in this respect. There is something for everyone; there is nothing for anyone.

Prodigality. A prodigal person is one who "spends excessively," who "squanders his possessions." The correlates of "disinterested" and "generous" oppose it, term by term, to "mean person" and "stingy person." Also, in the "figurative" sense, which is always revealing, objects of value are substitutable within the same class as avarice: one can be prodigal with compliments, with good words, with tenderness, and so on. Prodigality thus would be an antonym of avarice when viewed in terms of the whole set of its meanings.

The configuration now is seen as a semantic microstructure. In the first instance each junction utterance produces programs that in turn can be translated into the form of prototypical processes (Figure 9).

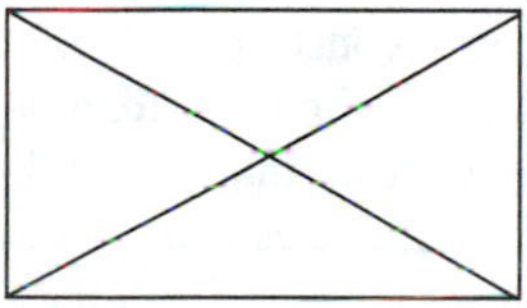

Figure 9

The prototypical processes could be reformulated in more general terms as being archipredicates of the elementary utterance, each one being characteristic of one of the forms of junction (Figure 10).

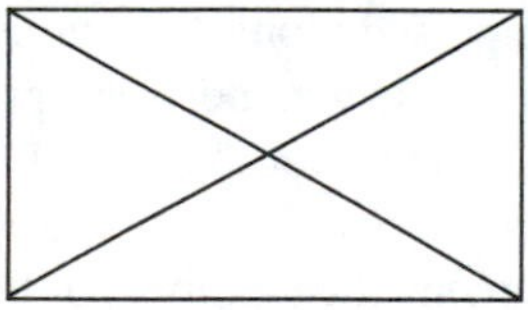

Figure 10

The two roles that we find in the configuration, thematic and pathemic, are defined in relation to one of these archipredicates. Initially a judgment of excess or moderation is made concerning that archipredicate. We thus end up with the semantic microsystem of the configuration we have conceived of (Figure 11).

As with any construct, as soon as you leave off empirical observation and the

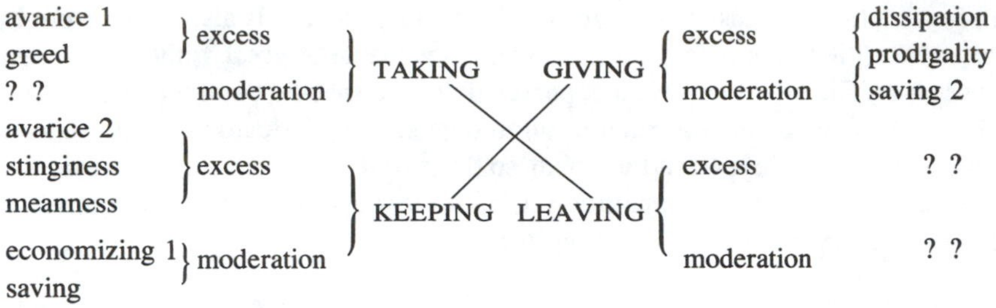

Figure 11

givens of its parameters in order to establish a model, positions appear that have no equivalent in the lexicon. As defined within the system, they are thus predictable in those discourses in which the configuration appears. In our case we have moderated conjunction–the subject takes what is his due and is content with his share–and excessive nonconjunction, a form of ascetic disinterest that could cast into doubt the very principle of the circulation of values.

On closer examination the two antonyms, "prodigality" and "dissipation," including their "figurative" meanings, also transgress the rules of general exchange. These rules, which we always reconstruct through presupposition, stipulate that the overall quantity of goods is limited and that each one's share is also limited. Thus, the value of goods flows from that very relative scarcity. To be prodigal is to act as if each person's share, and especially one's own, were not limited. On the one hand, this compromises the equilibrium of the exchange system, and on the other it casts into doubt the value of value–that is, the assigning of value. This is indeed confirmed by the fact that the two antonyms have to do only with goods that, correctly, might be considered to be the "fixed" share accorded each person: one can squander an inheritance, a fortune (i.e., nonrenewable goods), but one cannot squander a salary or income, which is renewable. Likewise, we have seen that dissipation destroys the object: literally, the share disappears as share and can no longer be passed along to anyone. This leads retroactively to these questions about avarice. One who desires a great income or a bigger salary will eventually be considered "ambitious" but will not be labeled a "miser." The "passion to accumulate" has to do with nonrenewable goods, which are part of a fixed distribution system among the members of the community. Although they are contraries, avarice and prodigality violate the same rule: the miser moves in on other people's shares and the prodigal person destroys his share. In contrast, the "saver" and the "economizer" know how to husband their shares.

Once again, in the passional configuration we are examining, the semantic investment of objects is of little importance. However, their syntactic properties define and modalize them with a view to eventual junction with the subject and are therefore determining. Such is the case with the features we have called "nonrenewable" and "partitive." But on the other hand, the appearance in the configuration of objects that do not usually comply with these syntactic properties, such as compliments or tenderness, shows us that such properties modalize junction and not the objects themselves. How might tenderness manifest itself as someone's share other than because some subjects consider as a value only what legitimately is their due in the exchange system and its intersubjective distribution? Here we are touching on the assignment of value, on the criterion that decides value. We can see that at this level, dissipation and prodigality show us another modulation of community tensions and of the circulation of values, a foolishness (whence "spending foolishly") that disperses and upsets the exchange system. We have yet to define the notion of "share" within the framework of this exchange system and its circulation of values. We will come back to that.

Generosity, Disinterest, and Largesse. Generosity is a "disposition to give more than one has to." Intensity is not interpreted here as an excess, and moral judgment is positive. If, as is the case, it is not thought that the threshold of dissipation is reached and passed, it is doubtless because the social observer can see himself as a possible beneficiary of the gift in question. Like "largesse" and "liberality," generosity is defined from the point of view of attribution—that is, of an eventual conjoined subject within a program for the transfer of an object. This social observer who sets himself up as a potential receiver, one who is already present in avarice and who is virtualized in the case of dissipation and prodigality, is thus linked to the whole ensemble of the configuration by becoming the delegate of an enunciative praxis, by being the witness to something that is usually called "passion," "disposition," or "action." He is the delegate of a collective enunciation to the extent that it is he who institutes perspective, and it is he who serves as a referent by which one can know if a beneficiary other than the subject is possible.

However, in this case, in order to understand the role of this social observer, it is not enough just to note the change in point of view. If he is unable to recognize himself as the eventual receiver benefiting from prodigality, it is because there can be no receiver of destroyed objects. If he sees himself as a receiver of an act of generosity, it is because the generous subject increases other people's shares, and thus at the same time his actions imply a receiver, even when he does not, in his generosity, destroy his own share. Contrary to what one might expect, and structurally speaking, the generous subject acts along the same lines as the economizing subject: spending is controlled, his share is safeguarded, others' shares are respected. This unforeseen synonymy can likely be explained in terms of the superimposition of two vestiges of social practice—that is, two different moments in society's action of mapping out its cultural and passional universe. Connotations that have fallen out of use and that were once attached to certain accepted meanings for "generosity," "liberality," and "largesse" operate in much the same way: at certain levels of society, at another time, the role of facilitating the circulation of goods was devolved; more recently the role of containing and slowing down that process of circulation has been defined.

As we saw in earlier instances, the semantic investment of objects is not relevant here. All that counts is respecting others' shares, at the syntactic level, and the activation of modulation, at the level of valencies. If economizing and saving are valorized despite their "slowing down" effect, it is undoubtedly because they are seen to have a regulating role within an "accelerating" environment. Likewise, if one evaluates generosity positively, despite its "accelerating" tendency, it is because of its regulating role in a "slowed" environment. The modulations underlying each figure of the configuration thus correspond to a certain state of affairs, a state of affairs vis-à-vis the tensions that are at play within the configuration as a whole. The "semiotic styles" of the miser, of the generous, and of the prodigal subjects would thus be seen as resulting from a selection through social practice of the inflections they bring to the dominant modulation in the state of affairs and which are brought into play through the mediating action of their modalized and stereotyped doing.

Furthermore, generosity presupposes "disinterest" (not acting out of self-interest), another antonym for avarice. Disinterest can be defined as a "detachment from all personal or self-interest." The disinterested subject would be to the generous subject what the "attached" subject is to the miser, a homology founded on a like relation of presupposition. And this same relation might, *grosso modo*, be homologated vis-à-vis the relation between competence and performance. Detachment and attachment, by virtue of their virtual nature, would involve only competence, in particular a volitive and deontic competence with there being no perspective concerning a moving on to any given act. Generosity and avarice, on the other hand, by virtue of the actual nature of the inducted competence and of the predictability of their doing (giving, accumulating, holding on to), would include either performance or competence grasped in terms of a moving on to carrying out a given act. We might note, for example, that if generosity is defined as a "disposition to give more than one has to," liberality (another version of disinterest) is a "disposition to give generously"; that is, it is a "disposition toward a disposition."

We may seem to be proceeding by apparently tenuous deductions in the series of presuppositions that order passional competence, and we must therefore say that the variations in lexical mapping that we see when examining the definitions of generosity, disinterest, and liberality are of a strictly syntactic nature. Nonetheless those variations show that there does exist a *modal sequence*.

The first stage in the sequence, defined as "attachment" or "detachment," has to do with a relation vis-à-vis values, a manner of relation that is sufficiently general so that it can be defining. It can thus, for the subject, define a way of being in the world ("attached" vs. "detached"): from the point of view of the generative trajectory, this first stage is responsible for the assignment of value. From the point of view of the syntactic trajectory, this first stage includes the modalization of junction, independently of objects. The second stage is truly a substitute for competence, something we have called a "disposition." The final stage covers the various forms we see when there is movement on to the performance of an act. These forms are identified as "attitude" or "behavior." They are:

Attachment/Detachment → Disposition → Attitude/Behavior.

Although nothing authorizes us to generalize from this sequence, it nonetheless brings to light the process by which the impassioned actor is constructed. One gets the impression that the accumulation of features that characterize that subject throughout the discourse in question is not a matter of chance. It seems that the passional roles (detachment, disinterest, generosity) organize and set themselves in motion, with the whole thing being founded on a modal syntax. The passional trajectory thus would include an aspectualization of the actor, one that would amount to the discursive form of his "inner life."

Construction of the Model

The Microsystem and Its Syntax

Following the lexical semantic analysis we have just carried out, all of the posts on the square of junction are now occupied and the configuration for avarice has now been reduced to its microsystem: disinterest is on the same side as nonconjunction, and generosity, in keeping with its dictionary definitions, occupies either the position of disjunction or that of nonconjunction. Further, the relation of contradiction between accumulating avarice and disinterest is confirmed by the contradiction existing between attachment and detachment that characterizes them. Our distribution is illustrated in Figure 12.

avarice 1
greed
??? . . . (moderation)

avarice 2
stinginess
meanness
saving
economizing 1

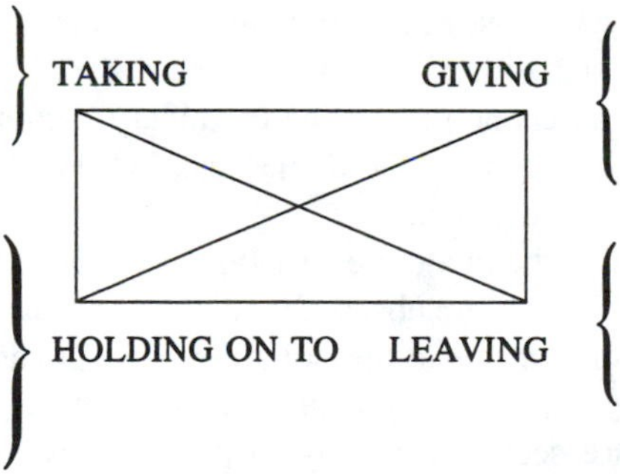

dissipation
prodigality
economizing 2
generosity 1

??? (excess)
generosity 2
disinterest
liberality

Figure 12

NB: The figures for excess are in italics, and those for moderation are in bold face.

The four main positions thus obtained define four fundamental attitudes shown by human beings vis-à-vis objects of value. Around these attitudes there are four main types of goal images, which, in turn, will appear as intended projects within eventual programs. The logicosemantic organization of our model uniquely clarifies the syntactic sequences we had already reached intuitively. We saw that accumulating avarice presupposes hoarding avarice. Likewise, generosity in terms of gifts presupposes generosity defined in terms of disinterest. What is antecedent to and subsequent to our passional and modal variations can be explained by the relations and transformations that we see in the microsystem. Thus mean miserliness is transformed into accumulating avarice by the relation of implication. This is what Balzac shows, in his own way, when he states that "avarice begins where poverty leaves off."

By building on the interdefinition process that characterizes such a semantic microsystem we can reconstruct its unlexicalized positions. Excessive nonconjunction would be a presupposed criterion for prodigality—that is, a scorn for all goods that would in itself constitute a transgression of the collective axiology and would also presuppose the absence of any value-assigning system: a form of nihilism, and from the point of view of the social observer, another failure to see, it would be the inverse of the process of going after "little things." Further, this scorn for values, because it is truly "displayed," becomes linked with the "admission of interest," which allows us to consider "excessive nonconjunction" as being the contrary of mean miserliness.

As for "moderate conjunction," it would become another form of disinterest, a form of acquisition that would consist only in satisfying one's needs. In effect, a disinterest that did not allow for satisfying those needs seen by everyone as legitimate would be considered excessive and would bring us back to the case we have discussed; disinterest is *moderate*, and rightly so, in that it allows for indispensable acquisitions. The balance we envisage here is the same as that we have already seen in the case of economizing: avoiding spending without allowing for indispensable spending demonstrates avarice; avoiding only unnecessary spending is being an economizer. The dictionary definitions do not establish a parallel between economizing and disinterest, but we see that this can be easily deduced within our microsystem.

It thus appears that the moderate variations and the excessive variations of our configuration constitute two subsets that almost completely exclude each other within the microsystem, this to the point that we can easily separate them from each other. This would in no way violate the principle of interdefinition. In effect all the relations are seen exclusively to prevail between the variations found within one subset: between saving, economizing, generosity, disinterest, and moderate acquisition on the one hand; between avarice, mean miserliness, stinginess, dissipation, prodigality, and excessive disinterest on the other. Once they are separated these two microuniverses reveal what is particular, respectively, to each. Excess and moderation, as is the case for the socioeconomic forms they translate, can be interpreted at the level of elementary structures as being two types of taxonomic distribution and two different types of syntactic functioning.

From a taxonomic point of view, we see that in the subsystem for moderation, the parasynonyms are curiously situated in schemata of contradiction: economizing 1 and economizing 2 in one case, disinterest and moderate acquisition in the other. Since moderation, and rightly so, consists in distinguishing between necessary things and unnecessary or superfluous things, and since it also consists in maintaining a balance between spending and not spending, acquiring and not acquiring, the development of the category these contradictions are supposed to produce is relative, gradual, and here seen as an alternative with a variable time span. On the other hand, in the subsystem for excess, the parasynonyms are located on the deixis in a relation of presupposition (avarice 1 and 2, prodigality and scorn for goods): the relations of opposition here are strong and irreducible.

From the syntactic point of view, the difference is even more striking. In the microsystem for moderation, one moves across deixis and schemata without interruption; the syntactic trajectory is unbroken and seems to obey the fluctuations of some external set of demands instead of the imperatives of some axiology or other. In effect, to go from saving to generosity, one need not change one's system of values. All that is needed is to change one's point of view and then move from the position of beneficiary to that of giver. In the subsystem for excess, on the contrary, we cannot go beyond its schemata without a complete upheaval of the value system. Only its presuppositions can be engaged without upheaval. On the other hand, in order to transform a hoarding miser into a prodigal person, or an accumulating miser into an excessively disinterested person, we need a conversion of a whole other kind of importance than in the case of the preceding subsystem. Let it be added that it seems completely impossible to transform a miser into a generous person—that is, to move from the subsystem of excess to the subsystem of moderation.

It would seem that the microsystem for avarice includes at least three different antonymic layers: weak oppositions, balanced alternatives within the domain of moderation; strong oppositions, reversals of the tendency toward excess; and absolute oppositions between the subsystem of excess and that of moderation. One can understand that once we combine all these kinds of oppositions (avarice with generosity, for example), we will obtain a maximal effect of antonymy. These different forms of antonymy, as we have seen, have to do with different semiotic levels.

Twofold Modalization

If we review our analysis, we see that avarice brings into play two distinct types of modalization. As far as attachment is concerned, we have only attachment to things, junction with the object; but we immediately note that the subject can have an affection for desirable objects (money, life) *as well as* for undesirable objects (death, solitude). Wanting, among other modalities, here is at play on two different registers: on the one hand, as a *modalization of the object of value*, with the object being seen as desirable or nondesirable, and on the other as *modalization of junction*, with junction being seen as desirable or nondesirable. Disinterest (taking a disinterested stance), for example, necessarily includes these two modal impacts: on the one hand, objects are classed as desirable in the collective system of values—because we would not consider as disinterested a person who is detached from objects that have no value—and on the other hand, junction with these same objects is considered to be nondesirable by the individual subject. Potlacht, for example, a codified version of dissipation, could be understood as a passion of destruction applied to objects that are considered to be desirable.

This twofold modalization has the effect of guaranteeing the individual subject's freedom of choice in this "hell of things" that the collective group offers him and codifies for him. The passional effect is not the result alone of the modalization that directly concerns the impassioned subject, but rather of their confrontation with each other. In effect, neither dissipation nor disinterest can be considered a passion if the objects concerned are not, in themselves and for the group, desirable. In the case of meanness, the *wanting-to-be* applied to junction is in opposition to the modalization of the objects in question, which are considered to be nondesirable: the passional meaning effect, and above all the codification through usage of these phenomena seen as passions, can in part be explained by referring to the opposition between these two modalizations.

But these two modalizations are not different only in terms of the syntactic instance—object or junction—that they affect, or just in terms of their exposing feature, positive or negative, but also in terms of their respective degree of intensity. So it is that avarice, for example, is characterized by a *wanting-to-be-conjoined-with* that is marked by a degree of intensity that is stronger than the desirability of the objects concerned. One can therefore imagine a gradated axis for the two modalizations. It would stretch between the two extreme poles of positive and negative desirability. Thus, meanness would bring about a confrontation between a maximal positive desirability of junction and a negative desirability vis-à-vis the objects concerned. Or again, generosity would include reconciling a maximal positive desirability vis-à-vis the objects concerned with a negative desirability vis-à-vis junction.

This gradation of the axes of modalization raises certain problems. In effect, if we could simply explain it in terms of the instance of their being set into discourse, their "gradable" nature would simply be an epiphenomenon that results from aspectualization. However, these graduated confrontations bring axiology itself and our very definition of values into question. We must once more refer to a system of social regulation of desires and of the circulation of goods. Modalization has the function of regulating, among other things, the relation between individual subjects and the collective axiology. This latter is present in two different forms: on the one hand, as a system of objectal values that projects various instances of wanting or having-to onto objects, and on the other, as a network of codes of good conduct and proper practice that allow one to know under what conditions the junction of an object with a given subject will not block circulation within the community as a whole.

Now we can understand the overmoralization contained in the dictionary definitions of stinginess and meanness. They relate at the same time to both modalizations: the transgressing of rules of proper practice, which are applicable to the modalizations of junction, and also the transgressing of the systems of values themselves, systems that regulate the modalization of objects. We can also understand why avarice and saving, although they are both founded upon a *having-to-be* (of attachment in one case, usefulness in the other), are nevertheless opposed to each another when considered in terms of moralization: in the case of "avarice-attachment," the *having-to-be* is a modalization of junction, one that can be imputed to the individual subject. In the case of "saving-usefulness," we have a modalization of the object that can be imputed to the collectivity in which the subject figures. The false synonymy of the two roles, just as that of the two cases of *having-to-be* subtending them, can be understood only in terms of the two modalizing instances and requires that we recognize that moral judgment and the projecting of codes of proper behavior can affect one or the other. The analysis of avarice and the field it covers leads us to consider the modalization of the object as being of the order of ideology – collective ideology in the case of the configuration we have established – and the modalization of junction as being the source of energy for passions, strictly speaking.

The Object and Its Various Levels

The distinction between the two types of modalization, although it is somewhat enlightening, only increases the scope of the problem. In effect, it leads us to recognize new forms of continuous variations that are regulated by axiologies having to do with the proper use of junction and not just with the investment of objects. That is why it seems necessary to come back to the different modes of existence of the object, because the relevance of those modes in the passional domain is not yet secure.

First, we can take as given that the semantic content of objects, the investing process that results in their becoming part of a system of values, is not relevant for the analysis of passions. The objects that figure in someone's avarice, greed, or even generosity can vary widely without the passion itself being affected.

On the other hand, certain syntactic properties, of a more general and abstract order than semantic investments, have provided us with a taxonomic base for our description. Thus the /hoardable, inconsumable/ feature, as is the case with the due "share" for each member of the collectivity (covered by the /partitive/ feature), allowed us to understand certain specific aspects of the objects in circulation in our configuration. These features, which we have designated as syntactic, are independent of the semantic classes to which the objects of value can belong. In a general way, it indeed seems that these syntactic properties serve as mechanisms for a quantitative yet tensive evaluation of the modulation of the continuous. Thus, the notion of "share" refers us to the /partitive/ feature. Since the principle of general exchange requires both a free circulation of objects and a permanent schema for fixing the distribution of fair shares, we can conclude that what is at play is the maintenance, within the group as a whole, of the "partitive" nature of objects in order that each person can keep his or her fair share without that share then becoming an "integral" or "integrated" unit.

Our usual thinking about syntax has led us to consider the syntactic object strictly as the object of the subject's interest, as the target whose trajectory is regulated by protensivity. Inscribing the object among other objects, inscribing a "thing" within the world of "things," cannot fail to raise the question of demarcational borders, as is the case with any pictural semiotics, for example. What are the extensions and margins of objects, as far as the level of epistemological preconditions is concerned? The solution may be sought by applying the category of "totality" to our thymic mass. It would thus be seen as a "cake," the pieces of which are distributed according to the requirements of the subjects. The recursivity of this category, which brings the rational construction of objects within the generative trajectory, reappears in the pathemic trajectory and allows us to account for a circulatory syntax that underlies any given passional microuniverse.

On the other hand, an examination of our dictionary definitions showed us that modalizations in these cases were of variable intensity and thus required study in terms of a continuum. The properties of the object themselves include quasi-aspectual variations: thus a partitive unit can be "open" thanks to generosity or "closed" because of saving/economizing. The opposition between partitive and integralizing is also one of degrees and stages. In the case of avarice it seems that an integralizing unit is constructed when there is a "closing," and as a response to there being an obstacle to the free circulation of goods. A twofold modulation is at play, one that is both cumulative and retensive. Furthermore, even if one can "metaphorically" imagine what a "fair share" of knowing might be, or of tenderness or compliments, a syntactic definition of the object considered to be of discontinuous extension is hardly satisfying.

These aspects of the passional universe we have examined lead us to try a continuous and tensive representation. To the extent that, at the discursive level, social norms are applied to a process of *circulation*, we are led to suppose that, at a deeper level, the coming into being of the collective group requires that any tensions within that group be regulated. It indeed seems that, within the configuration we have been studying, dispersive and cohesive forces are interacting and that the very coming into being of the collectivity depends on a relation between forces that favors the latter ones. At this level of abstraction we can represent general exchange – the circulation of goods, among others – as an aspect of social coming into being, a continuous flow whose modulations would tend to stabilize or destabilize the collective protoactant.

Two "logics" are at play in this social coming into being: a logic of forces, those of change (cohesive and dispersive), and a logic of positions, those of the units and of the totality that we should see against the background of an *interactantiality*. The various passions we have seen up to now come into play in this "flow," either to help produce cohesion or to help produce dispersion. Avarice, for example, maps out an island of slowing pace and resistance and thereby brings about the appearance of a "place" that deflects the flow and whose borders become opaque and impenetrable to change: in that phenomenon we can see an echo of what political economy says about hoarding and accumulating profits. Saving, on the other hand, is born of a slowing modulation that tempers excessively rapid change and maps out an individual, transparent, and penetrable place. As we have seen, the generous person acts in an opposite direction, to the benefit of change. Dissipation and prodigality, however, presuppose a dispersive acceleration that threatens the flow in another way, by preventing the forming of any place whatsoever. The flow in that case, having no route to follow, wanders off and evaporates. Cohesive coming into being would thus be threatened in two ways, by slowing down or by accelerating. Furthermore, two thresholds appear: the threshold at which an integral unit is created, on the one hand, and the threshold at which a partitive unit disappears, on the other. Any movement beyond either of these thresholds threatens the partitive totality.

Social becoming is seen against the backdrop of phoric tensivity; the "positions" that appear and disappear, according to the modulations applied to them, are valencies. Thus what allows any object in the world, whatever its syntactic or semantic properties, to take its place in our configuration is the *style of the modulation* that takes it on. From the point of view of the social observer the only objects that are assigned a positive value are those that participate in a "cursive" style, one that favors cohesive forces. From the point of view of the miser, it is instead a "suspensive" style, of the cumulating and retensive kind, that characterizes objects worthy of being sought after. These "semiotic styles" thus prefigure modalization as it is put to use by passions.

In effect, each of these styles is, on the one hand, converted and integrated into the modal syntax where it brings about specific meaning effects and, on the other, called on as an aspectualization at the instance of setting into discourse. For example, the "maintaining" of coming into being, the cursive modulation of the flow, prefigures the *being-able* that will be able to modalize the social subject and the objects she seeks. The islands of resistance and slowing prefigure the *wanting* and the *nonwanting* of the miser. The deflection of the flow onto "nonvalences" is an initial modulation of what will later appear in such modal setups as the *wanting* and *nonwanting* of the stingy person.

Existential Simulacra of the Subject

As opposed to the microsystem that allowed us to establish a local typology for passional forms, we can state that each of the groups of antonyms and parasynonyms can in part be defined in terms of varieties of junction, as long as we interpret utterances of junction, covered by the archipredicates "giving," "leaving," and "keeping," as things sought after by the subject and not as utterances attested to in the utterance. That is why, since the expression "modes of existence of the subject" is already used to designate the different statuses of the subject of a state within the rational narrative trajectory, we have chosen to call the different positions the subject assigns to himself within his own passional imaginary sphere "existential images." We propose a basic model, one that can take on the elementary syntax of the semiotic square (see Figure 13).

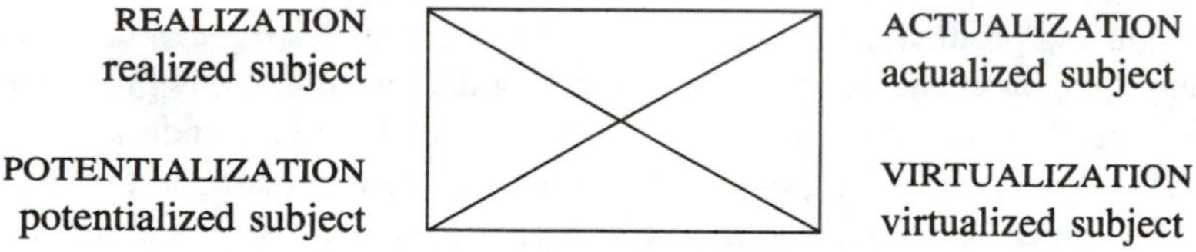

Figure 13

The trajectory of the existential images will constitute one of the syntactic bases of the dynamized modal mechanisms and of passion. Thus, the retensive miser is a potentialized subject (nondisjoined) who, by becoming an accumulating miser, is transformed into a realized subject (conjoined). Likewise the disinterested person is a virtualized subject (nonconjoined) who becomes actualized (disjoined) when he enacts generosity.

The modalizations that overdetermine the trajectory are not necessarily isotopic: the transformation of one modality into another modality is a separate and distinct problem whose principles we have discussed before and whose concrete enactment we will discuss later. The trajectory of the existential roles governs only the successive positions that the subject projects on the passional simulacrum as his "being." Thus we are dealing with a case of the *appearing of being*. The subject who has been potentialized by avarice, who "does not want to spend," is characterized, keeping in mind the attachment that links him to objects, by a *having-to-not-be-disjoined*, and, keeping in mind his desire to accumulate those objects, he is characterized by a *wanting-to-be-conjoined*. The modalizations of the accumulating miser thus come about thanks to a twofold transformation:

1. not being disjoined → being conjoined
2. having to → wanting to

Through the modal forces that affect it, the impassioned subject constructs, thanks to the first transformation, an imaginary scenario in which he successively occupies the positions of potentialized subject and realized subject. Intermodal syntax is what can account for the second transformation, against the backdrop of the modulations governing becoming.

The trajectory of these existential images allows us to account for the specific trajectories of each impassioned subject and, in particular, the way in which the passional imaginary puts the various avatars of junction into perspective. In effect, the impassioned subject has as the object of his focused desire the *goal image* that constitutes the last existential image of the trajectory. This is why the prodigal person cannot, in the first instance, be anything more than a possessor who is conscious of possessing, according to *knowing oneself to be*. The dissipation to which he abandons himself cannot be envisaged unless he is free to dispose of his goods according to *being-able-not-to-be*. Its existential trajectory will be as follows:

realized	→	virtualized	→	actualized
(conjoined)		(nonconjoined)		(disjoined)

We can see these roles from the perspective of disjunction, but in this case disjunction presupposes both nonconjunction and conjunction. We will use the term "existential trajectory" for the completed trajectory. This latter trajectory is constructed, through presupposition, out of the existential images that the impassioned subject acquires through simulacrum. Further, the trajectory of modal roles regulates transformations taking place between the contents of modalization:

knowing	→	being able	→	wanting
(knowing how to be)		(being able not to be)		(wanting not to be)

The difference between the two trajectories can be interpreted as a twofold imaginary process. On the one hand, when we speak of his existential trajectory, the impassioned subject brings into perspective the various eventualities of his relationship to objects of value, one of the eventual positions being able to regulate the whole chain. Thus the miser puts the whole chain in a position of being regulated by nondisjunction, that is, by potentialization: his only reason for accumulating things is to hang on to them. On the other hand, because of intermodal syntax, the subject modifies his way of acceding to objects of value. In so doing he has to function in accordance with the underlying tensive modulations. One of these modulations is also seen as a regulating force, thus putting the whole matter into the perspective of only one modality: the miser thus is an impassioned subject of *wanting*, which controls both the *knowing-how* and the *being-able* that are involved.

The difference can be further clarified: by fantasizing about his eventual potentialization through the whole series of other existential roles, the miser constructs his goal image. However, the linking together of those modalities, which are transformed one into the other, defines his disposition. The superimposition of these two—the existential trajectory that is organized into a goal image and the intermodal syntax that produces a disposition—constitutes the syntactic base of passional simulacra. To the extent that the existential trajectory is imaginary only in that it is a function of the modal charge that affects junction and suspends its narrative effectuation, we can say that the transformations that modify that modal charge translate the fluctuations in the relations between the subject and his goal image.

In semiotics it is not the usual practice to treat the predicate and its modalization separately, in a modalized utterance. We see, however, that from a syntactic point of view and from within a passional universe, their respective autonomies can be envisaged. The example offered by the configuration of avarice is quite clear on this point because the existential images are in and of themselves sufficient, independently of their associated modalizations, to differentiate syntactically between the main passional positions of the subsystem. Furthermore, if we accept the hypothesis according to which intermodal syntax results from modulations of tension, it cannot be confused with an existential trajectory, which, for its part, results from transformations taking place between the discontinuous positions of being, between positions obtained by projecting the category of junction onto the semiotic square. The question of their being superimposed on each other is a real one, especially since intermodal syntax, to the extent that it is a product of the tensive space of feeling, is in a way predisposed to enter into the passional imaginary of the subject, whereas the existential trajectory grows out of a passional readjustment of the syntax of the junction utterances.

The difference between these two phenomena can be clarified through an examination of what is meant by "transformation" in each case. In the case of the existential trajectory the changes of states are arranged according to a discrete logicosemantic principle and are controlled by an operator, the impassioned subject, who elects one of them to be the end term of the trajectory. It is thus from this final state, which is the key to the goal image in question, that the whole chain can be reconstructed through presupposition. Thus the generous person has to be realized, then virtualized, before being actualized.

In the case of intermodal syntax, however, things are different. Modalities here build on each other, are multiplied, and are transformed through transitions or syncopes, all the while obeying the tensive principle that sustains them. Further, nothing prevents the regulating modality from being in the middle of the chain as well as at its beginning and end: intermodal syntax cannot be reconstructed through presupposition. Avarice begins when there is an attachment to something, a kind of necessity that links the subject with the object—that is, a *duty*. It continues with a desire that we can identify as an effect of *wanting*. It must benefit from an ability, because the miser is one who not only wants to accumulate things and hang on to them but also knows how to go about this; that is, he has a *knowing-how*. It is *wanting* that controls the whole process, because on the one hand it changes the attachment involved into a possessive attachment and on the other hand it changes the ability required into a truly compulsive guile. Intermodal syntax is thus neither discrete nor linear: *duty* engenders *wanting*, which in turn modifies *duty* retroactively. *Wanting* is accompanied by a *knowing-how*, with the two modifying each other reciprocally.

The superimposition of the two sequences can happen only within modal mechanisms, thanks to the role of usage that freezes them in their state of stereotyped blocks. Taken separately, each modal predicate can be explained, simply, as being the overdetermination, by a modality, of a predicate of being or of doing. But as soon as junctions and modalizations combine in arrangements that possess passional effects, they, in a parallel way, become part of two syntaxes that obey different rules, and their association within a single configuration demonstrates that the modal mechanism as a whole has been recognized as belonging to a passional taxonomy.

Simulacra and Modes of Existence

If we now examine the modes of existence of the ordinary syntactic subject, we find the same positions, but they now designate the position of the subject within the narrative trajectory, outside the passional simulacrum. What we have here is a question as to the articulation of simulated utterances of junction that are part of the passional imaginary universe and that we have called "existential images" with real or effective utterances of junction. These latter are attested to by the utterance, because, even if our subject is capable of projecting simulacra that include imaginary transformations, it is no less true that his "adventures" continue, in a way that parallels the things he imagines. It is a matter of knowing what happens when the subject moves from one threshold to another.

Modes of existence, conceived of as states, presuppose instances of doing that produce them: *virtualization*, brought about by a sender or a manipulator, produces a virtualized subject; *actualization*, brought about by a helper that gives the subject knowing and being able, produces an actualized subject; *realization*, finally, results from the principal performance and produces the realized subject. There remains *potentialization*, which, to the extent that the system for modes of existence obeys the rules of elementary syntax, should take its place between actualization and realization. In effect, the model we have proposed is shown in Figure 14.

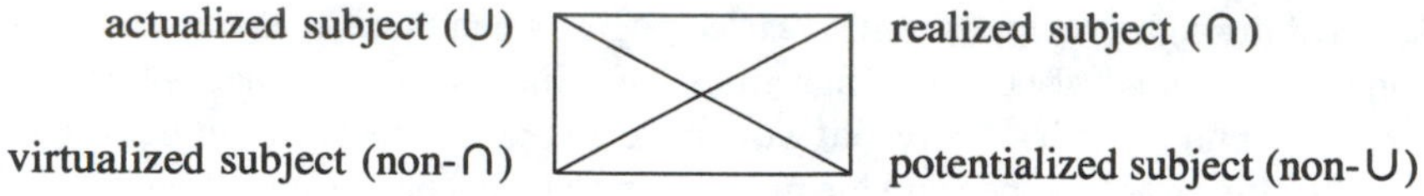

Figure 14

The sequence for modes of existence would be as follows:

virtualization → actualization → potentialization → realization

Of the four modes of existence for the syntactic subject, the "potentialized subject" position is the only one that has not yet received a narrative interpretation. It has been introduced in a strictly deductive way and appears, within the narrative trajectory that was established starting with concrete analyses of stories, to be a syncope within the chain of presuppositions. a black box whose very existence would not up to then have seemed necessary for us to understand narrativity. It is as if, from the point of view of the semiotics of action, *potentialization* was not relevant or needed in our reconstruction, through presupposition, of the positions that precede the realization of doing. One possible explication would involve conceiving of this position in terms of an open door, within the narrative trajectory, opening on the imaginary and on the passional universe. Potentialization alone would be able to sustain this passional unfolding, and there would be several reasons for this.

First, a passional disposition cannot replace a given competence unless it is situated between a competence of the classical type and performance: before performance because in a way it is presupposed by competence, and after ordinary competence, which in a way becomes part of it. In fact, curiously, the miser knows straight off how to save, the sadist how to inflict suffering, and the person in despair how to lament: it is as if the disposition in question, when it is introduced into the "effective" (actional) narrative trajectory, allows for a skipping of the apprentice stage. Hence, once it has been established as a competence whose purpose is a doing, the modal sequence can be interpreted as the "being of doing," a state of the subject that can be sensitized.

Next, potentialization, which might be seen as a required suspension of the narrative program between acquisition of competence and performance, could be defined as the operation by which the subject, now qualified for action, becomes able to *represent himself* in the process of doing – that is, to project a simulacrum of the whole actantial and modal scene that characterizes the passion in question. With all modalizations in place, the imaginary path they open can be seen in terms of and in the form of the existential trajectory. This allows us to understand, among other things, why passion often appears in the narrative unfolding in terms of a shying away from performance: once he has been manipulated or persuaded or made capable, the impassioned subject takes refuge, or finds himself carried away into his imaginary, before renouncing action or, instead, rushing into it. This is how fear works, for example, or, as we shall see, jealousy. The goal image that is introduced at this point into the narrative trajectory is to doing what a recipe is to the preparation of a meal: everything is in place in the representation the subject has of his doing; everything is presentified and can thus be set into discourse as is. The parallel continues because, just as the gastronome can stop at the stage of the discursive contemplation of the recipe, the impassioned subject can, without proceeding to action, savor the idea of a passional enactment.

"The Dairymaid and the Pot of Milk": Investment or Dissipation?

Now that he has reached this stage where he can represent to himself the doing and the trajectory as a whole, the syntactic subject is able to project, in the form of existential images, an imaginary trajectory. This is what the story of Perrette is all about (La Fontaine's country girl, as she carries a pot of milk, anticipates all of the riches that will flow from her sale of the milk: reinvestment of the money, further profits, and so on—very much counting her chickens before they hatch. Of course she spills the milk . . .).[2] She sets out a whole series of existential images and associated predicates: selling, making a profit, buying, giving a little, making more profit . . . Yet we know the result when reality reestablishes its rights: an all-too-sudden movement is enough to make the pot fall and lose all its milk, and the dream evaporates. La Fontaine's text is clear in the matter of competence. Perrette is an actualized subject, competent in every way to arrive in the village that is her destination and realize the transaction she is anticipating. But she is not thereby a realized subject, and La Fontaine presents her right at this intermediate phase, potentialization, which allows all kinds of fantasies. In the event, these fantasies lead to a self-representation of the doing in question and to the construction of an existential trajectory of "impassioned speculation." Perrette's trajectory is schematized in Figure 15.

virtualization → actualization → potentialization → (realization)
[mandate from husband] [precautions]
↳ IMAGINARY SPECULATION → FAILURE OF PERFORMANCE

Figure 15

At the discursive level, the change in register is accomplished through a disengagement: Perrette's fantasizing is presented in terms of a "story or account of thoughts" that begins as a condensed indirect discourse:

> Our Milkmaid, thus accoutred, thought
> What price her milk would fetch, and laid it out.

and continues as direct discourse:

> 'I'll rear the chickens in the yard,' said she.

The disengagement allows, starting with the series of modes of narrative existence, the passage to the series of existential images of the passional simulacrum. Most of the time, this is not so clearly marked in La Fontaine's fables and, in those cases, if one wishes to identify the passional simulacrum, one must make do with the veridictory shifts or aberrations that accompany it. From the point of view of the introductory discourse that is the starting point for the disengagement, the imaginary of the impassioned subject is situated on the *axis of seeming* in relation to the junction utterances that have been in fact attested to and that are situated on the *axis of being*. Conversely, from the point of view of the impassioned subject, the existential trajectory that he projects has to do with being, and the utterances of the introductory discourse are for him in the mode of seeming. Whatever perspective one adopts, the impassioned subject, at the discursive level, undergoes *veridictory tests*, which are often the only observable index of a passional functioning. So it is that the stingy person, from his own point of view, would seem to be no more than a careful economizer, but the verdictory test to which he is submitted by the social observer, anchored within the introductory discourse, identifies his impassioned character. Likewise, Perrette's fantasy might today pass for a simple "intended investment," but a moralist's comment on it highlights its impassioned character: veridiction sustains moralization, and behind moralization is sensitization:

> All, wise and fools alike, there lures beset
> Each mortal has his waking dreams.

But now that the object of value has been destroyed, Perrette is no longer a "simpleton," as is pointed out by La Fontaine, and the "lures beset" is thus now a *dissipation*.[3]

Passion and Veridiction. In Balzac we find comparable veridictory tests, since he is an expert on bourgeois, peasant, and even aristocratic avarice. In *Les illusions perdues* Mme de Bargeton leaves Angoulême and goes to Paris. That is sufficient to bring about a distinct change in her:

> The customs of the provinces had ended up influencing her, she had become meticulous in her accounts; she was so organized that in Paris she would be thought of as avaricious. (*Les illusions perdues*, p. 262)

The transformation is explicitly formulated in terms of a veridictory transformation, between "*having become* meticulous" and "*passing for* avaricious." In the discursive context, often termed "provincial," Mme de Bargeton's being is transformed (it "becomes") through the effects of habit. A simple economic competence, sustained by a collective axiology, is transformed into a thematic role that defines the modal being of the lady in question, a role that is set by repetition and that is identified as a socioeconomic role within the "provincial" taxonomy. But within the Parisian discursive context, the same manner of being is given a passional appearance. This implies that the social observer adopts a different taxonomy and as a consequence changes the passional effects that grow out of modal workings. Within a single discursive universe, a given instance of doing that presupposes a single competence can be perceived at two different cultural instances as either a socioeconomic role or a pathemic role. The change in status is accompanied by a veridictory transformation. In the case of Mme de Bargeton, three moments or instances are necessary: on the one hand, the instance of reference, the subject of enunciation who attests to what in fact is Mme de Bargeton's behavior (spending modestly, as is the case for all provincial nobility), and on the other hand, two instances of evaluation: one provincial and the other Parisian.

The veridictory tests that allow for the discursive articulation of the two series of utterances of state (modes of existence and existential images) in a way determine the introductions and withdrawals of the passional simulacrum and, in the simplest cases, facilitate the segmentation of those discursive units in which the passional dimension is more important than any others. So it is with the inner discourse of Perrette in "The Dairymaid." It unfolds entirely within the mode of illusion (seeming + nonbeing), between the disengagement that allows the simulacrum to be introduced and the engagement that corresponds to the pot's fall and the spilling of the milk. In the narrative text, veridictory tests are often accompanied by enunciative identifying features that allow one to textualize passional simulacra in the form of "stories or accounts of thoughts," impassioned discourses set into the introductory discourse.

Reengagement of the Tensive Subject. When Perrette drops the milk, the calf she had bought in her imagination evaporates. She had been "transported" by her own fantasy. Perrette introduces an element into the configuration that dictionaries ignore: the body, the sentient body of the impassioned subject. Modal descriptions, even veridictory descriptions, of the passional simulacrum are not enough to explain the importance of the body in the configuration of avarice and of dissipation.

To understand this we must come back to modes of existence. So far we have thought only about their narrative interpretation: when projected onto the trajectory of the narrative subject, the series of modes of existence organizes the different avatars of junction. But the same series can be projected onto the trajectory of theoretical construction, from the preconditions of signification to discursive manifestation. Indeed, the very notion of "mode of existence" comes from the distinction between the *ab quo* and the *ad quem* instances, an operational, working, abstract distinction that at the same time describes the narrative trajectory and the trajectory of theoretical construction. Nonetheless, in the case of the theoretical trajectory, modes of existence are no longer those of the narrative subject but rather are those of the *epistemological subject*.

While doing our first thinking about a semiotics of passions, we were led to recognize, at a stage that precedes the trajectory of the epistemological subject properly speaking, a tensive phase where that subject is prefigured by a "near subject, a sentient subject." Then there is the phase of division into discrete units and their categorization. Here that subject becomes a *knowing subject*. Setting into place the surface narrative syntax converts the subject into a *subject of quest*. Finally, at the stage of being set into discourse, the subject can be assimilated with the *discoursing subject*.

In conformity with the chain of presuppositions that regulates the trajectory of modes of existence, the discoursing subject being the subject of the *ad quem* instance is said to be *realized* because he has succeeded in moving the whole length of the trajectory, up to discursive performance. The subject of a quest is located at the level of surface semionarrative structures and is said to be *actualized*. He presupposes the knowing subject, the one who sets into place our "elementary structures," the *ab quo* term of the generative trajectory, which can be considered, therefore, to be *virtualized*. Now what is to be done with the *potentialized* subject?

This subject, it must be remembered, is deductively located between the actualized subject and the realized subject: to what instance might an epistemological subject that is situated between surface semionarrative structures and discursive structures correspond? The only plausible answer—and the only answer that is consistent with our preliminary proposals—would be as follows: the potentialized subject is the subject of enunciative praxis, an instance of dialectical mediation between a semionarrative instance and the discursive instance. As potentialized narrative subject this subject can put to other uses the competence acquired with a view to performance, in particular, imaginary uses. If the imaginary of the narrative subject consists of passional simulacra, the imaginary of the epistemological subject, the imaginary of the theory itself, can be nothing other than the tensive space of phoria, a space for which we have sketched out a "near subject," a sentient subject.

In the general economy of the theory, then, *potentialization* would be the mediating praxis that, by bringing together the products of the generative trajectory and those of phoric tensivity, freezes them and holds them in reserve as "potentialities" for usage, along with the "virtualities" of the schema.

The potentialized subject would then represent, in the trajectory of theoretical construction, the only instance in which the body has full legitimacy as something that can constitute meaning effects. Since semiotic existence results from the mutation of the products of perception (what is exteroceptive produces interoceptive phenomena through proprioception), it retains a memory of the body. Once it has been divided into discrete units and categorized, the only thing it retains concerning all that is proprioceptive is retained in terms of a polarization of the thymic mass euphoria/dysphoria. Enunciation alone, through the potentialization of usage, can once again appeal to the body's ability to "feel" and to the body itself as such.

Thus we need a reengagement of the sentient subject if we are to bring into discourse the somatic effects of passion. The "transport" that carries away Perrette the dissipator is the lexical manifestation, in classical French, of this reengagement. One of the significant indexes of this reintegration of the tensive subject into discourse has to do with the apparent inability of the discoursing subject to master syntactic linkings and series. The effect of tensive modulations is felt, trajectories are lost, and syntax seems subject to the effects of oscillations and changes in the equilibria of tensivity. It is as if, instead of demonstrating programmed transformations, aspectualization is what regulates the linking in series of predicates. Semiotic style would then be of greater force than any logic of action. So it is that Perrette, an impassioned discoursing subject, seems no longer able to control the story of her future transactions: she oscillates between anticipated sales and purchases, speculates vaguely, and seems unable to complete her plans. She surrenders in a way the last word to a somatic "transport." What could be called "style" here is thus a sentient subject who claims his rights through the intermediary of a tensive modulation that is frozen or set, and is potentialized.

Two Cultural Phenomena: Sensitization and Moralization

Sensitization is the operation by which a culture interprets a portion of its modal arrangements that can be considered deductively as being passional meaning effects. In language, sensitization is manifested either by condensation, thanks to the lexicalization of meaning effects, or through expansion, in the form of syntagma that include one of the generic terms of the nomenclature and a succeeding series that enunciates a behavior, an attitude, or a doing. In discourse, sensitization is recognized concretely, among other reasons because of the gap between thematic roles and pathemic roles, strictly speaking. It can also be recognized concretely because it is impossible to reduce a disposition to no more than a simple competence. This is so because when there is movement from disposition to act (that is, when the disposition is enacted), its effects are not all exhausted.

Moralization is the operation by which a culture offers a modal mechanism or arrangement that is in tune with a given set of norms, an arrangement that is conceived principally in order to regulate passional communication in a given community. Thus, whether it is of individual or collective origin, moralization signals that a passional configuration has been inserted into a community. It is manifested in language by the presence of pejorative or ameliorative elements, usually demonstrated by judgments concerning excess, insufficiency, or lack of moderation. These usually are found, in their condensed manifestations, in lexemes that denote passion. In their expanded manifestations, they are found in the glossing commentaries that define them. In discourse, moralization can be recognized by the fact that a social observer is given the responsibility of evaluating a given meaning effect, and that she is likely, in order to make such judgments, to give herself an actantial role within the configuration.

Sensitization

Cultural Variations. Different cultures, places, and epochs treat the same modal arrangements differently, and we see this in the configuration for avarice. Generosity, for example, has known avatars of this kind. In the first place, the modalization that regulates it and defines its modal isotopy has changed: starting with *being-able*, which once subtended that generosity that was linked to "greatness" and to "courage," and, more generally, all understandings of generosity that imply the "great resources" of the subject, we have moved on to a *wanting*, in the sense that the generous person is one who "gives more than he has to," the "more" being here the manifestation of an endogenous motivation that is independent of any obligations. Next, *wanting-to-be* itself was successively treated as a "quality" ("the quality of a proud soul, someone born into the right circles"), as a "sentiment" ("the sentiment of solidarity with humanity that leads one to show oneself to be benevolent, generous, quick to forgive, or spare an enemy"). Finally it was treated as a "disposition" ("the disposition to give more than one is required to").

The sensitization of the modal arrangement for generosity reached its maximum development in our classical age, when it was accompanied by extreme, positive moralization. This was because this "quality" was the criterion by which one was accepted as being of noble birth. It defined the "hereditary" being of the subject. This sensitization then weakened gradually because, in that generosity that was classed as "disposition," people recognized at the most a competence that was inscribed as a "tendency" on the part of the subject and that tendency was no longer seen as a "sentiment" or a "passion."

Nevertheless, its last meaning, that of *disposition* in the sense in which we use it metalinguistically, is now in place: it presents itself as a programming of the discoursing subject, as set permanently into the being of the subject, with no specifying of the isotopy that supposedly should invest it (economic, social, military, or affective?). The underlying modal arrangement is thus given a syntax, and the transformations that take place between modalities—transformations of the *knowing-how-to-be* into *wanting-not-to-be*—can be considered in such a way that the behavior of a generous person can be predictable in all circumstances. In other words, everything is set up in such a way that the passional meaning effect can appear within discourse. This is not so, however, in the case of contemporary lexicographical discourse, because that disposition is not considered to be a passion by the culture in which it is found.

The setting into place, at the semionarrative level, of an intermodal syntax, and its being brought into discourse in the form of an aspectualized disposition is thus not enough to produce a passional meaning effect. It is no more than the necessary condition; sensitization must do the rest. For example, unless sensitization is brought into play, that which had to do with the goal image of the generous person—that is, the placing into perspective of the whole existential trajectory around disjunction—would be likely to produce, as a meaning effect, simply a moral attitude, without any affective component whatever.

Sensitization is thus the first realizing stage in the process of setting passions into discourse. Enunciative praxis first selects and then potentializes modal segments by building on their manner of sensitization in earlier instances of their practice. But at each new discursive occurrence, these modal segments must be sensitized once again so that they can be realized in discourse as passions. Recategorization is thus always possible.

Sensitization in the Act of Taking Place. Sensitization thus defined is perceived only in terms of its effects. This happens once enunciative praxis has accomplished its task, when the passional meaning effect has become a stereotype and the stereotype has, in turn, become a passional primary element within a given practice. Its effects presuppose a process, operations that have to do with setting things into discourse. What can we say about this sensitization seen "in the act"? We might, by way of an answer, come back to Mme de Bargeton's adventures in Paris. When the Baron Châtelet has made arrangements for Mme de Bargeton in Paris she is disturbed and worried. This luxury scares her, and despite her considerable wealth, she is afraid she will not have enough and will end up in debt:

> At the moment [Lucien] left Mme de Bargeton's place, Baron Châtelet arrived, returning from the minister of external affairs, splendidly dressed as though he were going to a ball. He had come to inform Mme de Bargeton of all the things he had done for her. Louise was *worried*, this luxury *frightened* her. The customs of the provinces had ended up influencing her, she had become meticulous in her accounts; she was so organized that in Paris she would be thought of as avaricious. She had taken along a bond from the ministry of finances for almost twenty thousand francs, thinking that this sum would cover her excess expenses for the next four years; she was already *worried* about not having enough and getting into debt. (*Les illusions perdues*, p. 262, our emphasis)

Mme de Bargeton becomes a miser in the eyes of a Paris observer: it is the result of a sensitization that would appear to proceed exclusively by a series of reclassifications of modal arrangements and that would have an effect only within passional paradigms. But, as it happens, Mme de Bargeton is really affected by the contrast between her saving ways and the way she was being encouraged to live in Paris. Her new passional status is thus not just the effect of a veridictory test and of an external judgment. It results from a discursive operation that transforms her being and produces pathemic effects, not just in the judgments made by an observer, but on her syntactic trajectory as well. Balzac's comment thus highlights sensitization as it is in process and demonstrates the way in which a socioeconomic role is sensitized within the discursive series itself. A thematic role that has had a brutal change in discursive context is transformed into disquiet, alarm, and fear. Sensitization is thus not just an abstract operation that is necessary for our theory of passions. It is, further, something that can be observed in concrete discourses just as is the case for other operations pertaining to discursive syntax.

Sensitization therefore takes its place both within the general economy of our theory, as a process of explication, and, descriptively, within the discursive trajectory pertaining to the construction of the impassioned subject. Vertically, in a way, it constructs cultural taxonomies that process modal arrangements in such a way as to manifest them within discourse as passions. Horizontally, sensitization takes its place within the discursive syntax of passion as an independent process. So it is that Mme de Bargeton is classified as a miser within the culture of the Paris of her time. This legitimizes a new discursive interpretation of her competence, but she is also transformed, with the result that pathemic events appear in her trajectory. That is why it is correct to use the term "pathemization" for sensitization when it is conceived as being an operation that belongs to discursive syntax. In fact, from a genetic point of view, pathemization would precede sensitization when the latter is conceived as a cultural instance. It can be just a single, isolated occurrence, but it can also enter into general practice. If that occurs, the modal sequences it affects are identified as passions in that practice, and enunciative praxis can carry out its task. Sensitization as an enunciative operation is thus secondary.

The Sensing or Sentient Body. Beyond those questions of method that are associated with any cultural relativism, we can legitimately ask if it is indeed appropriate for semiotics to attempt to explain the nature of this cultural phenomenon. Is there any way of avoiding having ontological—indeed, metaphysical—answers to this question? That epistemological minimum that is our protection is threatened by all this. The vocation of semiotics of passions is to describe, even explain, the discursive effects of sensitization, but it is certainly not legitimate for it, without any "by your leave," to take credit for observations that other disciplines can and do make on the subject. It is, however, quite permissible for semiotics to investigate these other observations and try to benefit from them.

In the vein of extra- or parasemiotic explanations, one might for example conceive of sensitization as an operation of psychosomatic origins. One might think that certain modal arrangements act on the soma as if on a "location that welcomes them." This hypothesis raises more problems than it solves, however, because we would then have to show how cultures can determine which are the "welcoming locations" that are specific to them. In the cases of the "passions of asthma," for example, such a hypothesis would be tempting because, of course, it would make the semiotic analysis compatible with the genetic and allergenic explanations of this disorder. But this hypothesis would not be able to stand up to an examination of the concrete discourses in which the family and friends of the asthmatic adopt the same sensitized modal apparatus as the sick person himself, without, for all that, sharing his "welcoming location."[4] Cultural relativism also requires us to set aside a solution that would consist of a direct appeal to biological forms because these latter characterize the species as such, and not its culture.

On the other hand, to the extent that it formally articulates the body, images of the body, and sociocultural determinations, the concept of a "social habitus" that Pierre Bourdieu once proposed would seem quite appropriate.[5] Pierre Encrevé has shown, in his introduction to the French translation of William Labov,[6] just how useful it can be. The "articulatory posture" that is typical of a given social group, and which for example leads that group to pronounce such and such a diphthong in a "tight" way or in a "lax" way, can be explained in terms of a certain response vis-à-vis the tone of the muscles in question to a larger "postural schema." The postural schema in question would be seen as a kind of image of the body as it should be if it conforms to its social habitus. In this case, the postural schema would be a motor or physical schema that has been set into practice and that is characteristic of a given sociotaxonomy.

However, these sociological concepts attach too much importance to things being acquired through "experience." Nothing allows us to state that cultural sensitization is more a matter of experience and less an innate phenomenon. To the extent that sensitization overdetermines the process by which exteroceptive and interoceptive semes are made to be homogeneous through the proprioceptive, it transcends the opposition between the innate and the learned through experience. But we have a sorry lack of information concerning the way in which the body can intervene in the process. We have found it enough, given our axiologies and the opposition between euphoria and dysphoria, to believe that proprioceptivity acts uniquely through attractions and repulsions. But there is nothing that says that the body is unable to produce more complex elementary symbolizations that, without yet being semiotic phenomena, would prepare the way for the sensitization of signifying forms. Research carried out in anthropology and in medical semiotics may well give us some answers in this area.

It remains true that the very notion of a "schema of sensitivity," indeed that, more trivially, of a "welcoming location," constitutes a way into the investigation of passions. In the trajectory of the construction of the impassioned subject, at the level of discourse, sensitization would be neither the first nor the last word on passion. From an epistemological point of view, if the cultural relativism inherent in our acts of grasping the signifiers of the natural world could be explained by the presence of "schemata of sensitivity" within the human imaginary, semiotic existence itself would be affected. From a syntactic point of view, if we can postulate a "favorable or welcoming location" for the manifestation of passions, the trajectory of the impassioned subject does not begin with sensitization.

The Passional Constitution. One might think now of the Greek concept of *hexis*, which signifies both "manner of being," "constitution" (in the medical sense, for example), and the "habits," either of the body or of the spirit.[7] Benveniste points out that the corresponding verb, *ekho* ("having" and "possessing"), is an inverse "being (something) to," which explains why the verb itself, in its intransitive uses, and above all the noun derived from it, are able to designate both learned ways of being ("habits") and innate ones ("constitution").

As a working hypothesis we might then consider the sentient *hexis* as a cultural overdetermination of biological forms. It is translated by a specific articulation of proprioceptive phenomena and projects schemata of sensitivity onto semiotic existence. The dispositions and goal images evoked in realized discourses would find, or fail to find, an echo in those schemata of sensitivity and, thereby, would produce, or fail to produce, passional meaning effects. Sensitization in this case would presuppose, at the level of the preconditions of signification, a "constitution" of the sentient subject.

On the other hand, if we agree that sensitization can be grasped both through its effects within enunciative praxis and as a discursive operation, we can legitimately wonder whether the constitution of the impassioned subject might also be considered from two different perspectives. Up to now, we have examined, by way of a hypothesis that would be difficult to verify, only the eventuality of a "predisposition" of the sentient subject in the trajectory of the theoretical construction, starting with the idea that proprioceptivity might be constitutive of the impassioned subject. Now we can inquire into what might be the discursive form of a constitution "in the act"; that is, we can wonder how, within the syntactic trajectory of the subject, this location that is favorable to an enactment of passion is set up or created.

In the configuration of avarice, we repeatedly find figures that, without themselves being passions, appear as presupposed conditions, as, indeed, the terrain or location on which sensitization can take place. Thus the sensitization of the modal arrangement of avarice can be conceived of only if a certain "attachment" links the subject to objects. Likewise, generosity presupposes a form of detachment. Attachment and detachment come into play when the modal arrangement is not in place and, a fortiori, when it has not been sensitized. Both characterize the relation between the subject and the world, independently of any object of value or even of any system of given values. In a sense, attachment and detachment seem to define two different ways, for a subject that does not yet know any objects of value, of entering into a relation with the signifiers of the natural world, once they have been interiorized. In the absence of objects or of systems of values, the subject would have to do only with "the shadows of value" that fiducia offers him, and attachment and detachment would represent two extreme positions on the continuous gradation of fiducia.

In the configuration of most interest to us now, attachment and detachment occupy a position in the syntactic trajectory of the subject and not only within the theoretical construction. They are in effect presupposed by the true passional figures and can be manifested in discourse just as sensitization can.

Mme de Bargeton would not have become a miser, and would not have been alarmed by the way of life in Paris, if she had not in fact been subjected to some preparation for it all in advance. For if the change in her location is enough of an explanation, for the social observer, of her transformation into miser, it cannot alone explain the appearance of new passions (worry, alarm, fear) in her discursive trajectory. In other words, the sensitization we observe merely actualizes in discourse a property that the subject already has and had already before sensitization took place and which is of the same nature as "attachment" or "detachment." On closer examination, we find a trace of such a property: "The ways of the provinces had eventually had an effect on her." This explanation of Balzac's cannot be seen simply as a setting into place of a thematic role through repetition. In effect, the "ways" are codified "habits" that have been integrated into a culture and are not to be confused with repetition. It is a fact that the thematic role of "hunter" is constructed by apprenticeship and repetition. But it does not for all that bring about a "habit" and "mores."

Here we once again come upon *hexis*, which allows us to say that Mme de Bargeton is "constituted" or predisposed to be a miser before in fact becoming one and that sensitization strictly speaking, having been brought about by the change of discursive context or location, has its source in this initial, earlier, state. Habit is, of course, only one of the possible forms (acquired, in this case) according to which the impassioned subject is constituted.

Sketch of a Pathemic Trajectory. The phenomenon of *constitution* can be seen, independently of its "acquired" or "innate" nature, as a general predisposition of the discursive subject vis-à-vis the passional trajectories the future holds in store for him. They define his manner of access to the world of values and preselect for him certain passions rather than others. If we travel back along the discursive syntax, starting with passional manifestation, we thus successively come upon: *sensitization*, which is applied to a *disposition*, which is preserved in a *constitution*. In the other direction, we can argue only in terms of probabilities: Mme de

Bargeton could have undergone the influence of the mores and habits of the provinces without acquiring a disposition for avarice. That disposition might never have been sensitized if the change in location had not occurred. The discursive syntax of the impassioned subject thus can provisionally be set forth as follows:

CONSTITUTION → DISPOSITION → SENSITIZATION

Moralization

From Ethics to Aesthetics. In the configuration of avarice, many ethical judgments mark the activity of a judging actant. These judgments moralize certain kinds of behavior that, in themselves, might be neutral. The person who saves represents an unmoralized role, or is one who is positively judged, and the miser is negatively judged. Behavior that is deemed to be "in one's selfish interest" is judged negatively in the configuration we have studied, but it is judged positively in political economy, ever since Adam Smith, among others, and is also judged positively in pedagogy, where it is a key to success.

Moralization can borrow other ways than those of ethics or justice. Dandyism reorganizes the passional universe around a *knowing-how-to-be*, while opposing it to bourgeois values, which are seen to be organized essentially around utility.[8] In this sense, all passions are judged in terms of the "bearing" or "manner" that makes it possible to control their manifestation. Judging *knowing-how-to-be* is thus based on an aesthetic of daily life. In the same way, but with reference to other things, the *honnête homme* must, in seventeenth-century France, demonstrate a quality that, for lack of a better term, was referred to by the paraphrase: "The 'honnête homme' doesn't get irritated over anything." Here we are dealing with a *knowing-how-not-to-be* that is judged positively, thus permitting one to refrain from expressing one's passions, and which also is part of an aesthetic project applied to inner life.

It follows that moralization introduces a more general relativism into the passional universe, one that causes a problem. In the dictionary definitions, moral judgments establish certain thresholds on a scale of intensity, a scale that has its orientation and that allows conclusions to be reached as to excess or insufficiency according to whether or not the case in point is below or above the threshold in question. Desire, attachment, sentiment, or an inclination is thus qualified, in the configuration we are examining, as "lively," "excessive," "base," and the like. But one quickly reaches a dead end because, for these same dictionaries, "passion" is already defined as such in terms of excess: to moralize in terms of excess or insufficiency would thus amount to simply recognizing that such and such a modal arrangement belongs or does not belong to a passional register, thus simply paralleling sensitization. From the point of view of the social observer, moralization presupposes and covers sensitization, but that is no reason to confuse the two.

Socialized Passions. In order for us better to understand moralization, we can first inquire into the question as to who is responsible for it. Usually, when in semiotics we find a judgment being made on the doing or on the being of the subject, we look for traces of a judging Sender, and we believe that his judgment of doing belongs to the final stage of the canonical narrative schema. But here we are not dealing with the canonical narrative schema, and the trajectory of the impassioned subject is set in a simulacrum that prevents us from treating it as a classical narrative trajectory. Further, judgment can involve passional forms of competence, or disposition itself, before any movement is made toward enactment: one would speak of "wrong thoughts" or "inappropriate leanings." If the doing of the saving person is judged only in terms of a doing, from the point of view of his effectiveness and appropriateness to the moment, such is not the case for the miser. He is judged according to the existence, in his competence, of an excedentary passional disposition. Thus Mme de Bargeton, even before having had the time to spend or save a single franc in Paris, is judged according to her apprehension alone, that is, on her ability to imagine herself spending or saving. It is no longer either her doing or being that is judged, but rather a manner of doing or a manner of being. The nuance is sometimes tiny, in practice, but it makes all the difference in the world. It has to do with a certain modal arrangement and the way in which it is manifested.

As a consequence, the person responsible for the judgment cannot, in the strictest sense, be a Sender-judge whose only task would be to judge the success or degree of conformity of a given doing. We have seen the judging actant being confused with a frustrated Receiver (stinginess, dissipation) or with a fulfilled Receiver (generosity). Such observations lead one to think that the judging actant can be any of the potential partners of the impassioned subject in the configuration. But given that any passion is in theory subject to judgment and moralization, since the judging actant belongs within the configuration as legitimately as the impassioned subject, this amounts to saying that *there is no solitary passion*. All passional configurations must be intersubjective, including at least two subjects: the impassioned subject and the subject who takes on the responsibility of moralization.

The intersubjective, or more generally, interactantial, nature of passions is limited neither to setting into discourse nor to the intervention of a social observer. The analysis of the modulations that underlie the configuration of avarice has identified cohesive and dispersive forces between which unstable equilibria and disequilibria indicate the place for collective and individual values. When the protoactant is cut away from the tensive space these adversarial forces are freed. We can interpret them as prefiguring the actants involved: we can speak of *interactants*.

When we reach the point of enacting discourse, if the configuration is organized exclusively from the point of view of the impassioned subject, sensitization alone is manifested. If the configuration is organized from the point of view of a social observer, moralization appears, at the same time presupposing and masking sensitization.

The Stratification of Moral Discourse. Further, after having noted the instability of the observer actant, we might wonder if that instability results from the nature itself of the judgments. In fact, this instability is in large measure explained by the superimposition of the criteria for judgment. In dictionary definitions, for example, we see that such and such a passion can be negatively judged because it is based on an erroneous opinion (such as vanity or pretension), or because it is simply excessive (e.g., pride). Another passion might be judged positively because it is based on a correct opinion (esteem). In both cases, the one judging establishes his judgment on veridictory considerations (falsity for vanity, but also for stinginess, secrecy for hypocrisy). He bases himself on epistemic considerations in other cases (sufficiency or presumption) and on aspectual ones in yet others (excess). But, whatever might be the modal category in whose name the judgment is enunciated, the factor that seems to bring on the judgment itself is always of the order of "too much" or "too little." The miser and the avid enthusiast want with too much intensity. The dissipator spends too much; the stingy one saves in excessively petty ways; the mean, tightfisted one displays his stinginess too freely. The vain one and the proud one have an excessively good opinion of themselves. The ass and the presumptuous one enact their traits too ostentatiously.

It is as if the tensive underpinning of the passional universe comes back to the surface, taking on the appearance of a modal or aspectual category. Ethical judgments seek out modalizations (veridictory, epistemic, volitive, deontic, etc.) and aspectualizations and then project on them scales of intensity, marked by threshold points, as if to reactualize tensive modulations on those same scales.

The social observer therefore has direct access only to ethical roles. These roles, according to individual cases, cover epistemic roles, veridictory roles, deontic roles, all usually reformulated as pathemic roles. Nonetheless, it would seem that beyond all of these roles, the social observer is most interested in the notion of moderation or mesura. Given this fact, the judgment made of passions brings to light a criterion underlying all superimposed axiologies, one that has to do, as we have already suggested, with regulating the process of becoming.

Once the diversity and degree of stratification of the systems of reference for moralization have been recognized we can better understand the role of the observer himself. His "instability" is of itself functional. Thanks to the variations between the points of view we have adopted, and the fact that between the kinds of syncretism the judging observer can enter into with the actants of a given passional configuration, the subject of enunciation can cause variations in shading or lighting, from one passion to another. He can explore their combinatory potential and their taxonomies in such a way as to highlight the modal arrangements that are canonical in a given culture. This can also allow for them to be adjoined, with a view to moralization, to those axiologies that are specific to such and such a partner of the impassioned subject.

Instability in evaluation and the apparently random superimposition of axiologies of reference should not stop us from envisaging moralization as an autonomous dimension of discourse, because, despite appearances, the conditions for that autonomy are all there. Moralization is the responsibility of an actant who, while belonging to the passional configuration, is not thereby any less independent of the impassioned subject. Further, moralization is not at all dependent on the orientation of the existential trajectories involved or on thymic polarization. On the one hand, avid desire (realization) and dissipation (actualization) are both condemned equally. On the other, careful saving (potentialization) and unselfishness or disinterest (virtualization) are both equally valorized. Sadness can be very moral – when, for example, it demonstrates a sincere mourning – and an absence of reaction, athymia, can be as violently condemned, as in the case of Meurseault in *L'étranger,* by Albert Camus, as it is recommended to the *honnête homme* of French classicism.

Ethical roles are thus also independent from existential images, as they are from modal roles, and from pathemic and thematic roles. This independence is translated by the existence of an isotopy that would be shared by them and would be specific to them: the isotopy of moderation, mesura. Ethical roles then would be, in a given culture, the terms of a connotative taxonomy that is coextensive with that of sensitization, but with a different segmentation. The moral overdetermination of passional modal arrangements "perverts" in a way the taxonomy of pathemic roles by redistributing them in terms of *vices* and *virtues*. This can be explicit, which means the role will in discourse be considered a "good quality" or a "fault," or implicitly, thanks to the projection of "ameliorative" or "pejorative" semes. The whole group of these distortions, in a text or in the corpus of a text, will appear to be a *coherent deformation of the passional universe* that can be constructed, on analysis, as a *moral isotopy*. The recurrence of the same criteria of judgment (i.e., of the same type of scale of intensity, of the same judging actantial position) thus guarantees a homogeneous reading of the moral universe of the subject of enunciation.

This doubling of the area examined allows us to envisage the study, within the framework of languages of connotation, of moral discourse. This is a discourse that has to do with moderation and excess, with lucidity and illusion, with discretion and indiscretion in passional manifestations and, more generally, has to do with the respecting of implicit rules and codes that pertain in a given culture. The study of moral discourse, paralleling that of passional discourse, brings us to a classification of cultures to the extent that, if the pertaining modal mechanisms remain constant, the sensitization and moralization that affect them constitute two variable classes by which cultures—locations and epochs—are distinguishable from each other.

The Moralization of Observable Behavior. When moralizing passion, one judges not only a certain way of doing or of being, but also a certain way of being impassioned. This is because in vanity, for example, an initial ethical role is defined, in a way independently of passional manifestation, starting from a veridictory judgment (overrated opinion), and a second ethical role is defined starting from the passional manifestation itself (extravagance). Moralization in terms of moderation or mesura thus presupposes that the discursive trajectory of the subject will be completed, that its consequences will be manifested and observable in the form of *figures of behavior*. In our two examples, stinginess and vanity, condemnation is aimed most particularly against the showing off of these figures of comportment. This "ostentation" might be interpreted as a confrontation (intersubjective) between a *wanting-to-cause-someone-to-know-how* (in the case of vanity) and a *not-being-able-not-to-cause-someone-to-know-how* (in the case of the stingy person) of the impassioned subject on the one hand, and the *not-wanting-to-know* of the judging observer, or at least of the interactant whose position he adopts, on the other. Moralization here effects yet other modalizations, but only those that concern the informative properties of passional behavior. What we have, in fact, are interactive modalizations belonging to the pair informer/observer.

Mme de Bargeton cannot escape this rule: after the sensitization that brings to her a great variety of secondary passions that are grafted onto avarice, despite herself, she manifests repugnance when forced to make great monetary outlays. She physically flinches at Châtelet's information concerning her rent and other costs:

> She was already worried about not having enough and getting into debt. Châtelet informed her that her apartment cost only six hundred francs a month.
>
> "A pittance," he said, in seeing Naïs *flinch*. "You can have a carriage for five hundred francs a month, which in all corresponds to fifty louis. All that remains for you to worry about is your wardrobe. A woman who goes out in society cannot do otherwise. . . . Here one only gives to the rich." (*Les illusions perdues,* p. 262, our emphasis)

Her flinch is exactly what the observer, Châtelet, wants. He launches into a kind of moral lesson *à la parisienne.* Retrospectively we now can understand that a judgment of avarice, echoed by the subject of enunciation, is in fact made by Châtelet himself in the enunciated interaction: the social observer in this case enters into a syncretism with one of the partners of the impassioned subject, not within the configuration of avarice, but in that of seduction, which here is implied in the configuration for avarice. The flinch is the final message to come out of the passional trajectory, a message that is put into circulation through interaction and that is susceptible of inspiring manipulative strategies on the part of the partners. The nature of Châtelet's response, the moral lesson in economics, explicitly inscribes this "flinch" in a moral isotopy.

The example we have chosen is made up of two segments: the manifested behavior and the moralization that follows it. The behavior manifests a conjunction of the impassioned subject with a thymic object (dysphoria, in this case), and the moralization sanctions this conjunction. The passional behavior of this case belongs to a class of somatic manifestations of passion: blushing, paleness, anguish, flinching, physical tensing, shaking, and so on. We can agree to call such manifestations "emotions." The effect at the surface level of discourse of a somatic "irruption," an irruption that often characterizes emotion, comes from the engagement operation on the tensive subject that we have postulated in order to justify our installing the passional simulacrum within discourse. By calling on the modulations of feeling and becoming in the discursive chain, this engagement prepares the way for the somatic irruption of emotion. It is at this precise moment of the passional trajectory that the sentient subject remembers he has a body.

Sketch of the Pathemic Schema (continued). Now we can envisage in its totality, by way of a working hypothesis, the pathemic schema that the study of avarice allows us to construct and that we suspect organizes discursive passional syntax in general.

Moralization comes at the end of the sequence and has to do with the whole of the sequence, but more particularly with observable behavior. It presupposes pathemic manifestation, called *emotion*, whose appearance within discourse tells us that the thymic junction has been accomplished, by giving to the body itself a self-expressing role. *Sensitization* is presupposed by emotion: it is thymic transformation par excellence, the operation by which the discursive subject is transformed into a suffering subject, feeling, reacting, being moved or touched. It itself presupposes this discursive programmation that we have called "disposition" and that results from calling on modal mechanisms that are energized and selected by practice. It brings into play an aspectualization of the modal chain and a "semiotic style" that is characteristic of doing. Finally, *constitution* determines, at the head of the sequence, the being of the subject so that he will be receptive to sensitization. This stage obliges us to postulate at the level of discourse a determination of the discursive subject that occurs before any competence or disposition on his part. This is a determinism—social, psychological, hereditary, metaphysical, or whatever else—that then presides over the setting up of the impassioned subject.

The passional simulacrum, which is by definition reflexive, since the subject projects onto it his own existential trajectory and his modal disposition, does not, for this very reason, cover the whole sequence. The simulacrum is entered with disposition, and left with emotion. Constitution, because it presupposes a kind of external necessity over which the impassioned subject has no control, and moralization, because it sets into play an external evaluation or judging, are transitive stages in the sequence and do not belong to the passional simulacrum, strictly speaking. All of these propositions must of course be made more precise and validated ultimately, keeping in mind their eventual generalization.

Final Remarks

From the point of view of theory as from the point of view of method, the study of moralization presupposes a study of sensitization. Indeed, to the extent that we agree that moralization comes into play at the end of the trajectory, it is also what signals the end of that trajectory to us. From the perspective of the construction of the actor, moralization is the final stage: all ethical judgments presuppose—rightly or wrongly, no matter—that the actor has "proved himself" and has shown what he is capable of. Moralization then includes within itself both a *terminative* and a *completed* feature. It is as if, at the moment when ethical judgment is brought to bear, the actor were to be arrested in his development, frozen in the last image that the judgment has selected to be his ethical role.

On the other hand, the moral judgment having to do with figures of behavior presupposes a subject's disposition, one without which the figures in question might be seen as accidental, having no relation to the being of the subject. Moralization can cover only observable behaviors that presuppose a disposition. For that to happen we must first recognize the existence of an intentionality of passion, existing in the form of a goal image and of a sensitized modal arrangement. For all of these reasons, moralization presupposes sensitization, and that is why the study of moral discourse must be founded on a knowledge of passional universes.

In their roles as procedures that are constitutive of cultural taxonomies, sensitization and moralization thus also play a role in the regulation of intersubjectivity. In effect, by classifying actors in terms of the pathemic and ethical roles they might play within communication, these two procedures allow us to predict the behavior of individuals. In social or interindividual relations, a knowledge of passional and moral taxonomies allows each person to anticipate the conduct of others and to adapt hers as needed. The subject identified as "grouchy," "miserly," "spendthrift," or "credulous" is ripe for manipulation, because, the syntax of her trajectory being known in advance, strategies and counterstrategies can in large measure be programmed from the outset in any given case of interaction. Pathemic roles and ethical roles cannot be constructed by presupposition, basing oneself on performance. They can only be kept "as a block or package" in the memory of a given culture. They present us with the "instructions for use" of the subject, and the observer/manipulator knows which modal key to play when. Sensitization and moralization are thus not only procedures for description. They are in fact operations that are available to the actants of both the enunciated and enunciation. Thus the cultural taxonomies they help to construct are what is at stake in strategies of communication. They are what in large measure is responsible for the exchange of simulacra, and the one who has mastered the passional taxonomies of interaction can act in such a way as to influence those exchanges.

Setting Avarice into Discourse

When we construct the configuration of avarice we are also establishing the semionarrative underpinnings of a passional universe and recognizing the importance of the process of setting it into discourse. Having noted that most theories of passions were no more than part of specific discursive universes, it seemed unreasonable to produce one more theory, one that, under the cover of transcendence and deduction would have, like the others, rationalized and systematized a taxonomy linked to a specific culture. But the price paid, as far as method is concerned, is not negligible. Starting with discursive manifestations, and basing ourselves on a small number of theoretical hypotheses, we must progressively identify what belongs to universals and distinguish it from what is part of the process of setting into discourse.

This is not the moment for redoing the theory of discourse, but only to remind ourselves of the way in which the various instances we found in our study of avarice and its configurations are articulated with each other. First, at the level of phoric tensivity, a small number of modulations determine "semiotic styles" within the framework of a general principle of the circulation of value. Next, at the semionarrative level, existential trajectories, as well as sensitized modal arrangements, that are frozen and have been kept "stocked" under the rubric "primitive," constitute the syntactic basis for passional meaning effects. Finally, at the discursive level, the calling into play of preceding entities results in goal images and dispositions that come together to form passional simulacra.

Enunciative Praxis

The main difficulty, in the treatment of passional universes, has to do with the fact that we cannot ignore the factor of cultural instance. It intervenes at many points and at all levels. We met it, of course, at the discursive level, with the two operations of sensitization and moralization characteristic of enunciative praxis in the area under study. But we also met the factor of cultural instance at the semionarrative level because of the selecting process it carries out among the various modal arrangements that we can conceive. But, and this was not expected, it seems that it is also manifested at the level of tensive preconditions. The modulations that are characteristic of the configuration under study in effect seem unable to be separated from a quantitative component, so that what is at stake in connection with the tensions we see between cohesive and dispersive forces is found in the stabilization of a collective actant. Further, the process of becoming is here the object of a restrictive interpretation that reduces it to a principle of circulation of values within the community. Also, neither sensitization nor moralization receives a satisfactory explanation unless reference is made to such and such a phenomenon that is proper to the epistemological level, as would be the case among others, for instance, for a "sensitive" *hexis*.

Up to now we have been saying, by way of a working hypothesis, that enunciative praxis might resolve all of these difficulties. It can, in fact, thanks to its movement back and forth between the semionarrative and the discursive, explain how connotative taxonomies that have been developed in the first instance by practice are ultimately integrated within *langue* by setting primitive (in the Latin sense) or primordial units into it. But it seems that culture intervenes in another way, too. If we agree that semiotic existence is constituted through a homogenization of the interoceptive and exteroceptive through proprioception, we then thereby posit the existence of the macrosemiotics of the natural world, which in a way are waiting for a subject so that they can become signifying. Now, the "morphologies" of the natural world are not just physical or biological. They are also, among other things, sociological and economic. That is, they are specific in a way to given cultural areas and historical epochs. In other words, the signifiers of the world that are integrated into semiotic existence through perception are not all "natural," and the horizon of being that lies behind phoric tensivity is in part culturally determined, indeed economically determined, as in the case under study.

Thus, in the configuration for avarice, it seems that the tensions involved are already, even before the categorization and formation of the relevant syntactic actants, partly inflected by what we have called the "circulating fluctuations of value." This circulation can be seen as the traces left behind, on the ontic horizon, by the socioeconomic determinations that are implicated. Nothing prevents us, however, from thinking that this inflection is the result of practice and enunciative praxis. In effect, enunciative praxis cannot act on the presence of cultural originals at the semionarrative level except by stereotyping the products that result from setting into discourse. The items brought into play are selected, shaped by practice, and stored in the semionarrative memory. One can imagine that the same goes for the tensive level, because it is also the object of convocations within discourse. This is how we have conceived of *semiotic styles*.

If we now come back to setting into discourse itself, we make the distinction between two orders of phenomena. On the one hand there is a group of phenomena that is relatively well known in semiotics, such as actorialization, aspectualization, and on which the study of avarice and its configuration shed new light. On the other hand, we see another group of phenomena that is less well known or even misunderstood, such as the canonical pathemic schema or passional simulacra, about which it seems prudent to gather more information before taking a position. This is seen as particularly true in the light of our study of jealousy. We already have a provisional assessment of the usefulness and role of the first group.

Actorialization: Thematic and Pathemic Roles

Actorialization is a process that consists in projecting, through disengagement, any actors who have the status of "not-I" and who are to receive syntactic investment in the form of actantial and modal roles, as well as semantic investment, in the form of thematic roles. It is within this very general process that it is appropriate to interpret the appearance of pathemic and ethical roles.

In relation to actantial roles, whose linking together obeys a succession of tests and modalizations, the pathemic role appears globally as a segment of the actantial trajectory, a segment that is given its dynamics by the text's intermodal syntax. Enunciation, when the point of setting into discourse is reached, can resort to these ready-made and stereotyped segments in order to manifest those zones in the actantial trajectory that have been sensitized.

In relation to thematic roles, which, against the background of a thematic trajectory, we can encatalyze starting with the dissemination of semantic contents, the pathemic role will be a sensitized segment of the thematic trajectory, one that is already in and of itself a stereotype. In both cases the actor is invested with segments of sensitized and moralized roles. Nonetheless, the distinction between thematic and pathemic roles is often a problem and warrants a more careful examination.

Given the preceding analyses we can note an initial difference, one that has to do with the orientation of the processes of construction. Between the miser and the saving person there is no difference in competence if one examines only the contents of the modalities in question. However, a difference appears as soon as one takes the process or activities involved into account. For the analyst, the competence of the saving person is exclusively retrospective: the saving person is one about whom we know only after the fact, given the results obtained, that he is able to moderate his expenses. On the contrary, the competence of the miser seems to be prospective to the extent that the miser is one about whom we can predict, before any results are seen, that he will not spend.

Things are more complex than that, however, because the thematic role also includes a discursive programmation of the actor and therefore also has a predictability factor. The difference, rather too subtle a one to be operative, has to do with the fact that the pathemic role is prospective at the very moment of its construction, whereas the thematic role becomes so only after its construction.

We might, more felicitously it seems, inquire into the aspectualization of both types of roles. The competence of the saving person is manifested only if the situation calls for it, when the opportunity to realize a saving presents itself. The competence of the miser is always able to be manifested, independently of the narrative situation – for example, in a set of facial expressions, in a set of gestures or movements. This is because the pathemic role affects the actor as a whole. The thematic role is iterative and the pathemic role is permanent. That is why, in the description of the miser, we seek manifestations of passion in his face, in his expressions. Nobody would dream of examining the expressions or face of a saving person in the search for evidence of his saving competence.

The explanation for all of this is quite simple. Manifestation of the thematic role strictly obeys the dissemination of the theme in discourse, whereas the manifestation of the pathemic role obeys the logic of passional simulacra, an imaginary dissemination that is independent of the theme.

This distinction should allow us not only to differentiate between the two types of roles, but also to note the passage from the thematic to the pathemic in discourse. When the recurrence of a role appears to be anarchic (that is, as soon as it no longer obeys the dissemination of the theme), we can say that we are dealing with a pathemic role. The saving person becomes a miser as soon as his resistance of the circulation of values intervenes within the discourse in question in an "unseemly" way and when that was not to be expected. This aspectual feature has as much to do with the permanence that is characteristic of all dispositions as it does with the obsessional form that a passion such as avarice can take on.[9]

As in apprenticeship, recurrence of doing and modal recurrence are constitutive of the thematic role. It is by repetition, by the control and situational application of the acts of doing, that the saving person learns his role.

NB: We must distinguish here between "recurrence" and the aspect we call "iterative." The miser is a "permanent" role whereas the angry person's role is "iterative." In this case it is a matter of the internal aspectualization of the role, and the "permanent/iterative" opposition has a distinguishing value vis-à-vis the two figures. But the miser and angry grouch both, as stereotypes, demonstrate a functional recurrence that allows us to identify their roles as a *class of behaviors*. It is functional recurrence that allows for predictability in behavior. In a way, and in another context, classes of behavior, both thematic and passional, are homologous with Propp's functional classes.

The productive recurrence of stereotypes would also allow us to redefine certain terms from among the passional nomenclature of natural languages. For instance, we might redefine "character" and "temperament." "Character" derives directly from functional recurrence: it is always defined as a class, in terms of a permanence of one type of thematic and passional responses to situations that vary and, in this sense, character, as a stereotype, reduces the modal arrangement of the actor to a small number of modal isotopies and roles. "Temperament," on the other hand, being founded on equilibria and hierarchies between several roles and several modal isotopies, might be defined as the domination, by one pathemic role, over others. Just as we find controlling modalizations in given modal arrangements, we would find, in the total group of roles engaged in by the same actor, a modal segment that would, with regard to that total trajectory, be a controlling segment. We are not attempting to save on the use of terms from the passional nomenclature. Rather we are noting that because actors accumulate modal arrangements and several types of roles in the course of given discourses, we can envisage "macroarrangements" within which directing phenomena can appear.

Further, thematic and pathemic roles show a hierarchical relation that is basically founded on presupposition. When a pathemic role presupposes a thematic role, recurrence is, from a semantic point of view, coherent. That is, it is isotopic, and the stereotyped and sensitized modal segment is substituted for the modal segment that is only stereotyped. Furthermore, the pathemic role sees its semantic virtualities reduced by the thematic role. Thus, to say that someone is "hungry for honors" amounts to restricting the pathemic role of the miser by attaching a social thematic to him. When a pathemic role does not presuppose a thematic role, recurrence, from the semantic point of view, is in large measure aleatory (that is, anisotopic); all of the semantic virtualities of the role can then be actualized.

Other associations can be envisaged, ones that are more complex, but also more revealing. Machiavellianism, for example, supposes on the one hand, a sequence of behaviors and of strategies founded on competence, on the political isotopy, and on the other hand, a passional disposition. The thematic sequence here is a given form, a sophisticated but stereotyped one that has to do with *knowing-how-to-do* and *being-able-to-do,* and with the first of these regulating the second. The disposition implicated here is that of distrust. Instead of substituting itself for the whole of the thematized modal segment, in the way the miser substitutes himself for the saving person, the passional disposition of the Machiavellian subject sets itself into the thematic trajectory and occupies only a part of it. Thematic trajectories of the political type include a stage at which the subject is susceptible of being modalized by *believing*. In the case of Machiavellianism, distrust replaces belief. This is not an isolated example: most of the configurations we see in concrete instances of discourse display mixed roles and imbrications of this type. The difference in the case of the miser is, perhaps, in the last analysis, purely lexical: in instances of the embedding of roles and of trajectories that, in realized discourses, are equally complex, lexicalization retains, on the one hand, only the sensitized segment (miser) and, on the other, the whole of the trajectory (the Machiavellian type).

There is a fundamental question in this connection: in this agglomeration of roles (modal, pathemic, thematic) that are articulated with each other, what becomes of the subject? Is the actor that covers several of these roles able to produce a "subject effect"? If we limit our considerations to associations between roles, subject-actors would all be potential schizophrenics, but aspectualization reestablishes a certain coherence. Setting into discourse, through disengagement, allows for the unfolding of an autonomous discursive universe. But this disengagement is pluralizing, and there must be engagement if any homogeneity is to be reestablished. Recursively, as with the modulations of becoming, discourse is prey to cohesive and dispersive forces. The cohesive force that allows the actor to find his homogeneity one way or another is, in this case, aspectualization. In effect, beyond the more or less regulated agglomeration of roles, a process of the construction of the actor is seen, one that might take the form of a passional sequence—that is, of that preliminary canonical pathemic schema we believed we had recognized. Constitution, disposition, sensitization, emotion, and moralization would then be interpretable in terms of opening, setting things in train, and development and installation of pathemic roles, and would subsume all underlying agglomerations of roles. We will come back to this.

Aspectualization

We can in a general way identify two aspectualizing processes: demarcation, which establishes plateaus and limits along a continuum (cf. perfective/imperfective), and segmentation, which tends to establish stages along a discontinuum (cf. inchoative/durative/perfective). But things undoubtedly become more complex as soon as, in the instance of setting into discourse, we call on continuous and modulated entities and on discontinuous and modalized entities. The pathemic schema, for example, aspectualizes the process according to a discontinuous mode. But, on the other hand, as we have just suggested, it reintroduces continuity and homogeneity, where the different stages of modalization of the generative trajectory (such as disengagement) had brought about a destruction of roles.

Thus, the aspectualization of passions takes several forms. Without attempting an *in extenso* treatment of the whole question, we can at least underline the lessons learned in the course of our study of avarice and its configuration. There we see at least four different plateaus or stages of aspectualization. The first is the functional recurrence of thematic and pathemic roles; this stage is excluded because it does not belong to the sememes we analyzed and instead is part of the procedure that constructs those sememes. Next, we noted an aspectualization that proceeds by the segmentation of the stages of passion, but that is not yet sufficiently established. There remains, on the one hand, the aspectualization of the occurrences of passion, which in a way is responsible for regulating the continuous and discontinuous aspects of passional manifestations in discourse and, on the other hand, the internal aspectualization of each occurrence, which in a way is constitutive of passion as such, independently of its occurrences in discourse.

Scansion. The aspectualization of the occurrences of passional behavior gives emphasis to manifestation: we can distinguish between strong passions (those of the choleric, angry person) and emphatic passions (those of the miser). In the case of milder figures, recognition of the passion is enough to predict behavior: recognizing a miser gives one a maximum of predicting power. In the case of figures enacting strong, emphatic passions, we distinguish predictable passions from those that are not predictable. Some will be *frequentative*, and knowing what their period of manifestation is allows one to predict behavior. Others are *punctual*, that is, unpredictable.[10] One and the same sensitized modal arrangement can receive each of these aspectual forms. Thus, the modal apparatus for anger can appear as either durative and mild and unemphatic (i.e., irritable) or as punctual (i.e., furious). In fact, any pathemic role can receive any of a panoply of degrees of intensity, but our lexicon grants this to only some of them.

The category of passional emphasis (scansion), to the extent that it puts the occurrences of passional behavior under the control of an observer who aspectualizes, plays an essential role in interindividual and social regulation. Beyond its descriptive and distinguishing role within analysis, we have to note that once this category of passional emphasis is integrated into a cultural taxonomy as one of the defining characteristics of pathemic roles, it makes it possible for any subsequent partners of the impassioned subject to predict instances of passion, the affective crises, and stases of that subject's trajectory.

Rhythm. The internal aspectualization of each occurrence gives a certain rhythm to passional manifestation, one that regulates the tensions and the nontensive factors of the passional process itself. This rhythm (pulsation) includes, among other things, the classical triad "inchoative/durative/terminative." In a way, rhythm is nothing other than the discursive form that intermodal syntax takes on. It is what allows us to explain how modal arrangements can become dispositions in discourse.

But, in another way, rhythm can also undergo shifts, and these variations then play an identifying role among passions. Thus, among the variants of "fear," we note, as distinguishing aspectual features, *anteriority* in "apprehension," *inchoativity* in "being struck with fear," *durativity* in "terror." In fact, in the series "apprehension–struck with fear–terror," the aspectualization of passion is inseparable from the trajectory of the antisubject himself because the impassioned subject is in this case an observer who aspectualizes as a result of the perspective according to which he perceives what is happening. According to whether or not he perceives the threat prior to its occurrence, or perceives it inchoatively or coincidentally, he experiences one or other of these passions. This should not surprise us because usually the aspectualization of pragmatic programs is a function of the various turns taken in the interaction between subject and antisubject. This is a feature that merits further study so that we might generalize from it: the variations of tensions that we observe in the aspectual component of discourse can often be explained in terms of variations in the equilibrium between antagonistic forces.

The variations in tensions and moments of nontension that are regulated by passional rhythm are inherent also to the existential trajectory that the passional subject adopts for himself. The miser, for example, experiences tension in a context of nonconjunction, a more intense tension in a context of disjunction, and a maximum tension in a context of nondisjunction (he hangs on to things). Then he experiences nontension in a context of conjunction (he accumulates). Such variations in a general way echo the tensive modulations of becoming.

In fact, it seems more and more difficult to maintain aspectualization at a given level of the trajectory for our theoretical construct. A lot of research suggests that we are dealing with a case of semiotic determination that is of a very general nature, probably of a nature as general as that of the semiotic square. As with the constitutional model, whose place can be fixed within deep structures and which in practice keeps moving away from that place, aspectualization seems to cover properties that also escape from their assigned loci. That is why we have provided, at the level of preconditions to signification, a whole group of tensive modulations that prefigure discursive aspectualization itself.

Intensity. The concrete analysis of a passional configuration such as that for avarice reveals, at all the turning points of the structure in question, the category of intensity. Intensity belongs to the procedures of aspectualization. On the one hand it is one of the forms by which tensions and moments of nontension are distributed within the unfolding process. On the other hand, it implies an observer actant who can compare intensities, apply gradated scales through the setting into perspective of the phenomena in question, and establish plateaus along those scales. Further, all we need, in order to recognize that these demarcations have accomplished their tasks, is to find excess on one side of a demarcation and insufficiency on the other on a given scale that identifies the varying intensities of a given passion.

We have already noted, in the area of avarice, that the intensity of desire always pointed us to a certain sharing in the circulation of goods within a given community and that this was usually accompanied by certain modulations of the movements within that society. This means that intensity is a discursive form that manifests semionarrative or tensive entities that, in and of themselves, have nothing "intense" about them.

This fact is as obvious in the cases of other configurations, for example, in the case of "esteem–admiration–veneration." Esteem is defined as a sentiment born of good opinion one has concerning someone else's merits and value. Admiration is a sentiment of joy or delight when in the presence of someone one judges as being superior in attractiveness or greatness. Veneration is a great respect made up of admiration and affection. It often is of a religious nature, in which case worshipful adoration is mixed with fear. For the enunciatee, the receiver, of an instance of discourse in which these three passions appear successively, the effect produced is one of growing intensity. But a closer examination reveals that intensity covers structural changes here. In the case of esteem, it proceeds by enacting comparisons with other individuals (presumed or real) in order ultimately to make a conclusion as to the person's merit or value. Admiration compares the person to the whole group of people who belong to the same category. One is moving from a relative superlative to an absolute superlative. Finally, in the case of veneration, the evaluating observer himself, who is respectful and fearful, and thus dominated, makes of himself the humble, unworthy person against whom the venerated one is compared. The apparent graduation in judgment depends on a series of discontinuous variations in the reference term, and the variations in intensity successively cover a transitive and relative superlative (esteem), a transitive absolute superlative (admiration), and a simultaneously transitive and reflexive superlative (veneration). Intensity would thus appear to be a meaning effect showing quantitative variations within the actantial and modal structure of the configuration. It remains true that intensity translated them into discourse along a continuous and tensive mode.

Undoubtedly we must distinguish between the identifying function of intensity and its constitutive function. It is identifying when it allows us to differentiate superficially, for example, between esteem and admiration. In this sense, intensity gives information the partners of the impassioned subject can use to identify immediately the pathemic role that they will have to take into account in this instance of interaction. Because of intensity, the impassioned subject becomes informative vis-à-vis his observing partner. This observation is true of all intensity. An intense blue is, among other things, a blue that attracts the eye just as a "terrible sorrow" is, to begin, a sorrow that draws the attention of even the most inattentive observer. Thus, intensity appears as a perceivable manifestation of a causing-to-know that is supposed to alert the partners of the impassioned subject.

But this superficially identifying function has an effect on variations in the constitutive intensity of passion, an intensity that allows us to note the difference between what is passion and what is not. In this sense, intensity manifests the sensitization of the modal arrangement.

In order to understand how discontinuous phenomena—changes vis-à-vis the observer's position, as in avarice, generosity, or dissipation, and changes vis-à-vis reference, as in esteem, admiration, and veneration—can be manifested in a continuous and tensive way, we likely must come back to the modulations of becoming. We have already suggested that the intensity of the desire of the miser might be interpreted as a disequilibrium between collective and individual forces of cohesion and forces of dispersion: the constituting of an individual and exclusive locus to the detriment of collective cohesion is in this case the very source of the effect of intensity.

We might generalize on this observation, but with the appropriate caution. In the series "esteem-admiration-veneration," the respective loci of the judged subject-object and of the impassioned observer evolve in opposite directions. As the locus of one is confirmed and assured, the locus of the other is weakened. Although this is not explicitly and categorially translated by modal variations, we can see that the relation between these forces is inverse and that this inverse effect might eventually be made explicit through transfers of power and knowledge. The phenomenon we are trying to pin down is thus outside of modalization and categorization. It is as if, in intersubjectivity, any emergence of passion can threaten the place of any of the interactants, as if the passion in question set them back into a presemiotic stratum where the identity of each one is still unstable and depends on the identity of others. An interactantial identity is one that is to be shared, and each individual identity would then be established at the expense of others.

We again meet the idea that intensity, just as aspectualization, is born of variations in the equilibrium between cohesion and dispersion, a struggle in which the stabilization of actantial loci is at stake. At this point this seems to be the only plausible explanation that might allow us to reconcile a quantification that is seen in variations in equilibrium between adversarial forces, and variations in intensity that manifest discontinuous changes. Such a hypothesis opens new perspectives for us in our attempt to understand how archaic axiologies begin to take shape in a presemiotic space.

Let us return to excess, defined as "too much quantity," a violation of the limits of moderation. Intensity here occupies one plateau, a border beyond which something changes. In the area of avarice, excess appears as a destructive disequilibrium. Excess in holding on to things imperils circulation within the community. Excess in spending imperils individual "loci," and insufficiency vis-à-vis the objects that are desired creates phenomena of illusion that are the source of a society's losing its normal perspective. Likewise filial or amorous veneration can be considered as excessive as soon as it imperils the very identity of the impassioned subject. One might say the same of an excess of despair or of authority. Each time an interactantial arrangement attains a certain degree of stability, any passional figure that could cause it to regress to an earlier and less stable stage will be considered as excessive.

The ethical judgment that then appears in discourse just reformulates the regression that is threatening interactantial becoming. We often note that excess signals, at the discursive level, a change of isotopy, which is generally not the case with intensity. Thus, between an ordinary sorrow and an "intense" or even "violent" sorrow, the only thing modified is the equilibrium between euphoria and dysphoria. But in the case of an "excessive" sorrow, a border has been crossed and we have moved into another isotopy, an isotopy, for example, such as that of affectation or pathology. Whatever the final interpretation, it is interesting to note that it will always begin by an interrogation on the status of the subject or of his veridictory status (he shows or does too much of this or that) or even of his very status as semiotic subject (something is missing). The change in isotopy that we see at the surface and the crossing of a border both go back to a profound destabilization of interactantial arrangements.

In the case of intensity, we are dealing with a becoming that is in the process of taking place. We are dealing with protoactantial arrangements that seek to become stabilized and where sensitization is literally embodied. On the other hand, in the case of excess, we are dealing with a becoming that has already taken place but that is threatening to regress. We are dealing with destabilized protoactantial arrangements. The social observer, taking a position against this threatened regression, moralizes passional manifestation in order to reaffirm a state of affairs at the expense of a state of feeling.

Chapter 3
Jealousy

The first objective of a study devoted to jealousy was to have, alongside a passion that at first might be taken to be a "passion for an object" (i.e., avarice) an intersubjective passion that potentially would include at least three actors: the jealous person, an object, and a rival. Of course avarice eventually showed itself to be intersubjective, at least implicitly and especially at the moment of moralization. But jealousy offers the advantage of making explicit, beginning with the lexical manifestation of its configuration, and a fortiori within discourses, a passional scene with several roles, an interweaving of strategies, an interaction with its own history and becoming.

In the discursive trajectory of the miser, in effect, intersubjective relations appear only at the moment of judging. They are, of course, fundamentally the mainspring of the "movement by which value is circulated." At the discursive level, however, they tend to be downplayed in favor of relations vis-à-vis an object. Thus it is only in the light of moralization that we see that riches have been accumulated and hung on to at the expense of others. Conversely, we see jealousy against a background of a complex and variable intersubjective relation that is by definition present along the whole of the passional trajectory: fear of losing the object is understood here only in terms of the presence of a rival, at least of a potential or imagined rival, and the fear of a rival is born of the presence of an object of value, which is what is at stake.

Right away we note that the passional trajectory is, in this instance, a function of the twofold relations between three actors, the whole being directed according to the perspective adopted by the jealous person. Jealousy can in this respect just as easily be a distress and a *suffering*, as it can be a *fear* and an anguish. This depends on whether or not the decisive event in question takes place earlier or after the passional crisis. If the event—the junction of the rival with the object—is anticipated before its actual occurrence, the relation of *being rivals*—S_1/S_2—comes to the fore and awakens fear: in this case there is a need to watch the other person, intercept his actions, keep him away from the object, and, finally, take exclusive possession of the object in order to exclude the rival. If the event is perceived after the fact, it goes without saying that, for the jealous person, there is nothing much he can do vis-à-vis his rival other than to seek revenge. On the other hand, the relation of *attachment*—S_1/O, S_3—now comes to the fore. The jealous person directs his attention toward the object about which one now inquires as to which of the two, the jealous person and his rival, it prefers and whether or not it can be trusted. Now and only now is the suffering in question fueled by fiduciary and epistemic variations.

This scenario is, however, no more than a variation in perspective, along the axis of anteriority and posteriority. It presupposes a unique actantial arrangement that has to do with setting into discourse. On the one hand it focalizes the effects of a given syntax, because the forms that jealousy takes change at the same time as do those of the instances of junction involved. On the other hand, it presupposes a consistent configuration. The description of this passion as such begins with the description of the constants that underlie the setting into discourse and its variations.

Further, because lexical analysis has shown its limits and its presuppositions, it will from here on be strictly ancillary, and our construction of jealousy will, in the main, take its items from what moralists have to contribute, as well as dramatists and novelists. In fact, thanks to a "growing" study of passion, and based on many and varied textual facts, we can seek to enrich our syntactic models and grasp the organization of a configuration in its entirety.

The Configuration

Attachment and Rivalry

A first approach, one inspired by lexical semantics, will consist of allowing ourselves to be, for the moment, guided by dictionary definitions. It seems useful, in order to get a preliminary idea of what jealousy is, to know to what more vast configurations it belongs. According to the definitions, to its correlates and antonyms, it seems that jealousy is at an intersection of the configuration for *attachment* and that for *rivalry*, these two corresponding to the relation between the jealous person and the object (S_1/O, S_3) and the relation between the jealous person and his rival (S_1/S_2), respectively.

All definitions of jealousy take into account, directly or indirectly, an antisubject who threatens ruthlessness or has already acted ruthlessly. For example, an antonym such as "debonair" is explained, among other ways, in terms of "complaisance" and "peaceableness," which amounts to confirming the "combative" and "offensive" character of the jealous one and thus, the at least potential presence of a rival on his turf. On the other hand, the jealous person is above all—and by the very etymology involved—someone who is "particularly attached to . . . ," who "is absolutely determined to . . . ," and that is why jealousy has also to do with desire, zeal, and envy. Attachment is also present in the antonyms in question, this time in a negative relation: "indifferent" is explained in such terms as "insensitive" or "detached," for example.

But we must note that these two configurations are, if not closely related, at least carefully articulated within jealousy. Through a sort of alternated presupposition, attachment is reinforced by rivalry and rivalry is intensified by the motivating attachment involved. What results from this articulation of these two largely autonomous configurations is far from negligible. On the one hand, rivalry will never be, for the jealous person, joyous and all-conquering. It will instead appear as sad and bitter, always seeing the prospect of losing the object. On the other hand, attachment will by its nature involve worry and concern, because there is the threat of the rival. At the very moment when all that counts is a relation with a loved one, for example, worry keeps alive the fear of a more or less imagined threat from the antisubject. That is why Proust has us note, in connection with the love Swann declares for Odette de Crécy, that when a lover does all to keep his love for himself alone, he is no longer thinking about enjoying what, at the beginning, was his delight. The intersection of these two configurations is thus more than a simple semantic compounding or a linking up of isotopies. Each one is considerably modified under the influence of the other, just as, within a fixed modal arrangement, each modality is modified, in terms of its meaning effects, by the influence of the others.

One of the possible explanations is likely to be found in the actantial arrangement that we have postulated from the start: the $S_1/S_2/O\text{-}S_3$ triangle does not represent an arithmetic addition of two dual relations, but rather *an interaction*. Thus the jealous person is a subject that is torn between two relations, each of which seeks to possess him totally, but to neither of which he can commit himself totally. He is preoccupied by his attachment when he is fighting for something, and conversely he is obsessed by rivalry when he has succeeded in getting into a position to love something or someone.

Initial Generic Configuration: Rivalry

Rivalry and Competition. "Rivalry," according to the *Petit Robert*, is the "situation of two or more people who are in dispute over something" (especially such things as first place or first rank). "Situation" refers us to an actantial and narrative arrangement, independent of any passional manifestation. This appears to be the syntactic kernel of the whole configuration. We note the existence of an archetypic polemical relation, one that is ultimately organized around an object (the "something"), but most often around a qualification of the subjects, "superiority," which could be interpreted as resulting from a comparison of modal competencies.

"Competition" (concurrence), "rivalry" between several people or forces in pursuit of the same goal, specifies rivalry by attributing to the rivals this same object-goal with parallel narrative programs. In rivalry, the object is no more than an empty locus, a "something" that interaction between two rivals has put at stake. It is only with its correlates that the identity of the object is made clear–although only allusively–in terms of "result" or "advantage." So it is with the French near synonym for "concurrence," namely "competition," which adds to the above a "simultaneous seeking"–that is, a temporalized and aspectualized discursive trajectory.

The category of junction and the polemical structure here give us a very particular articulation: junction is just a variation on the polemical structure because the "object" is nothing more than the fact that the rivals have set their sights, identically, on the same goal. In other words, this empty locus, on which the rivals have set their respective sights, is something brought to life by their desire to attain it, and the convergence of their efforts brings an object into being. This is also what is presented by the simultaneity of the trajectories, a simultaneity already noted in connection with competition: the aspectual superimposition is not a discursive accident. It is the sign signifying that the rivals have identical goals.

Emulation. "Emulation," "a sentiment that leads one to seek to equal or surpass someone in merit, in knowledge, in work," is an old synonym for "rivalry" and for "jealousy." It brings a new element to rivalry. Far from following the same route as the two notions of competition we have reviewed earlier, in whose cases the object is brought into being, emulation focalizes on the comparison between the competence of S_1 and S_2. This competence can be grasped as such, as a *knowing-how-to-do* or a *being-able-to-do*, or through an ethical judgment that transforms it into "merit." The object that emerges from this rivalry is a modal object, and therefore what is at stake here is the very being of the subject in the rivalry.

Nonetheless, merit has become, in contemporary language, "merit in terms of something else," a merit that is measured with reference to an object of value that has been acquired or is expected to be acquired. Setting one's sights on the object is again at play, but it is subject to a condition, that of competence and recognition. Indeed, the merit of a given subject is evaluated along the whole of its trajectory: not only is the result obtained judged, but also the subject's manner of being, his manner of doing, his conduct through the course of various peripeteias, and his attitude in the face of the obstacles he encounters. Thus defined, merit seems to be based on the same modal effects as passion: it is a form of competence; it is not exhausted when the performance is realized; it is not reconstructed by presupposition, starting with competence; it appears as a "modal surplus" that characterizes the being of the subject beyond or within the competence required for the realization of the program.

Further, emulation, through merit, radically separates the polemical doing associated with qualifying and deciding tests, from the attribution of the object, associated in turn with glorifying tests. It is only at the moment of recognition, for which a Sender is responsible, that the subject receives the reward he deserves. This two-stage distribution confirms the twofold interpretation the modalizations of competence can receive: on the one hand, in terms of efficacy and need—they so appear, through presupposition, starting with success or failure; and on the other hand, in terms of the manner of doing or of being of the subject—which is how they appear when ethical judgment is implicated.

Emulation finally brings a last element to the configuration for rivalry, and it is important. Defined as a "sentiment that leads one to . . . ," it is the first figure, in this whole set up, that accedes to the rank of passion. At the very moment when the emulated person's merit seems to be based on a "modal surplus" that is like the surplus seen in the case of passional effects, our nomenclature makes of it a pathemic role that includes a sensitized competence, which should lead us to persist in our idea that the ethical, as the passional, appears in discourse as soon as the modal effects of being seem to become dissociated from competence vis-à-vis a certain doing. Further, the modal and actantial arrangement is placed *into the perspective of only one object*. Rivalry and our two versions of competition, which partake of no particular setting into perspective, are treated not as pathemic roles but as "situations." For there to be emulation, S_2 must have passed his tests, then S_1 must equal or surpass S_2, which makes S_1 the "emulated person" and S_2 the model or subject of reference. Rivalry or competition is thence no longer symmetrical: we are no longer dealing with a pair of processes that are aspectualized into simultaneity, but rather with an unfinished process, S_1's process, in relation to another subject, S_2, whose process is treated as finished. This latter finished process shows S_1 what degree of competence he must attain. Emulation is meaningful only if rivalry is seen in terms of S_1's perspective, and this is how it becomes a passion.

Envy. In the dictionary definitions, we find two forms of envy. On the one hand, it is a "sadness," an irritation or hate that opposes us to someone who possesses something we do not possess. On the other hand, it is seen as the "desire to enjoy an advantage, to enjoy a pleasure that is equal to someone else's." In this case it seems that the configuration for rivalry has to choose between the polemical relation and the object relation. What is particular to envy is that it can manifest only one of these relations at any one time. It must be made clear in this regard that the choice is necessary only because of the ever sharper actualization of the object (something or other, an advantage, a pleasure). The figure covers two sememes that were complementary in our preceding figures and that seem to become exclusive of each other in this figure.

Nonetheless, in each of these sememes, the third actant has not "disappeared," nor has it been blotted out. It has been relegated to the second rank because it is a *mediator vis-à-vis the focalizing relation*. In the envy of the S_1/S_2 type, the O object actant mediates S_1's envy with regard to S_2. In the S_1/O type of envy, the S_2 actant mediates S_1's desire. The mediating role might be interpreted, in this case, from the point of view of the S_1 subject: through O, S_1 sets his sights on S_2 and, through S_2, S_1 sets his sights on O.[1] These mediating roles are conceivable only if the actantial arrangement in question has not yet stabilized. It would seem that, in the protensive goal setting of the impassioned subject, the interactant can still hesitate between the status of object and that of subject. This means that, for S_1, the locus of the object identifies itself as being this side of the rival, and the locus of the rival identifies itself as being this side of the object. Mediation thus supposes as a condition that the S_1 subject is susceptible of representing an "internalized" actantial scene to itself, one in which actantial roles can still be exchanged.

Interactantial mediation will be seen in discourse in two complementary directions: on the one hand, we see added to the first setting of perspective that we noted in connection with emulation, the one that sensitizes the whole of the arrangement (orientation in the direction of S_1) another perspective, which is also set up in terms of the perspective of S_1, which focalizes either the rival or the object. On the other hand, the relegating of the other actant to a mediating role is translated as an intensification of the focalized relation: mediation by the object intensifies rivalry, and mediation by the rival intensifies the desire for the object. Once again, intensity is, in discourse, nothing more than the manifestation of the instability of the underlying actantial arrangement.

From Umbrage to Jealousy. "Umbrage" is a "sentiment of defiance," a "fear of being eclipsed, thrown into the shadows by someone else." What is unique to umbrage is obvious when we compare it to envy or emulation. In the case of envy, nothing much is left because the object recedes into the background, and desire is no longer manifested. As for emulation, it seems that umbrage reverses its structure: instead of seeking to surpass or eclipse someone else, the subject fears being surpassed or eclipsed. Emulation presupposes a superiority on the part of the rival; umbrage apprehends it. The underlying phenomena are the same: it is the configuration for rivalry, lacking any defined object, but perceived according to the perspective of only one of the subjects. The only thing to have changed is the discursive form in question. On the one hand, while emulation takes S_2's competence as its reference, umbrage takes S_1's competence as its reference. One might indeed imagine a unique situation that might incite umbrage on the part of the subject of reference and emulation on the part of the other subject. This is thus yet another variation in perspective. Emulation here is constructed within the perspective of the one who seeks to surpass someone else, and umbrage is constructed within the perspective of the one who is susceptible of being surpassed.

"Jealousy," in this configuration, is the end point of the series of specifying steps and articulations that we have already noted in the preceding figures: it is the most complex of them all. It is based on the $S_1/S_2/O$, S_3 actantial arrangement. It is also based on the perspective of just one subject, S_1. It can focalize either on the relation of rivalry, whereupon it narrows to "fear," prospectively, or it can focalize on the object relation, in which case it narrows to "suffering," retrospectively. Further, it will more and more become like umbrage, as opposed to emulation, because its perspective will always be that of the person who fears being surpassed or who suffers from having been surpassed. In other words, the competence that is the reference here is that of the jealous person, and when the system is reversed and the competence that is the reference becomes that of the rival, we leave jealousy and enter the domain of emulation.

Point of View and Sensitization. In the configuration for avarice, variations in point of view were imputable only to moralization. Indeed, since we could oppose the two moral variants of disjunction, prodigality and generosity, based only on a change in point of view (nonreceiver/receiver), it seemed that ethical judgments were based on the observer's discursive transformations. This was true to the point that we could say that the difference between a nonsensitized thematic role such as saving and a sensitized pathemic role such as avarice had nothing to do with changes in point of view.

However, in the configuration for rivalry, one to which jealousy belongs, it is sensitization that is predicated on variations in point of view. What is at play is as much a matter of narrowing of focalization as it is one of changes in point of view *stricto sensu*. The narrowing and changing of point of view are at play on several levels of the configuration, and are seen as a series of perspective settings that overdetermine each other.

The first perspective setting is the one that reorganizes the $S_1/S_2/O$, S_3 actantial triangle from the point of view of S_1 alone, thus producing the "emulation–envy–jealousy" series. The latter thereby finds itself being distinguished from the series of nonpassions. The frontier that has thus been crossed, thanks to the fact that the whole arrangement is now reoriented according to the perspective of only one of its actants, is that of sensitization strictly speaking: it is thanks to this orientation that we can recognize the sensitized arrangements.

The second perspective setting is the one that, within the point of view of S_1, puts either the S_1/O relation or the S_1/S_2 relation in the forefront. In emulation, the S_1/S_2 relation wins out, thanks to a focalization/occultation of the underlying narrative arrangement. In effect, the polemical relation and the attribution of the object are syntactically dissociated, the one preceding the other, the one being shaded out by the deployment of rivalry and relegated to the role of ultimate reward for the rival that wins. Against this setting into perspective of the syntagmatic deployments of narrativity, we have a paradigmatic perspective that allows us to identify two different envies and two different jealousies: in this case, the shaded-out relation is not relegated to a narrative segment other than the one in question, but is instead kept in the background of the focalized relation.

Since perspective setting here is part of the sensitization of the actantial and modal setups, it can be treated both as a discursive operation that is found within the trajectory of the impassioned person, and as an explicative procedure, within the trajectory of the theoretical construction. On the one hand, as discursive operation, the perspective setting takes the figure of a pathemic transformation, all the more intense for the fact that the perspective is complex, and therefore moves through the classical operations involved in the constructing of points of view. On the other hand, as a procedure that is part of the theoretical construction, it has a role in enunciative praxis and will as needed refer back to the tensive analysis of an as yet unstable interactantiality. The mediation we have identified in envy and jealousy is played out against both backdrops: as a figurative and actorial arrangement, and as a manifestation of the tensive instability of the interactant. The blocked-out relation continues to be manifested both as "mediating" and "intensifying" in connection with the focalized relation.[2]

Once it has been concretely adopted by an *emboîtement* of perspective settings, the protoactant's procedure of scission, which we have anticipated in terms of a tensive precondition, defines itself more precisely. After identifying an interactant that will allow it to represent itself vis-à-vis an "other" (this is the birth of "self for self"), it will seek, by orienting the element of protensivity, to bring about either an object or a subject, in the background behind this interactant. The realization, within discourse, of these variations of tension, and above all their manifestation as distinct meaning effects, requires that there be an observer that can call on them in the form of variations of perspective. The impassioned subject, whether he be a jealous or an envious person, is the "focalizing" discursive subject.[3]

Watching the Jealous Person. We might point out here that jealousy specifies an observer actant responsible for the orientation of the actantial arrangement in question. The jealous person suffers from "seeing another person enjoy something," or he "is afraid of losing something." In the one case, it is S_2 that is focalized; in the other, it is O, S_3. But what is unique to jealousy is that, while it brings either one or the other actant to the forefront, it is always directed at the S_2/O,

S_3 relation. Whatever the perspective that has been adopted, the spectacle that offers itself to S_1 always involves the junction of rival and object. If an "other" is enjoying O or if O can be lost in a way that benefits that "other," beyond any variations in perspective, the same scene always brings about the same passion. Jealousy obeys the same distinctions as envy, but it does so against the backdrop of its own specifications.

If the basic spectacle of jealousy is made up of the junction of rival and object, the jealous person is, as an observer, excluded from that relation of junction. The envious person has to choose between two perspectives—S_1/S_2 or S_1/O, S_3—of which he remains, however, the main pole. For his part, the only choice the jealous one has is between two perspectives on S_2/O, S_3, with he himself remaining in the background. The choices are $(S_1)S_2/O$ or $(S_1)S_2/O$, S_3. This is why the jealous subject finds it impossible to segment its actantial arrangement any other way, and why the hated or apprehended scene is imposed on him. He himself, vis-à-vis his own passional simulacrum, presents as a virtualized subject, a subject without body and one that cannot accede to that scene.

This unique position within the actantial arrangement will, at the discursive level, be seen as the attribution of a specific observing position. The observer of jealousy becomes a "spectator," that is, an observer whose spatiotemporal coordinates refer to those of the spectacle offered up to him, but who can in no way figure as an actor in that scene. As we shall soon see, whatever the spatial or temporal position of the jealous one vis-à-vis the scene in which the rival and the object are conjoined, that scene is always "present" in his imagination—it is the product of the workings of his spatiotemporal determinations—but he is always excluded from the scene.

Second Generic Configuration: Attachment

Intense Attachment. Here we will limit ourselves to an examination of "attachment" strictly speaking, followed by that of its correlates, "possession" and "exclusivity." In the definition itself of jealousy, attachment is on the one hand associated with intensity, because it is "lively," and, on the other, with "the desire for exclusive possession."

The intensity of attachment would seem to overdetermine junction, because the dictionary makes it clear that it is a "sentiment that unites us." To the extent that attachment appears as a constant that underlies all of the various forms the relation between subject and object can take, it can be interpreted as *a necessity* that the variations of that relation do not affect, just as in linguistics a presupposition is considered to be necessary to the extent that the variations (negation, interrogation) that affect the posited element are irrelevant. Attachment appears to be based on a *having-to-be* that modalizes junction but not the object, whatever that junction might be. This is a *having-to-be* that in a way implicates the semiotic existence of the subject. It is as if, with attachment broken off, the subject had to regress to a presemiotic stage where nothing would any longer have any value for him.

We cannot see how intensity can directly affect this modality, since it is categorial: how can any self-respecting necessity be more or less compelling than any other necessity? The only possible answers to this are of a discursive or tensive nature. One can allow that certain necessities are hierarchically superior to others, that some are more urgent and have a greater priority. Necessity can have no other gradation, no differences in intensity other than those that require, when setting into discourse takes place, that there be a temporal and spatial distribution of programs as a function of their linear nature. The intensity of attachment can be recognized in particular either by the temporal antecedence of the programs in question or by their being ranked first in the figurative representation that the subject undertakes to carry out.

It is more difficult to grant that this figurative translation of intensity is not, to a greater or lesser degree, prefigured as immanence. As a manifested phenomenon it presupposes a manifestation. Maybe the solution is in the tensive modulations that prefigure modalities. Duty is prefigured, at this level, by a punctualizing modulation that suspends becoming, transforms it into a simple postponing delay, and it neutralizes all of the potentialities of that change. For the tensive subject, this means that its zones of valency are all unified: the whole group of the modulations of his becoming is reunified around just one valency, that of the object of attachment. In the tensive space of phoria, an intensity of *having-to-be* is thus conceivable, because the effect of the punctualizing modulation can be more or less widely felt. Further, the stronger an attachment the greater the subject's tendency to, figuratively speaking, be confused with the object of value. This can, in tensive terms, be translated by the fact that a greater intensity manifests a questioning of any actantial differentiation that has taken place.

If we now consider narrative actants and junctions, we see that the intensity of attachment is translated in terms of the degree to which the subject is invested by the object. This "degree" covers two phenomena: on the one hand the investment of the subject by the object is more or less solid according to whether or not that subject can welcome other objects. Just as there are "exclusive" or "participative" objects that can enter into junction with either a single subject or with several subjects at the same time, there are "exclusive" subjects and "nonexclusive" subjects who can receive either just one object, or several.

Here we are once again seeing the quantitative component that we already met in the case of avarice. We also are seeing its cohesive and dispersive effects. A subject that is "attached" to an object is, in this respect, a subject that is wholly and singly devoted to the object in question. On the other hand, the subject remains attached to the object, be he joined to or disjoined from it. In general we believe that the subject is semanticized by the object of value at the moment of junction. The attached subject is, on the other hand, semanticized by the object no matter what the mode of junction, and this in a way precedes any categorizing of junction in terms of disjunction/conjunction. This means that things remain at the fiduciary stage. Thus, among other things, it can be said that we can measure the intensity of attachment (and thus of *having-to-be*) by noting the importance of the narrative aleas experienced by the subject. Intensity here is thus a meaning effect pertaining to the way in which attachment resists the aleas of junction: resistance to loss, to absence, to abandonment, and to jealousy and satiety. Attachment that resists the destruction of the object, attachment beyond death, reveals the principle of intensity very well. It manifests a certain way of being of the fiduciary subject that is independent of the object of value.

There seem to be two kinds of possible relations between the subject and the object of value. It would not mean much to say that *having-to-be* modalizes junction with the object if all of the variations on junction were implicated. If we believe, however, that modalization here brings up a simulacrum, we can then say that *having-to-be* modalizes a simulacrum of realization. The simulacrum is initially shifted out so that it can be dissociated from the utterances of junction attested to elsewhere. It is then shifted in on the tensive subject so that there can be a direct appeal to the modulation that prefigures *having-to-be* and its extension can be brought into play. The way in which the new simulacrum resists an eventual return to welcoming discourse is a function of the extensiveness of that modulation. The disengagement and the reengagement allow us to understand why, despite the affective evolution of the relations between subject and object, attachment can remain intangible. The subject can thus continue to dream of conjunction with his object of value, beyond even death or the disappearance of that object.

Zeal. Zeal intensifies and moralizes attachment. They say it is a "strong ardor and desire to serve a person or cause to which one is sincerely devoted." Intensity manifests itself here as "warmth"; the sentiment has become a disposition to do (serve), and attachment is only presupposed. Further, attachment is reformulated as "devotion," which, if we set aside the fact that the relation is in this case intersubjective and hierarchized, amounts to signaling the exclusive investment of the subject by his object. The subject is "devoted"—indeed, "sacrificed"—to his object and the correlates of "fidelity" and "loyalty," once the moralization that overdetermines them has been suspended, confirm the independence of the *having-to-be* in question vis-à-vis any narrative peripeteia.[4] Further, these two correlates presuppose *trust* and thus remind us that, before moralization, *having-to-be* gives rise to expectation, and we are further, and more important, reminded that the modulation that prefigures *having-to-be* takes form against a fiduciary backdrop.

One might wonder why, starting with a common sememe ("intense attachment"), we on the one hand obtain a passion that is moralized positively, along with all of its correlates (zeal), and on the other hand obtain a negatively moralized passion (jealousy). This is all the more surprising for the fact that, in several European languages, all passional figures are completely unified around the etymon *zelos*, from which we get both "zeal" and "jealousy." We would further note that *zelosis*, derived from the verb *zelo*, brought together the signifieds "emulation," "rivalry," and "jealousy" without distinguishing among them. We can think of one hypothesis to help us understand in part what has happened. As attachment and zeal become more and more differentiated from rivalry, the mixed forms such as jealousy (and to a lesser degree envy) are negatively moralized, and the "pure" forms, such as emulation on the one hand and zeal on the other, are positively moralized. It is further proof of the predominance of moralization in any cultural reworkings of passional taxonomies. While the Greeks accepted that zeal for an object and rivalry can come together – indeed, they derived from each other – we seem to valorize their distinction.

Possession and Enjoyment. The exclusive possession claimed by the jealous person opens up two parallel investigations, one concerning possession and the other exclusivity. Frequently we understand "possessive attitude" to mean an exclusive attitude, but this contamination of one term by another is just one effect of their frequent association.

"Possession" is the "faculty of having the use of something that one has at one's disposal" and thus refers us to "possessing," "having use of," "having the enjoyment of." The subject in this possession is not a subject of doing that seeks conjunction, but rather a subject already in conjunction that seeks the enjoyment of the object. We also note a subject of doing, one that gives pleasure to the subject of state, but it is situated on the thymic dimension and no longer on the pragmatic dimension that brought about conjunction with the object. One chooses and buys a house (pragmatic dimension), and one enjoys it when one owns it (thymic dimension). Once the object has been conjoined with the subject, it in a way loses its pragmatic status and is transformed into a thymic object, an object of enjoyment and source of euphoria (or dysphoria: the house can be a success or a disaster). What is most important here has to do with the fact that since pragmatic conjunction has been accomplished and is not in question, it continues to be lacking something. For the story not to end here, a competent operator subject must appear on the scene.

"To have something at one's disposal" is, among other things, "to use" or "do with it as one pleases." The subject of possession is therefore above all, since we presuppose that he must have the object *at his disposal*, a *volitive subject* who, once in conjunction, can deploy all of his wanting capacity on the object. The study of possession seems to have clarified, in a new way, the modal surplus we always meet in the universe of passions. Even when it has been realized, the quest for the object does not exhaust one's "wanting to be conjoined with" and another form comes into play, the same one that explains why the miser wants to enjoy his treasures and why it is not enough for him simply to accumulate them.

More precisely, "to do with it what one pleases" is still a doing, but one that is on the thymic dimension. Nonetheless, the change of dimension is accompanied by the discrete emergence of a quantitative clause: "to do with it as one pleases" is also to master, totally, the object. The object figure is transformed into an image of the subject's *wanting* and is nothing less than that wanting. In fact, what we have is not even another wanting, a *wanting-to-enjoy*, for example, but, conversely, an enjoyment born of the fact that the *wanting-to-be* in question is coextensive with the object, that the descriptive object of value, because it is susceptible of belonging to any other subject, has now become the modal object that is characteristic of a particular subject.

Possession allows us to grasp, in its earliest stages, a process that we will often meet. It is one that seems to be the transformation of the object into subject. If enjoyment is the action of getting out of something "all the satisfactions it is *capable* of giving," the object is still considered to be a modal object, here a *being-able-to-do*. Enjoyment is, in a way, the result of a certain adequation between the wanting projected by the subject and the "being able" that seems to come from the object (the thing possessed is "capable" and "susceptible" of giving satisfactions). We have to take everyday metaphors seriously, and "figurative" meanings must be seen as eminently significant. On the one hand, in wanting to extend his wanting to the object in its integral totality, the possessing subject acts as if the least fragmentation of that object would constitute resistance to his goal. Thus, by modalizing a quantified version of his object, the possessor projects onto it a competence that is susceptible of transforming it into a subject. The least "part" of the object that might escape from his possession would make of it a resisting subject. On the other hand, the sharing of modalizations between the two actants supposes that it is the possessor who has "wanting," and the possessed that has "being able." A modal microanalysis shows that, once discourse has moved to the thymic dimension, the modalizations projected by the impassioned subject onto the object of value bring into being a competent subject. So it is that the object figure includes both a pragmatic object of value and a thymic subject operator.

Exclusivity. Exclusivity, just like the adjective "exclusive" and the verb "to exclude," includes a modalization, according to a *having-not-to-be*, and a quantification.

Any exclusion supposes a totality and a part of that totality considered as a unit. What delimits exclusion is a unit that comes out of a totality, an individual, a group, or a fraction. This unit can be extracted in a transitive way—one group excludes one of its members from its ranks—or in a reflexive way—a group or an individual affirms its exclusive rights to such and such a privilege. To be exclusive is to "refuse to share, to refuse any participation," so that exclusion can also concern the distribution of objects of value in a given society.

There are therefore two ways of sharing (or of refusing to share) objects of value in a community: either along the diachronic axis, each one being able to hope to have his share at one time or other, as long as the circulation of goods is not blocked, or along the synchronic axis, each one being able to participate at the same time in the enjoyment of available goods. If avarice and its antonyms disrupt the circulation of goods along the diachronic axis, exclusivity now is an obstacle to participation along the synchronic axis. The circulation of goods is based on the notion of "one's share," a share that corresponds to the "definite or specific partitive" of grammar. Participation supposes, conversely, a nondifferentiation of parts that corresponds to grammatical "indefinites." The objects here are, at any moment, of free access for all subjects. Exclusivity determines a single unit that has been taken out of the domain of participation and that corresponds to grammar's "singular defined."

Two questions remain: the status of the unit within totality and the status of objects vis-à-vis exclusive subjects. Exclusive subjects interrupt or put into question the process by which the collective actant is constituted. We can from the outset grant the existence of individuals that are treated as integral units in the sense that, as units, they include individuation features. The bringing together of the features they have in common transforms them into partitive units. The totalizing of these partitive units then constitutes a partitive totality, which in turn, because it presents, as a totality, individuation features that directly issue from the common features collected within the trajectory, can become an integral totality.

Exclusivity concerns "subject-units" that are individualized at the expense of the collectivity and that affirm, against the common constitutive features of that totality, differentiating features. This can be interpreted as *a resistance to the constituting of a partitive totality.* If applied to the distribution of objects of value within the community, this reasoning implies that a partitive unit, then any partitive totality, is to be defined in terms whose starting point is those objects of value that constitute a common feature. Thus, the exclusive subject would block the operation by unilaterally declaring the uniqueness of a given object of value. We have already met this phenomenon in connection with avarice, and its recurrence in the universe of passions is at the very least curious. Nonetheless, for the miser, it was a matter above all of slowing or of stopping the flow of the circulation of goods, and this slowing alone transformed his share (a partitive unit) into an integral unit. The exclusive subject, as we have suggested, invents his share and immediately appropriates it. Two operations are thus necessary: first, the creation of a partitive unit and then, its transformation into an integral unit. Neither jealousy nor exclusivity presupposes any form of circulation, because the shares in those cases are not yet part of the community in question.

If we now consider the status of objects, we see that nothing is solved by our calling them "participative" or "nonparticipative." We have already noted that it is not appropriate to speak of a participative character for objects of value as such. On the one hand, land can be parceled off or it can be held in common; on the other, knowledge can be jealously kept to oneself. The participative character of objects is nothing other than the meaning effect of the consensus reached by subjects in their regard with a view to the constitution of a partitive totality. All you need is for one of these subjects to refuse to agree (refuse to share) and his object will become considered "nonparticipative" and he will be seen as "exclusive." Individuals can assign status in this matter. One can be jealous of one's wife, of one's prestige or discoveries, but cultures also can show this jealousy – they decree that goods or women are to be held in common, or that knowledge is the exclusive right of clerks and sorcerers.

Exclusivity is based on a *having-not-to-be*, whether it be cognitive or logical. Two irreconcilable propositions are declared exclusive. In the epistemic, what is recognized as impossible is "excluded." In the juridical, a privilege or a right that is reserved for one person or group is "excluded." The withdrawal of a given integral unit from the partitive totality is regulated by a *having-not-to-be*, on two levels. On the one hand, it is the relation of the collective subject with the selected object of value that *should-not-be*. On the other, it is the relation between the single subject and the collectivity that also *should-not-be*. Exclusivity prepares the way for rivalry. In attachment itself, the collectivity brings itself into the equation negatively, as an actantial presence with which the subject establishes, through presupposition, polemical relations. Against the backdrop of this breaking of the consensus, this rejection of the partitive totality, we see a rival emerging. In this sense, the rival is nothing other than a concretization (actorialization) of this presence that is at the same time rejected and postulated by exclusivity.

This similarity to attachment shows us a surprising symmetry. Within the perspective of rivalry, the conflict between antagonists, initially seen as a quest for superiority, could then focus on an object whose appearance on the scene was in a way brought on by that antagonism itself. Conversely, from the perspective of attachment, the decision to withdraw the object from the community, to reaffirm the object's "originality in and of itself" and to refuse to recognize in it that partitive feature that is the basis for the collective actant, foretells the rival and stakes out the locus where the antagonist will establish himself.

In our concern to free ourselves from cultural taxonomies we should avoid choosing between two solutions: either conflict engenders the object or else the object engenders conflict. But the two solutions also presuppose an absence of consensus in the community, or more generally a difficulty in the constitution of the collective actant. In this respect, neither the object nor the rivalry is relevant. At the center of a dislocated actantial constellation cohesive forces work for harmony and a coming together in the form of a collective actant, and dispersive forces oppose this. The features of "participative" or "exclusive" are thus interactantial properties that belong to the collectivity for their development and that ultimately, in order to be manifested, will have to be mediated by either the object or the rival.

Here we are confirming a certain view of the passional universe, one that is neither specific nor likely universal, but only generalizable. The passions we are examining appear as configurations that regulate relations between an individual or a group and the collectivity, whose dynamics stubbornly call into play the constitution (in process) of the collective actant. This seems to be the only explanation for the recurrence of quantitative phenomena, and it is against the backdrop of the equilibria and disequilibria so created that we also see appearing *the foreshadowing of the rival* as well as *the foreshadowing of the object.*

Jealousy, at the Intersection of Two Configurations

If we now consider jealousy at the intersection of rivalry and attachment, several things must be done. First, as a mixed figure, jealousy might be the object of a study that would involve the variations in equilibrium between rivalry and attachment, following principles of variations of dominance within one and the same complex term. This would be an intercultural study, in which changes in cultural representation of jealousy, geographically as well as historically, would be seen as a function of the respectively different importance of the two configurations. We have already emphasized, with a brief allusion to "Greek" jealousy, what would be interesting about such a study. That is not, however, our intention. The intersection of these two configurations is not a simple juxtaposition. It engenders multiple interreactions. It would be useful to examine the effects of attachment on rivalry and those of rivalry on attachment. Further it would be useful, from a syntactic point of view, to study the distribution of the respective components of the two configurations, distribution around jealousy itself.

When we once again consult dictionary definitions, we see that they identify four sememes, each characterized by a generic term. We thus see a case of *attachment*: "lively attachment marked by umbrage"; a *bad sentiment*: "bad sentiment that one feels when seeing someone else enjoying . . ."; a *worry or concern*: "worry inspired by fear of having to share . . ."; and finally a *painful sentiment*: "painful sentiment that, in the case of the person experiencing it, is awakened by a worried love for someone, the desire exclusively to possess the loved one, the suspicion or certainty of the loved one's infidelity."

The difference between "bad sentiment" and "worry" is in large measure a matter of a variation vis-à-vis the perspective that differentially hierarchizes relations with objects and relations with rivals. The first sememe–with "attachment"–explicitly roots jealousy in the relation with the object, reserving for rivalry the role of superficial overdetermination (umbrage). The fourth adopts the same hierarchy while centering the whole of the passional arrangement on "love," a specific form of attachment, and then overdetermining it as a result of the effects of rivalry (worry, suspicion, etc.). Within this whole, the two options are thus realized: the first and the fourth sememe grant preeminence to attachment, the second and third, to rivalry. This allows us more precisely to observe the effects of "intersection" on each of the two configurations.

On the one hand we note, parallel to the appearance of "umbrage," the recurrence of "worry." Just as, indeed, umbrage also includes, in at least one of its accepted meanings, an indication of worry, we can suppose that this last figure is one of the important innovations of jealousy vis-à-vis attachment. The jealous lover is in the first instance *a worried person*. If we can trust the definitions of worry, the jealous one is going to know "agitation," perpetual lack of satisfaction, and "concern." This absence of repose, this trouble that is an obstacle to the peaceful enjoyment of the desired object, is in essence based on an oscillation between euphoria and dysphoria, so that the jealous person is neither truly euphoric nor truly dysphoric. The principle of that oscillation is to be looked for in the difficulty there is in polarizing the terms of phoria. Conjunction with the object is not enough to render the subject euphoric. Of course what prevents the subject from enjoying the object is rivalry. It is rivalry that takes the pathemic form of worry and umbrage, when it comes in contact with attachment, because, while overdetermining attachment, rivalry undergoes its influence and thus gives us an example of the mutations that occur within passional macroarrangements.

On the other hand, we see here the development of mistrust, suspicion, and fear. Here we have a brave combatant or a meritorious, emulating person who, as soon as he comes into possession of a jealously loved object that he feels he must defend, suffers apprehension. In effect, beyond his integrity, which he has to preserve, and beyond his superiority, which he has to demonstrate, he must also have this preoccupation with the object that he seeks exclusively to preserve for himself.

Distrust, suspicion, and fear are all based on a *fiduciary perturbation* that modifies the initial givens of attachment. Attachment, in effect, presupposes a *having-to-be* that is the basis for trust—not an intersubjective trust, since one can also be attached to an object, but a generalized trust, the possibility for the subject of giving meaning to his life. The emergence of rivalry on the horizon of attachment casts doubt on that trust, to the point that the relation with the loved object can be affected: under the influence of rivalry, attachment is transformed into mistrust.

Because he cannot peacefully enjoy the object, and because he is caught up in his combat with the rival, the jealous one flails about worriedly instead of acting, and he mistrusts instead of trusting. The distortions that each of the configurations can undergo, brought on by being overdetermined by the other, engender figures that are specific to their intersection, and they are the very figures of jealousy.

The construction of jealousy will come after we study those figures of overdetermination.

The Syntactic Construction of Jealousy

The Syntactic Constituent Parts of Jealousy

Jealousy is organized around a dysphoric event that can be located either prospectively or retrospectively, thus transforming the jealous one into either a fearful subject or a suffering subject. Further, according to whether or not he sets in the forefront the rival that is enjoying his object or the object that has escaped him, the jealous one will know umbrage or mistrust. These variations in the pathemic roles that are deployed at the moment of setting into discourse do not affect "jealousy in and of itself." Now is when we must construct that figure, starting with givens we have gathered from realized discourses. Further, within discourse itself, the passional simulacrum of jealousy, and in particular of the scene thereof that the jealous one provides for himself, is not affected by variations of perspective.

If, one last time, we look at the different varieties of jealousy, we see a strange and paradoxical indifference vis-à-vis junction on the part of passion. Of course the jealous subject, in his various pathemic roles, is not indifferent to the fact of being conjoined or not with his object. Nor is he indifferent to the fact that his rival possesses or does not possess the object. But the passion in question remains the same whatever the utterances called into play.
All combinations can be seen:

conjoined S_1/conjoined S_2 (seeing another enjoy an advantage that one would like exclusively to possess);
conjoined S_1/disjoined S_2 (the fear of having to share or of losing);
disjoined S_1/conjoined S_2 (seeing someone else enjoy an advantage that one does not possess);
disjoined S_1/disjoined S_2 (the fear that another person will obtain what one does not have but which one desires to have).

Nonetheless, jealousy is indifferent only to those varieties of junction that the subject knows at the moment when he is jealous. This is because jealousy admits a syntactic arrangement as a constant, an arrangement according to which the rival possesses the object and where the subject is deprived of that same object. But this arrangement is actualized by the passion in question itself, independently of the narrative situation in which the three actants find themselves, and it appears as the "existential" content of the simulacrum. The variations in perspective inherent to setting into discourse are thus in part the effect of gaps between these two types of junction—effective junctions and simulated junctions—and the construction of jealousy as such can be no more than the construction of the arrangement that is specifically of the simulacrum, simply, in this case, the discursive constant we identified earlier.

Worry. Worry seems more general than fear or umbrage, and that is why it will be considered as one of the fundamental syntactic constituents of jealousy. Fear alone presupposes only a knowing and a believing, an expectation that is modalized conflictually by both a *being-able-to-be* (eventuality) and a *being-able-not-to-be* (rejection). Conversely, worry introduces, with permanence and iteration, a stereotyped pathemic role, a constant vis-à-vis the passional competence of the subject. Circumscribed around fear, jealousy would be no more than a punctual and incidental sentiment, because fear is real only in terms of a coming event, one that is at play here in terms of an object of knowledge that mobilizes expectation. It is in a way a jealousy dictated by circumstances. Conversely, with worry, which by definition has no precise object, jealousy becomes a property of the subject himself, inscribed not within circumstance, but within competence, in terms of a manner of being of the jealous person.

Compared to umbrage, worry also conserves a generic position because umbrage is just an ephemeral phase of jealousy or worry, the phase in which the foreshadowed rival is perceived. From the syntactic point of view, therefore, worry regulates the whole chain and is in passing translated either by umbrage, when the rival is manifested, or by fear, when the dysphoric event is expected.

Worry can in particular become grafted onto the expectation of the event just as easily as it can onto the expectation of suffering itself. In this sense, it causes a complete phoric upheaval in the impassioned subject, an upheaval that engenders minimal "feeling." Further, if an agitated oscillation between euphoria and dysphoria prevents the worried subject from effecting a polarization that would make a true subject of quest of him, it brings him back, through a regression along the generative trajectory, to phoric tensivity, one that is anterior to categorization. Oscillation, in effect, cannot be interpreted as a trajectory between extreme positions. The worried person is not a cyclothymic person. What we have is a perpetual hesitation within a mixed figure who cannot fix his terms. That is why the worried person can be understood to be a subject that is immersed in tensive modulations.

The worried subject might pass for the stereotype of the impassioned subject because, since he cannot traverse the discontinuous positions within modal categories, within which he can in effect only "oscillate," the only trajectory that offers itself to him is a trajectory from one modalization to another—that is, within the modal arrangements in question. By preventing the subject from effecting the discontinuous transformations that modal categories usually offer, worry predisposes that subject to compliance to the intermodal syntax of the relevant passional arrangements. The worried person would thus be a prototype of the impassioned subject in another way too, one that is complementary to the preceding one. If we seek to identify his specific modal arrangement—indeed, his existential trajectory—we fail. Wanting, knowing, being-able, and having-to-do can also be the basis for worry. Realized, virtualized, actualized, and potentialized subjects can all, for different reasons, be worried.

Worry is no more than this oscillation that sets into place a simulacrum available for another passion. The oscillation brings about the shifting of the tensive subject with a view to his traversing more specific trajectories. Worry in a way prepares the way for other passions. It defines a certain *constitution* of the subject. It becomes particularized only as a function of the passions that subsequently invest the simulacrum and provide it with a modal arrangement.

So it is that, if worry can affect attachment, it becomes the worry of someone who has something to lose, that of a realized subject, and also a worry that disturbs *having-to-be*. We could speak of a "concern." In effect, concern is a hybrid figure that results from an encounter between attachment and worry. In language, the term itself can designate both the object that is absorbing and preoccupying the subject and the preoccupation itself—indeed, the moral suffering that can ensue. Concern thus borrows from attachment—the subject's being absorbed by the object, an integral and alienating investment of the subject—and from worry—submission to the oscillations of phoria. Concern appears as a worry that has taken on the modal arrangement of attachment.

Mistrust or Distrust. Mistrust and distrust are components of umbrage, suspicion, and fear. They exploit the fiduciary component that underlies attachment. Here we should identify two different occurrences of mistrust in the configuration. On the one hand, there is a mistrust that is presupposed by jealousy and has its source in rivalry. It is a mistrust vis-à-vis the adversary, and which, while being necessary to it, is in no way specific to jealousy. On the other hand, there is the mistrust that is awakened by jealousy, a mistrust vis-à-vis the loved one about whom one suspects infidelity, for example. Thus it precisely results from a disturbing of the confidence that is proper to attachment. This implied mistrust is not necessary to jealousy. It is just one of jealousy's eventual variants and can be, for example, suspended in a case where the jealous one accedes straight off to certitude and, so to speak, settles for suffering treachery. Let us for the moment examine the mistrust that is presupposed and that is inherent to rivalry.

As a start we must note that the fiduciary dimension is inscribed both within the modal definition of attachment and within that of exclusivity. On the one hand, *having-to-be* determines a fiduciary expectation that restricts the subject's horizon to only one object. On the other hand, *having-not-to-be* determines another form of fiduciary expectation—this time a negative one—thanks to which the subject can protect his territory. But confidence and mistrust emerge out of fiducia, the latter being a complex of tensive modulations in which valencies are defined. Once discretization and categorization of modalities have been accomplished, fiducia is converted into a fiduciary dimension. Nonetheless, the latter does not directly derive, nor in particular do confidence and mistrust, from modalities alone.

At an initial stage, alethic modalizations, whether they define themselves in the form of *having-to-be* or in the form of *being-able-to-be*, allow the cognitive subject to give out adequation judgments that, in turn, project modalizations that are called epistemic on those junctions that have been converted into objects of knowledge. The passage from a *being-able-to-be* to a *not-being-able-not-to-be*, for example, will at this higher level of articulation be reformulated as a passage from the "probable" to the "certain." It is epistemic modalizations that are then moralized in order to engender the fiduciary category. The ethical judgment that intervenes will then overdetermine each epistemic modalization as a function of a preestablished taxonomy. Certitude will appear, for example, in some cases, either as "confidence" or as "credulity." The whole package of these stages in the generative procedure in a way accounts for the way in which *believing* is constituted, starting with a generalized fiducia that is lacking in articulations, to the sophisticated structurations of the epistemic dimension of its moralization.

In the case of jealousy, "certitude" is always valorized, negatively or positively. There will be positive certitude before a passional crisis and negative certitude during the crisis itself. Positive certitude, born of attachment, is manifested as "confidence" or trust (and not as "credulity"). Negative certitude, born of exclusivity, is manifested as generalized mistrust, a kind of pessimism that is intrinsic to jealousy. The jealous person always prefers to "know," at whatever price, and he says so himself. This, seen from outside the passional simulacrum, is generally interpreted as a large capacity for *believing*.

When it is projected onto the semiotic square, the fiduciary dimension is organized as shown in Figure 16.

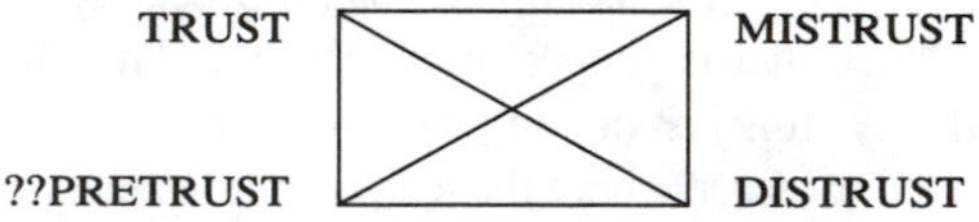

Figure 16

Coming back to jealousy, we see that *mistrust*, which is based on a negative certitude, can intervene only after there has been "proof," real or imagined, of the rival's triumph. It is thus the end result of the fiduciary trajectory in the case in which the event is still expected at the moment when jealousy is manifested, and it will be a point of departure for the trajectory in the case of an accomplished event.

As for umbrage, a figure by which the jealous person perceives at least a "foreshadowing" of an eventual rival, it simply brings about a suspension of confidence or trust—that is, *distrust* (S_1 has stopped trusting). This suspension is deployed in terms of "suspicions" by which, even if the subject does not truly know what he is dealing with (because he still lacks proof), he presumes that there is something to know. The suspension of trust thus proceeds not by the acquisition of a knowing but through the acquisition of a metaknowing, a knowing that has to do with the presence of objects of knowledge. Umbrage is a pathemic role of the jealous person, one that is brought about by a rival's doing. This doing plays an informative role in that it transmits a metaknowing. The polemical relation, in jealousy, is initially a hypothesis held by S_1, one that suggests to him the presuppositions that are associated with exclusivity and reinforced by worry.

We might think that trust, in this condition, is particularly fragile. It is of course required for attachment, since the subject must believe in the value of his object in order to believe in his own identity, but it is at the same time undermined by the rejection of participation, which is, in the case of jealousy, coextensive to attachment itself. It was obvious, once we had modally formulated the jealous person's pathemic roles, that a conflict was predictable, a conflict between the subject of *having-to-be* and the subject of *having-not-to-be*. These two modalizations are the basis for two roles of just one subject, attached and exclusive, and as a result the subject is in contradiction with himself. The contradiction arises from the fact that, to protect himself from any loss, the jealous person must be mistrustful, whereas in order to ensure that his attachment endures, he must remain trustful.

Beginning with the hypothesis according to which a rival is defining himself nearby, the jealous subject projects possible scenarios that result in his becoming distrustful in all matters pertaining to his attachment. These scenarios constitute the figurative staging of the S_2/O, S_3 relation. Next a proof is needed in order to transform one of these probable scenarios into a certainty. The jealous person's trajectory thus includes two fiduciary transformations, one involving the move from trust to distrust, the other the move from distrust to mistrust. The first, because of the conflictual situation that has been in place from the beginning, even before the crisis of jealousy, is enacted on the slightest pretext. The slightest fact, the slightest sign can compromise the unstable equilibrium of exclusive attachment, thus giving preeminence to the negative side of the internal contradiction. At this stage, the jealous person is a pure receiver of indexes and signs. Next the suspension of trust sets off a cognitive quest that is made possible by a metaknowledge. The second transformation will bring about a sorting from among the hypotheses. This sorting belongs to the sequence of jealousy and we will discuss it more fully later, with supporting texts. The complete trajectory is outlined in Figure 17.

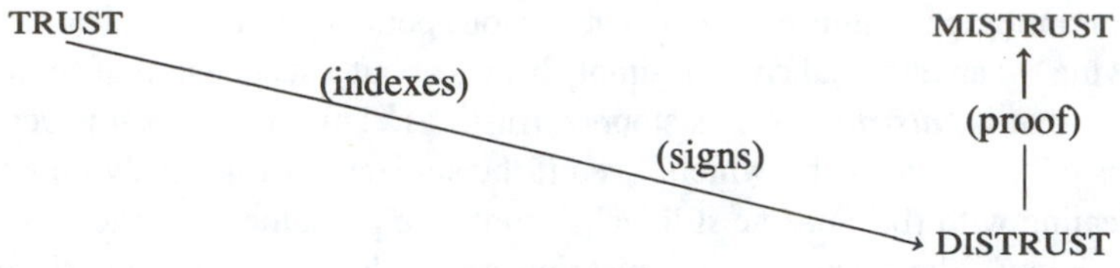

Figure 17

However, a worried subject whose identity is assured by his being reengaged on the tensive subject, cannot hope for such a neat trajectory. Although he is distrustful and suspicious of foreshadowed rivals he perceives around him, he remains trusting right up to the end of the trajectory, and sometimes beyond, with regard to the loved object. There is no end to the cases of the figure that we can imagine and that fall between trust linked to attachment and mistrust linked to the polemical structure. But the jealous person will always be torn between two fiduciary roles, because, within the passional simulacrum, his mistrust cannot be understood without attachment, and as a consequence it continues to presuppose that attachment. That is why, for example, when he is trustful on the one hand and distrustful on the other, the state in which he finds himself can never be described as being a "complex term." It is just an oscillation, a simultaneous assertion and negation that, echoing the phoric breakdown of worry, can only amplify that state. Tensive modulations have shaken the phoric mass, and the fiduciary dimension adds an instability born of the simultaneous assertion/negation of contraries. That is the first figure of autoengenderment, of autoamplification that we frequently find in realized discourses and that seems to characterize jealous passion.

Outline of a Model for Jealousy. Jealousy, in its most complex version, uses an actantial structure that is made up of three actants, S_1, S_2, and O, S_3. That structure is converted into a sensitized arrangement through three successive instances of setting into perspective. The structure is set into S_1's perspective, and then we have two parallel secondary settings into perspective: S_1/S_2 on the one hand, and S_1/O, S_3 on the other. A last setting into perspective is applied to the results of the two preceding ones, and it consists, in both cases, of reconstituting the S_2/O, S_3 couple in the form of a scene from which S_1 is excluded.

By way of an initial summing up, we might say that the relations of junction between these actants are modalized as follows: $S_1/O\text{-}S_3$ is modalized by *having-to-be* (attachment) and by *wanting-to-be* (possession). S_1/S_2 is modalized by *having-not-to-be* (exclusion vis-à-vis the community) and S_2/O, S_3 is modalized by *having-not-to-be* and *wanting-not-to-be* (exclusivity). All of these modalizations are of course projected according to S_1's point of view, which, by assigning an initial orientation for the whole arrangement, succeeds in sensitizing the pertinent modalities. Worry and concern, defined as "oscillation" and "absorption," can be interpreted only at the tensive level, as modulations. Summing up, "jealousy-in-and-of-itself" needs for its definition (1) the conversion of actantial structures into perspective arrangements, (2) sensitized modalizations based on tensive modulations, and (3) tensive modulations directly called into play within the simulacrum.

Two elements in this construction—attachment and worry—dispute the right to the status of presupposed; their syntactic roles are, however, quite different. The first gives the whole structure of jealousy, as configuration and trajectory, a modal capacity, which, even if it is based on a tensive phenomenon, is expressed at a given moment in the generative trajectory as the category of *duty* or *having to*. The second cannot receive any specific modal formulation, but it gives to the whole of the syntactic trajectory both a triggering motif and a semiotic style that, superficially, can appear to be aspectual. As a "triggering," it covers the reengagement on the tensive subject. As "semiotic style" it ensures the transitions between the different stages of the jealousy crisis and maintains a homogeneity beyond modal transformations and pathemic role changes. Attachment is thus the *modal presupposed* of jealousy and worry is its *phoric presupposed*.

Roles and Pathemic Schemata. We can say that jealousy comes in two forms: as part of a vast configuration in which it is just one conceivable passional eventuality, or as a specific passional event that until then has been intuitively designated as a "passional crisis" or "jealousy crisis," The *passional crisis* strictly speaking includes suspicion, which is a form of knowing whose object remains a secret—a metaknowing; it then includes the administration of proof and the staging of a decisive scene that leads to the acquisition of a certitude. From that certitude are born mistrust and suffering. This suffering can be, according to each case, either a distress (retrospective) or a fear (prospective).

Because of the complexity of its organization, jealousy does not belong to one configuration or to one pathemic system, but to several. It belongs to that of attachment, of exclusivity, of polemicocontractual structures, and of fiduciary passions, among others. Not only is jealousy not an isolated passion (because it belongs to microsystems in which it is just one among many positions), but, further, it participates in several pathemic constellations. The play of intersections and confrontations, which allowed movement from modal categories to modal arrangements, is reproduced here and allows us to move from pathemic structures, such as that for avarice, to *pathemic arrangements*, such as that of jealousy.

In the same way as the intersection of several modal structures engenders a modal arrangement, and therefore a pathemic role, the intersection of several pathemic roles engenders a pathemic arrangement. Just as is the case for modalities within a modal arrangement, pathemic roles are linked together and transform each other within a pathemic arrangement, thus defining a further degree of syntactic articulation of the passional universe. A passion such as envy, for example, might have been entirely circumscribed within the configuration for rivalry and within the microsystem of polemicocontractual structures. Anger, on the other hand, participates in several microsystems, just as is the case for jealousy. We could thus contrast "simple" passions with "compounded" passions. It seems preferable however, in order to avoid falling into taxonomies and the study of isolated passions, to stay with the expression "pathemic arrangement."

The construction of jealousy thus requires an initial establishment of pathemic microstructures against which backdrop its specific arrangement defines itself.

The microsystem for attachment, for example, which is regulated by the modal structure of duty, would appear as set up in Figure 18.

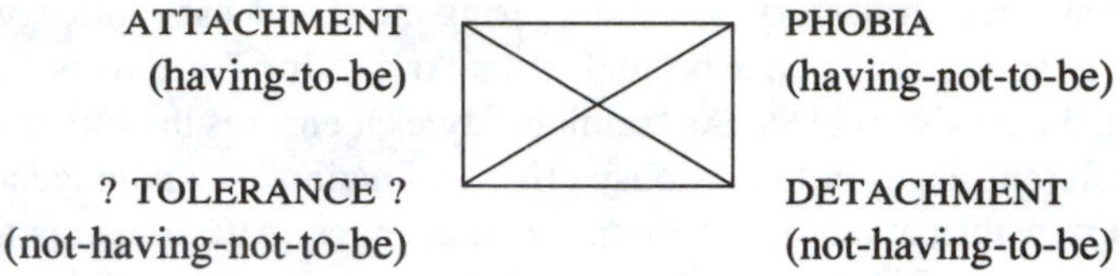

Figure 18

The structure for polemicocontractual structures, when applied to attachment, would, alongside jealousy (a passion of antagonism), bring out passions of discord such as "demandingness" and "harshness," passions of conciliation such as "indifference," and, finally, passions of collusion such as "complaisance," unless this latter's spot is taken up by "abnegation," in a differently modalized version.

If we now consider the system of the collective and individual actant, which is the basis for exclusivity, jealousy now takes its place in a microsystem whose distribution is based on a breaking down of the quantitative category; that is, it is based on partitive units (Pu) and integral units (Iu) and on partitive totalities (Pt) and integral totalities (It) (Figure 19).

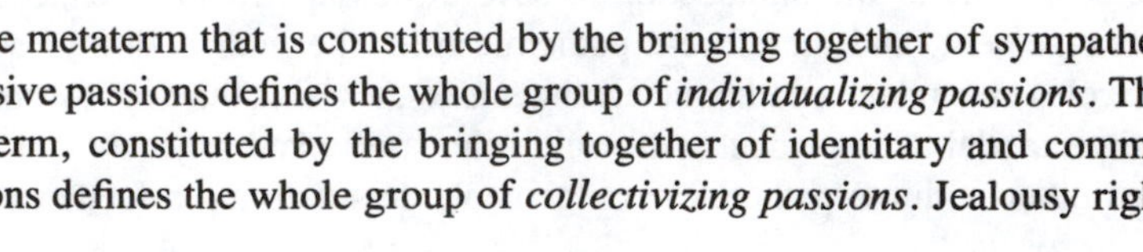

Figure 19

The metaterm that is constituted by the bringing together of sympathetic and exclusive passions defines the whole group of *individualizing passions*. The other metaterm, constituted by the bringing together of identitary and communitary passions defines the whole group of *collectivizing passions*. Jealousy rightly belongs with individualizing exclusive passions. "Compassion" is a sympathetic individualizing passion that characterizes the partitive individual subject because he shares, through that passion, a common feature with those he is like. "Conviviality" is a collectivizing communitary passion, and if one agrees to make of "public opinion" an impassioned subject, it can be just that within the framework of collectivizing passions, be they communitary or identitary. Finally, passions of the integral collective subject are those by which a whole group determines its identity. The "awareness of class" would be such a passion, but so too would all those national passions that, according to whether or not they are grasped or perceived from outside or from within, can pass either for outmoded stereotypes or as the leaven that gives life to a collective identity.

This brief look at some of the microsystems to which jealousy belongs does not claim to be exhaustive—that would make no sense here—but it does allow us to understand how jealousy is an "arrangement of arrangements." In each microsystem, the passions that occupy their various positions are based on sensitized arrangements. To the extent that jealousy participates in all of these microsystems, it articulates in a macroarrangement those specific passions that it brings together. Those are the articulations to which we now turn.

Jealousy, an Intersubjective Passion

Once the $S_1/S_2/S_3$ triangle is laid out, jealousy appears as a vast field for maneuver and passional event, of which certain developments can immediately be seen. Intersubjectivity here will be analyzed in terms of five types of interactions:

1. $S_1/O, S_3$ — the avatars of the love relation
2. S_1/S_2 — variations of rivalry
3. S_2/S_3 — the feared conjunction
4. $S_1/S_2 + S_3, O$ — the jealous one and his spectacle
5. S_1/S_1 — the jealous one as his own judge

All of these interactions imply confrontations, dominations, manipulations, and countermanipulations, which we will not yet systematically examine in detail at this time. Some of them are, within the framework of jealousy, more profitably looked at than others. To explore them, we will turn to the discourse of moralists and the problems that analysis of their discourse presents. Here we will meet Roland Barthes, Pierre Augustin de Beaumarchais, Jean de La Bruyère, Pierre Claude de La Chaussée, François de La Rochefoucauld, Jean Racine, and Henri Beyle (Stendhal).

Within the configuration, three actants have been initially defined in relation to the utterances of junction attested to in welcoming discourse. What is essential in these passional interactions is their capacity to bring about, within the configuration, a communication in which the message objects exchanged are exclusively or especially modal objects. They work within a simulacrum that is the result of passional disengagement, and even "infidelity," which, from another point of view, can pass for an eminently pragmatic transformation, functions within the passional configuration as a modal object. The first consequence is that the "actants" of the initial triangle will all be split into modal subjects and distributed over various roles that do not necessarily correspond to the initial segmentation. The second consequence, which flows from the first, concerns the status of these modal subjects in relation to the narrative actants represented by the "jealous one," the "rival," and the "loved subject-object." To the extent that what is exchanged in an instance of jealous communication is exclusively modal, the sensitization that is at work in the whole of the configuration influences the modal arrangements that are put into circulation. Within the macrosimulacrum pathemic roles appear. They are simulacra that the partners exchange.

NB: We are referring here to two kinds of simulacra: on the one hand passion inscribes itself completely within a simulacrum; on the other, the partners exchange simulacra that are sensitized modal arrangements. In effect, the significance is the same; only extension varies because jealousy presents as a pathemic macroarrangement (the first type of simulacrum) that includes many pathemic roles (the second type of simulacrum).

Already, the status of the rival in jealousy is uncertain. First, the fact that he is attested to or that he is not, be he a narrative actant in welcoming discourse or just a construct of the jealous one's imagination – none of this takes away any of his passional effectiveness. Then, all one needs is for S_1 to refuse to enter into the partitive totality for a virtual antisubject to be created by presupposition and for the faintest "foreshadowing" that might extend over the loved object to be able to give reality to this antisubject. Whether S_2 is an attested-to actant or a creation of S_1, the result is the same because the "rival," real or imagined, can, within the configuration, fill only the role that is assigned to him by the jealous one. He is nothing other than the simulacrum that S_1 projects starting with the modalizations of attachment, possession, and exclusivity.

For the loved subject-object, we have already noted the extent to which its status was profoundly modified by the modalizations projected by S_1: the *wanting* of the possessor converts him into a thymic and modal object. In fact, all jealousy needs is a desire to possess exclusively and a wished-for conjunction. In this respect, the object also has no other role in the configuration than those that the jealous one projects. He does so in the form of a simulacrum through which he pursues his own dream of exclusive possession.

We will finally show that the identity of the impassioned subject is itself entirely modeled or formed by interaction, and in particular by the modal arrangements that are created there, circulate there, and are exchanged there.

The study that follows thus concerns simulacra that are set up within jealous communication. It will also look at the transformations those simulacra undergo through the effects of the various strategies and manipulations to which jealous passion gives rise.

The Simulacrum of the Loved Object: From the Aesthetic to the Ethical

A Remaining Hope

> You reach a zenith of torment that is an extreme misfortune, poisoned with some remaining hope. (Stendhal, *De l'amour,* XXXV, pp. 122–23).

The only way out for the unfortunate jealous person is to no longer love, to break his attachment, because the trust that is intrinsic to attachment remains independent of the distrusts and mistrusts born of the rival's activities. It serves as an underpinning for all of the fiduciary transformations that are part of jealousy, but it is not affected as long as the identity of S_1 is not in question. In particular, the fiduciary breakdown brought on by S_2's entry into the lists—indeed, the marked preferences of S_3 for S_2—cannot affect the fundamental believing by which the subject assumes his semantic investment. The "hope that remains" thus supports suffering because it guarantees the preservation of the ultimate presupposition of jealousy. But already it appears that if everything begins and continues with this presupposed believing, everything can end with it also.

It has often been shown that the negation of a syntactic presupposition represents a questioning of the universe of discourse whose basis it is.[5] Now, attachment is the basic presupposition of the universe of discourse that constitutes the passional macrosimulacrum, the one that at the same time contains all of the others. The believing that accompanies attachment cannot disappear without the whole passional universe being destroyed. Thus the dissociation of the basic believing, this "remaining hope," from the various mistrusts that are linked to the aleas of the polemicocontractual structure implies a stratification of the macrosimulacrum in terms of passional subspaces endowed with a relative autonomy. The role of the jealous one already covers two distinct "fiduciary" subjects, attachment and exclusive possession. The enduring nature of the first, and its resistance to the avatars of the second, is the condition for passion to last and, with it, suffering.

Universality and Exclusivity

> Each perfection you add to the crown of the object you love, far from bringing you celestial enjoyment, will turn a knife in your heart. A

voice cries: this ever so charming pleasure is your rival's object of enjoyment. (Stendhal, *De l'amour,* XXXV, p. 122)

The cognitive doing by which the subject recognizes her object of value is here the usage program of a thymic doing. The "possessor" subject tortures the subject of the "enjoyment" state through the contemplation of the object. Stendhal finds here those strictly cognitive-thymic operations that are associated with the exercise of "possession." We recognize the operation by which the loved object is transformed into a modal object: the projection of *wanting-to-be* by the possessor. But, as an effect of exclusivity, this modal projection at the same time brings about the simulacrum of another virtual possessor, one who might claim her partitive totality rights. By displacing the scope of modalization from junction to object, she creates her own misfortune. By "objectifying" the expectation of enjoyment—that is, by situating it within the object—the jealous one grants it an autonomy that renders it accessible to the rival.

What is particularly in doubt now in the construction of the simulacrum of the loved object is its universality. An insoluble contradiction appears between the syntactic object that cannot be shared and a value that is recognized as universal, or at least general. We are led to see the jealous one both as an individual subject and as a social subject: the social subject, by constituting his object as "lovable," as a modal object inscribed within a system of value, creates the exclusive individual subject's misfortune. In the final analysis the contradiction resides in the opposition between universality and exclusivity. Universality is linked to partitive totality or, at least, pays homage to it, because the "perfections" that create the expectation of a "celestial enjoyment" obey axiological criteria that are common to all of the subjects of the collective actant, whereas exclusivity is based on an integral unity.

The contradiction between universality and exclusivity would make of jealousy a passion that is both, paradoxically, communitary and exclusive: by signaling her desire to reserve the object of value for herself, the jealous one presupposes that the object might be of interest to many others. We might also note that the contradiction takes the form of a conflict between simulacra: on the one hand, the simulacrum of the object, modalized independently and participating in the consolidation of the collective actant, and on the other hand, the simulacrum of the subject, including a kind of internal object, modalized differently. As a last resort, at the moment when she is semantically investing it, the subject inscribes the "internal object" within a system of value to which she subscribes but that is not, unfortunately, specific to her.

The aestheticization of the object is a valuable indication concerning the process of construction for the simulacrum of O, S_3. At closer inspection, we see that the loved object is not just considered here to be a particular object, one that is invested with the semantic values that are characteristic of an axiology. It is also presented as a potentiality of an object, a potentiality in which all kinds of contents can be invested. The very term "perfection," while directly alluding to canons of beauty that presuppose a semantic investment, is significant. Certainly, it refers us to a creative doing, a "divine worker" whose particularly successful creation testifies to her talent. But this reconstruction remains unsatisfactory because it is no more than a mechanical extrapolation, a catalysis of the kind used in instances of the emblazoning of the female body. What Stendhal's aphorism gives us, however, and what we do not need to extrapolate, is an aspectualization of the aesthetic object. "Perfection," in effect, whether it comes under a *knowing-how-to-do* or not, is an aestheticized figure of terminativity. If the reader remembers the inchoativity that is characteristic of objects of value in Eluard's *Capitale de la douleur* (see chapter 1), he will readily deduce that the "perfection" referred to by Stendhal manifests a valency.

This means that the jealous one comes together with original aesthesis, thanks to attachment. Because she is reengaged on the tensive subject she is in a position to refeel the tensive scission that we interpreted as the first upheaval suffered by meaning. The conflict between the two simulacra cannot be explained, however, in terms of a conflict between an exclusive and a "perfective" valency, because we cannot see why they would ever be in conflict. On the other hand, the "perfective" valency pursues its path along the generative trajectory: it is converted into a syntactic object, then a modalized object, and finally an object of value inscribed within a collective axiology. Conversely, the "exclusive" valency remains a valency and is directly convoked at the moment of setting into discourse in order to quantify the trajectories of the actors involved. The contradiction is born of a difference in procedure: exclusivity defines an "internal" object that belongs to the individual subject. This is true to the extent that exclusivity continues to be anchored directly within a valency that is accessible only to the tensive subject. Universality defines an object that, even if it also comes out of a valency, has been "externalized," semanticized, axiologized, and aestheticized throughout the length of the generative trajectory.

The opposition between the universality of value and the exclusivity of valency confers two distinct roles on the jealous one: a cognitive subject who takes on the job of aestheticizing the object and who claims participation in partitive totality, and a thymic subject who seeks exclusive possession. The first tortures the second by causing her to know that her celestial enjoyment is not exclusive. This moral "torture," as opposed to physical torture, is defined thus as a negative thymic transformation whose means are cognitive. Further, as a process, it presents itself according to an iterative and durative aspect. The passage to thymic dimension is grasped here from the point of view of the exclusive subject, the one who suffers. She in a way drags into all this the cognitive subject who decrees the universality of the object, thus confirming the "contagious" character, within interaction, of passional effects.

The Conversion of the Actant

> It is in vain that we impute jealousy to love; it is always a lack of esteem. (P. C. de La Chaussée, *Retour Imprévu*, act 2, scene 8)

Contradiction? How can one both recognize and not recognize? We have had a change in dimension: from an aesthetic of love we have gone, with La Chaussée, to an ethics of love. The aesthetic of love treated the loved one as an object; the ethics of love treats it as subject. That is why aesthetic and painful recognition concerns the *O* actant, and why lack of esteem concerns the S_3 actant.

Reference to aesthesis allows us to explain this transformation: the shifting in on the tensive subject actualizes this presemiotic and quasi-fusional stratum where the status or various statuses of the object are still barely definable and where the only difference has to do with an unequal distribution of intentionality (in its protensive form). In the many probable scenarios that the jealous one projects starting with his first suspicion, in certain of them the loved one takes on the figure of a competent subject that is susceptible of establishing an alliance with S_2. The "lack of esteem" is based on one of these scenarios.

At the passional level strictly speaking, this lack of esteem is the result of a generalization of simulacra and of a sensitization that becomes diffused within the whole of this set of interactions. We can represent the passional simulacrum, at the moment of jealous crisis, as an interactantial space that is integrally occupied by sensitized modalizations that can affect any of the interactants. Thus an object actant can seek out and take on those modalizations that are necessary for him if he wants to adopt a pathemic role in the simulacrum. The formulation of La Chaussée itself, by locating the modalization and moralization of *O*, S_3 within the perspective of S_1 (the lack of esteem), presupposes that the role of "unfaithful" is indeed a simulacrum projected by S_1.

The Simulacra of Rivals and Identification

The Merit of the Rival

> Jealousy is like an admission that is under the constraints of merit. (J. de La Bruyère, *Les caractères*, XI)

The person figuring in the jealous one's jealousy is evaluated in terms of a meritorious subject, as meritorious or less so than the jealous one. But, in this case, as opposed to emulation, in which S_2 is straight off posited as a reference for S_1 and where the rival is in a way a delegated Sender figure that designates, by his example, the goal that should be sought after and the trajectory to be followed to attain it, jealousy implies an "admission subject to a constraint," modalized by a *not-being-able-not-to-do*. The comparison of competences here takes as its reference, as in the case of "umbrage," not the rival's competence, but rather that of the jealous one.

The "constraint" in question can be nothing more than a presupposition: by fearing that the rival can win out over him and attain his goal object, the jealous one presupposes that his rival is indeed capable of that or, in the sense used by classical language, that the rival deserves it. In this sense, passional manifestation functions as a *causing-to-know* that proposes as an explicit message a "fear of losing" and as a presupposed implicit message an "admission concerning merit." But, in another sense, the admission is under certain constraints because it runs against the interests of the jealous person. For this latter, recognizing the merit of the rival amounts to increasing that rival's chances, by recognizing his *right to the object of value*, and his own reasons for being afraid. Finally, there is "admission," (that is, recognition of a wrong or of a lack), to the extent that, as a last resort, the jealous one presupposes his own inferiority. A good part of this interaction has to do with the respective weight of the respective merits and competences of S_1 and S_2.

From Emulation to Hate

> The jealousy felt by superior people becomes emulation; that felt by small minds becomes hate. (H. de Balzac, *Le contrat de mariage*, pp. 548–49)

The recognition of the superiority of S_2 plays the role of a contract for an eventual program of surpassment (emulation), and introduces into rivalry a positive moral component. But it can also turn off into pure conflict and rivalry is then negatively moralized. We have here an unstable equilibrium that can tilt in one direction just as easily as in the other. Balzac attributes positive disequilibrium to the moral superiority of the jealous person and negative disequilibrium to his "small mind." Competence is certainly at play here, one whose content remains to be determined. We do know, however, that it is this competence that sets up the simulacrum of the rival: be it a reference and example to be followed, by positive identification and attraction, or a hated enemy, through negative and repulsive identification. This competence that creates simulacra is, it seems, made up of two types of contents.

The first is an axiological content. In effect, the moralization that accompanies the two subsequent passions of jealousy – emulation and hate – indicates through presupposition that the jealous one should have respected a code shared by all. The second content is modal, and it regulates the process of identification. We can suppose that the superiority of the rival, having been evaluated in relation to the jealous one, claims a certain amount of competence for this latter. In other words, at the moment when the jealous one develops the simulacrum of his rival, he is for himself a simulacrum. Thus, the process of identification occurs through a comparison of two modal images: that of the person of whom the jealous person is jealous in relation to that of the jealous person.

The evaluation of his own competence by the jealous person, which is implicit and presupposed as soon as he begins this comparative process that is triggered by jealousy, can be called into question in a violent way, as we shall see, by the one of whom the jealous person is jealous, even if he does not appreciate being treated, just because of the jealous one's jealousy, as just any guy that comes along. Racine gives an example of just such an attack, in the preface to *Bérénice*.

The Presumptuousness of the Jealous One

> All of these criticisms are from four or five little unfortunate authors who have never themselves been able to elicit any excitement from the public. They always wait for the opportunities offered by the success of some work, in order to attack it, *not out of jealousy, for on what basis might they be jealous*? but in the hopes that someone might take the trouble to answer them, thereby dragging them out of the oblivion where their own works would have left them for life. (Racine, *Bérénice*, Preface, p. 20; our emphasis)

If the critics cannot be jealous, it is because they are too inferior, because they have no competence, no being-able-to-do, no knowing-how-to-do, and the sanctions imposed by the public are sufficiently clear on that point. This reasoning through presupposition allows us to define the modalities of competence by starting with the goal object, and the modal values in question should be adapted to the sought-after objects of value. The object of value that the critics are trying to deny Racine is literary glory (vs. "obscurity"), and it is thus clear that they do not have the required competence. The absence of competence among these subjects of doing brings about an irremediable disjunction of the subjects of state. Right up to the moment of the enunciation of this preface, the critics *could not* know glory. By refusing to give their names and answer them personally–that is, by refusing to conjoin them to the "glory" object of value–Racine modalizes them according to a *having-not-to-be*. It is this lack of competence, which has already caused disjunction, that in addition precludes their being jealous.

In order for S_1 to be jealous, she must present the same modalities as S_2, and the difference between the two competences must be gradual. For them to be compared, the two simulacra of rivals must be comparable: this is indeed a truism, but it is one that does not fail to resist analysis. The whole problem comes from the fact that S_1 and S_2 have to be modalized in a parallel way (in order to be comparable) and yet in a different way too (so that the superiority of one of them can be pronounced). The difference is thus gradual, indeed aspectual. The underlying rule might be defined as a "principle of an approached identity."

A nongradual interpretation, a categorial one, can be envisaged, however.

Identity and alterity belong in effect to one and the same microsystem in which a discontinuous trajectory can appear (Figure 20).

Figure 20

The principle of approached identity can then be interpreted, along a trajectory that leads from the "other" to the "same," as the grasping of a process of identification at the stage of contradiction, that is, at the "identical" position. The rival can be neither the "same" nor the "other." The comparability of the two rivals is thus interpreted as a presupposition on the square, and the comparison between the two can be seen as that implication that moves from the "identical" toward the "same." We can now understand why the jealous person that respects ethical codes would seek to bring about that implication herself, by equaling her model through emulation, and we can understand why the hate-filled jealous one would tend instead to come back, regressively, to the position of the "other."

The hypothesis according to which these competences should differ only in terms of degree remains cogent, as long as we aspectualize the process of identification described earlier. We would represent the two possible trajectories as shown in Figure 21.

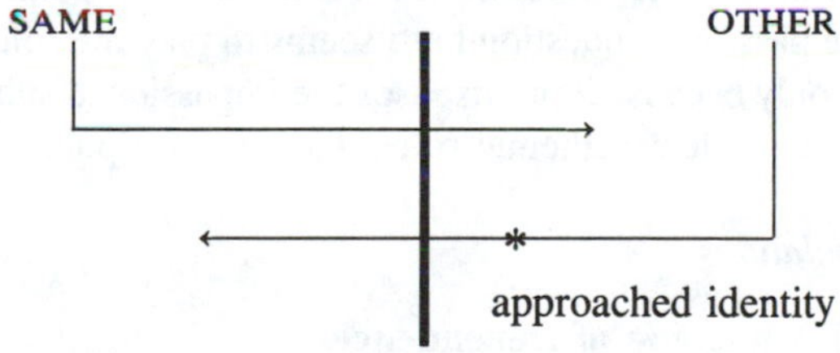

Figure 21

Then identification of the jealous one with the rival must thus be interpreted as a discursive process: at the moment of construction of the simulacra, the jealous person tries to capture the modal identity of the other, to appropriate it for herself. If she succeeds, she is an emulator. If she approaches the rival, she is an acceptable jealous person. If she fails, she cannot even claim the title of jealous one.

By establishing the rapprochement between S_2's merit—according to La Bruyère—and the competences needed for jealousy—according to Racine—we see, in both subjects, a "right." Because of her merit, which as we have seen is a moral evaluation of a competence that brings a reward, S_2 ***has the right to the object***. In other terms, once her merit has been recognized, her relation with the object is modalized by a *having-to-be*. For her part, S_1 has the *right to be jealous* only if she is comparable to S_2, that is, if her competence can be recognized as sufficient: we are thus back, albeit implicitly, to merit, that is, to a right to the reward won through qualifying tests. But then, if access to the object is regulated by the merit of each of the two, there can be no exclusivity: the object of value comes to all those who demonstrate adequate qualification, and partitive totality regains its legitimate place.

Now we can understand why the preceding admission is "constrained": it introduces into jealousy a system of values that is opposite to it, a universe regulated by contract, including a Sender that recognizes merits and assigns rewards, a universe where polemics must obey perfectly circumscribed rules of competition. Conversely, exclusivity is a strategy that rejects any contract and by which the individual subject withdraws from society. Once again, the universe of values that opposes that of the jealous person keeps bursting in upon her imaginary, thereby torturing her. We saw that, with Stendhal, through the simulacrum of the object—its universality—and here we see it in La Chaussée and Racine, through the simulacra of the rival and of the jealous one—rivals that are quasi-identical because of merit.

To sum up on this point, the expression "constrained admission" makes us think of manipulation: here we have the jealous person manipulated through simulacra that she herself constructs, and in particular the simulacrum she has of the rival. A *not-being-able-to-not-do* is transmitted to her, although we cannot say by whom: the passion in question here seems to play the role, indirectly, of "manipulator," if only because it predisposes the impassioned subject to splitting up into several independent pathemic roles that can manipulate each other.

Passional Manipulations

Request for and Admission of Dependence

> Jealousy may please some proud women, in terms of its being a new way to demonstrate to themselves their power. (Stendhal, *De l'amour*, p. 128)

Through his passion, the jealous one demonstrates his "attachment." It is true that passion, from the methodological point of view, is an obstacle to the reconstituting of presuppositions because it "predisposes" the subject in terms of a prospective orientation. But, as passion, and once it is recognized as such within a cultural taxonomy, it in and of itself presents a certain number of modal presuppositions that a partner of the impassioned subject can reconstitute. The fact that we can recognize attachment by interpreting signs of jealousy in a way proves that passion is of a syntactic nature, because hateful manifestations and aggressive ones and the various sufferings of jealousy cannot presuppose attachment in terms of its being a paradigmatic backdrop. The only explanation is that we have the presupposition of syntactic antecedents. In our case, the manifestations of jealousy, even aggressive or dysphoric ones, reactualize, in their capacity as presupposing factors, the presupposed phenomenon that we have seen attachment to be.

But, in the preceding quotation the attachment of S_1 to O, S_3 reappears after the fact in passional interaction, through presupposition, and becomes the basis for a strategy. It thus appears as a request for dependence on the one hand and an admission of dependence on the other. Once the *having-to-be* is put into circulation in the simulacrum, as is the case for all of the modalizations that find themselves in this situation, it can be used in the exchange that takes place between interactants. Projected on the relation that has been set up between the simulacra of S_1 and S_3, this *having-to-be* introduces a hierarchy that brings about a manipulation: S_3 will manipulate S_1 to get out of him this "admission of dependence" that we know jealousy to be.

It seems that we have a phenomenon that resembles attraction. The attraction a subject feels for an object presupposes that a cohesive force that is exterior to the subject attracts him to the object. Within the framework of what we have called minimal feeling, tensive force is primary, and it brings about both the source and target "effects," subject and object. But at the discursive level the subject, in order to rationalize this force, has to presuppose that another subject is responsible for it. In some instances this can be his "object," when it has become competent to attract.

Likewise the modalization that engenders attachment will be presupposed by the subject affected by it. The subject will suppose that it comes from another subject, possibly the "object" of attachment. Consequently, once modalization is introduced into the passional simulacrum, each of the partners can be led, from his point of view, to attribute responsibility for it to the other. Thus S_1 can believe that S_3 is requiring him to manifest the effects of attraction that he resents, and S_3 can believe that he is attracting S_1. Now, S_3 passes for a manipulator subject who, thanks to *having-to-be*, modalizes the relation between S_1 and his object.

The reconstruction that the impassioned subject undergoes within the simulacrum is thus not the same one as the one we can establish, from outside, analytically. From within the simulacrum, the jealous one's attachment, affected by umbrage, is in a way a love that remembers a past defeat, because attachment is reinterpreted as alienation, an alienation that can only be the result of some effrontery or other. We have to suppose that there has been some earlier test, preceding attachment, which, when the love is born, ends up producing the domination of S_1 by S_3 and which, at the moment of jealousy itself, closes out in a final reaffirmation of domination. Nonetheless, the jealous one is correctly defined as exclusive, possessive, captative. We must therefore suppose that the possessive actions by which he takes over the loved one make possible a reverse domination. It is banal to say that one becomes dependent on the objects one owns, as soon as one becomes passionately attached to them. Things clear up if we remind ourselves that the jealous person has concentrated his whole being – syntactic and semantic – on junction with an exclusive object of value and that that object can give way to a competent and independent subject. It is true that, on the pragmatic dimension, through conquest and appropriation, S_1 submits O to his being able and to his wanting. But, on the thymic dimension of possessive enjoyment, it is S_1 that is at the mercy of O, S_3.

The figurative trajectory of love, including the initial meeting, reciprocal seduction, and avowals of love, is the object of a rereading within the simulacrum, under the twofold influence of the modalization of *having-to-be* and new interactions that are established under the aegis of jealousy. This rereading reorganizes the testing trajectory that includes the three canonical stages: confrontation – domination – appropriation.

The most interesting phenomenon involves the dissemination of sensitized modalizations within the simulacrum and onto the partners in the interaction. It seems that, once they have been taken over by the simulacrum, these modalizations can be grasped by any of the interactants in order to enrich passional communication with a new figurative trajectory. So it is that what can be read from the point of view of the jealous person as "exclusive attachment" becomes, from the point of view of women who like jealousy, a flattering "dependence." This is a difference in syncretism, essentially, because each of the two partners gives himself, or attributes to the other, according to the individual case, the role of the modal operator that projects *having-to-be* on the S_1-O relation.

Another notable fact: once the passional interaction has been triggered by one of the partners, once the modal arrangements have been disseminated within the simulacrum, they become fixed on one or other of the interactants, according to strategies and changes of point of view, and they pathemize him. The competence of the manipulator subject S_3 is here just as passional as that of the manipulated jealous person, because the jealousy of the latter is echoed by the pride of the other. Stendhal makes it clear that women who can reinterpret jealousy as an admission of dependence are "women who have pride." They are thus "predisposed" to such an interpretation because it gives them a dominant position, and jealousy just reactualizes this disposition by offering it the already sensitized modal arrangement it needs. Communication within the passional simulacrum then takes the form of an interaction between the passional "dispositions" of each participant, dispositions that reactivate each other reciprocally, thanks to the power of contagion of the sensitized modalizations that circulate between the partners.

The substitution of pathemic roles for the ordinary competences of the manipulator and manipulated is characteristic of passional manipulation. To "causing-to-do" there is opposed a "causing-to-suffer" and "causing-to-enjoy." Instead of leading the manipulated subject to realizing a pragmatic program, the manipulator "impassions" him in order to have him realize a thymic program. In our modal arrangement, the being-able of S_3 is transformed into the duty or having-to of S_1 and the causing-to-suffer consists in projecting dysphoria onto the modalization of S_1. This is how attachment becomes a painful alienation. The causing-to-enjoy, conversely, consists in transforming the duty or having-to of S_1 into the being able of S_3 and in projecting euphoria onto the modalization of this latter. This is how jealousy *pleases* ladies, or so Stendhal claims.

Scene and Image

> "In the domain of love, the most painful wounds come more from what we see than from what we know." . . . "Here, at last, is the definition of image, of all images, it is that from which I am excluded . . . I am not in the scene." (R. Barthes, *Fragments d'un discours amoureux*, p. 157)

The central passional transformation of jealousy is presented by Barthes as a "spectacle" of the relation between rival and object, one that is presented for the viewing of the jealous person. This allows for the figurative deployment of the ends and means of the torture that is inflicted on the subject of state by the cognitive subject. The jealous one is a *spectator*, that is, an observer whose spatiotemporal coordinates are fixed in relation to the scene, but who cannot enter that scene as an actor. In the particular case of jealousy, this specific position is the result of an exclusivity installed by the jealous one himself. In effect, once the exclusion has been effected, S_3, O can be in conjunction only with one object at a time, and conjunction with the others is modalized by a *having-not-to-be*. In the arrangement that is presupposed by the jealous one, the conjoined subject is S_1 and the excluded subject is S_2. But, to the extent that sensitized modalizations are disseminated within the interaction, all we need is that, in one of the scenarios brought on by the suspicions of S_1, S_2 find himself in a relation with the object, and we will have exclusion being applied to the jealous one himself and he will then become the unfortunate one emanating from the partitive totality. In fact, the principle of the dissemination of sensitized modalization within the simulacrum comes back against the one who introduced it, and for the third time, the suffering that results originates in a cognitive doing of the jealous person himself.

The "image" or "scene" here designates *the figurativized passional simulacrum*—that is, a spatialized, temporalized, actorialized, and semanticized one. The fact that the spatiotemporal coordinates of the spectator can coincide with those of the scene, and that this is so whatever the spatial and temporal position of the S_2/S_3 couple in relation to the jealous one as actor, constitutes one of the explanations of the effect of "presentification" that the passional simulacrum creates, because, in whatever moment or place the jealous one finds himself as actor, the jealous person as spectator has to be *present at the scene*. But, from another point of view, this spatiotemporal engagement is no more than the figurative manifestation of the engagement back on the tensive subject. The result is that the simulacrum is, in relation to welcoming discourse, in an eternal present, and this explains its indifference vis-à-vis the adopted perspective. Whether infidelity is in fact perpetrated, expected, or even in the process of taking place, it is in any event presented in the course of the jealousy crisis.

Therefore there can be no better stage director than the jealous person himself. Even with respect to the scene itself, one that unfolds before his eyes, the actors are for him no more than simulacra that he projects and arranges at will. In a way, the jealous one is thus able to intervene in the feared and dreaded scene, not only as the "director" that stages in vivo the simulacra that haunt him.

Such an arrangement offers many possibilities for eventual cognitive trajectories. If S_1 is a spectator, the S_2/S_3 couple is an informer. Like any cognitive object, and a fortiori in the case of passional interaction where modalizations are disseminated, anyone who knows that he "knows that he has something to impart so that someone else can know it" can be transformed into a cognitive subject, and thus, eventually, he can dissimulate. Veridictory and epistemic strategies, like the polemicocontractual variations at play in the exchange of information, can flourish here.

Countermanipulation: Pretending to No Longer Believe

> Since others have power over you only insofar as they can take things away from you, or can cause you to hope for those things, things, that is, whose greatest single factor is passion, if you succeed in convincing them that you are indifferent, suddenly your adversaries have no weapons. (Stendhal, *De l'amour*, p. 124)

If a believing can trigger things, the cessation of a believing can halt everything. But here we do not have a not-believing, but rather a causing-to-believe-that-one-does-not-believe. The strategy is founded completely on the simulacrum of S_1 because the jealous one constructs not only the simulacrum of his partners in jealousy, but also his own, on which the manipulations of which he is the object are based. By modifying his own simulacrum, he can interrupt the course of manipulation or modify it. The "weapons" that the subjects in the love polemic have are modal weapons. Moving, in the mode of seeming, from attachment to indifference, the jealous person replaces a *having-to-be* with a *not-having-to-be*, and the various strategies of domination and cruelty of which he is victim temporarily lose—until the next countermanipulation—their modal support.

In this type of passional manipulation, what is at stake is not directly the quest for an object that has in fact been attested to in the utterance – it can be found there, of course, but indirectly – but rather control of a representation, control of simulacra. This control is acquired by intervening on those modal arrangements that are disseminated in interaction, in particular thanks to veridictory transformations that allow each of the partners to present to the other only those modal misrepresentations that he has conceived of for his own purposes.

Moralization

Scorn or Overestimation?

> You are reduced to scorning yourself in terms of being lovable: what makes the pain of jealousy so sharp is that vanity can in no way help you bear it. (Stendhal, *De l'amour,* p. 123)

> SUZANNE: Why so much jealousy?
> THE COUNTESS: As with all husbands, my dear, because of pride alone. (P. A. C. de Beaumarchais, *Le mariage de Figaro*, act 2, scene 1)

The jealous person, who has appeared both as a subject of state and as a cognitive subject that evaluates merit, here takes herself to be an object of evaluation and she moralizes her own modal arrangement. With Stendhal, she participates in her own indignity. With Beaumarchais, she overestimates herself. The contradiction is quite obvious.

"Lovable" – literally: "one who can be loved" – includes the modality of *being-able-to-be*. This modalization of being is then moralized, overdetermined by an ethical judgment that allows one to conclude that to be lovable is estimable, and not being so, reprehensible. The expression "scorning yourself in terms of your being [here not being] able to be loved" presupposes that the jealous one has already recognized herself as not being loved and then only, after that, as unlovable. We can see, in detail, how modalizations shift within the simulacrum because the jealous one initially posits that the object can fail to be conjoined with her and from that ultimately deduces that she herself cannot be conjoined with any object of the same kind.

"Pride" is based on an overevaluation of one's own competence that, if it does not directly formulate a *having-to-be*, nonetheless prepares its actualization. We have a knowing that has to do with the "value" of the subject, one the latter acquires by self-assignment of the role of a Sender that has the responsibility of measuring merits and distributing rewards in proportion to those merits. Conjunction then becomes a right.

Two explanations of this divergence between Stendhal and Beaumarchais come to mind. First, they do not take the same perspective. Poor esteem is constructed from one point of view, that of S_3, whose lack of affection is imputed to a lack of esteem. Then a second point of view, that of S_1, allows for confirmation of the first judgment and a moralization of it. Overesteem is constructed from one point of view first, that of S_1, who evaluates herself positively, then from a second, that of S_3, who rejects the first judgment, finds it erroneous, and moralizes that error. In both cases, the two same points of view are solicited and set one within the other, but with a hierarchical inversion such that, depending on the case, moralization is effected by, as a last resort, either S_1 or S_2.

Stendhal and Beaumarchais are not exactly speaking about the same thing. Stendhal defines underesteem starting with a *not-being-able-to-be-loved*, that is, starting with a modal arrangement that has been set up by the jealous one herself and in which the loved one has become an autonomous object in the eyes of the jealous one. Beaumarchais refers to a sense of dignity and superiority vis-à-vis a sense of what is one's right. The pride of the jealous one is built on a sense of "what is one's due" and thus comes back to a *having-to-be* and not a *being-able-to-be*. Beaumarchais thus refers to the modalizations that jealousy presupposes and not those that it implicates and sets up. This *having-to-be* is homologous to that of attachment. In Beaumarchais's text, however, it regulates the rights of the husband and not the attachment of an impassioned subject. The passional configuration receives a stereotyped modal block that defines the thematic role of the husband instead of a pathemic role. But once it is within that configuration and has been reactivated by passional interaction, the thematic modal block is itself sensitized and is also manifested as a pathemic role, that of pride. The difference is thus one of *procedure*, since the *having-to-be* has, on the one hand, attachment as its effect, if it is directly presupposed starting with jealousy, and on the other hand, pride, if it is convoked from the thematic role.

According to whether or not she reactivates a presupposed *having-to-be* or displays a *not-being-able-to-be* that she comes to within interaction, the jealous one will be one who has pride—pride in the style of "umbrage"—or she will be "reduced to scorning herself." The change in judgment is thus based not on some internal paradigmatic contradiction, but on a modal transformation, between a presupposed modalization and an implied modalization. The result is a certain internal contradiction, but a syntagmatic one that defines a *paradoxical arrangement* that results from an overlapping of two modalizations. In effect, thanks to the reactivation of all of the presupposed within the simulacrum, jealousy brings about a confrontation between the two modalizations and the two judgments that follow from them. On the one hand, that confrontation is a splitting apart, because the last modalization brings into question the first. But, on the other hand, it confirms the modal coherence of the subject because if the first modalization were effectively canceled out by the second, there would be no possible confrontation. Pride then appears as the manifestation of a subject that has not renounced her identity, despite all the aleas she has run into. From this we can see why one of the meaning effects of this paradoxical arrangement, based on the global presentification of modalizations, can be *an effect of recovered dignity.*

Honor and Hate on the Part of the Jealous One

> We are ashamed to be jealous, but we are proud of being capable of jealousy, and of having been jealous. (F. de La Rochefoucauld, *Maximes*, p. 313)

In his self-judgment, S_1 identifies the momentary and localized manifestation of passion—"being jealous"—and the ability—"being capable of jealousy"—eventually confirmed by precedents—"having been jealous." This distinction covers several others, of a different order.

First a temporal distinction: here and now, jealousy is shameful. At another time, or later, it will be or was not so; it can even be a source of pride. The subject of enunciation—the admission is, among other things, an enunciation—can admit only to a jealousy that he is not experiencing, that is, a shifted-out jealousy. He can in this case be part of a passional discourse (i.e., someone who speaks of his passions) yet cannot be part of an impassioned discourse (i.e., in which his passion is directly expressed). The positive moralization of a disengagement is not done in order to surprise, because it has to do with "a healthy distance" and that criterion is quite common in ethical judgments. But, in the case of jealousy, and likely in the case of most passions, it highlights a particular code of honor that warrants examination.

If the subject does not admit to jealousy without shame, in an impassioned and engaged discourse in which jealousy is directly expressed, it is initially because of "self-control," control that is in a way the passional version of the more general code of "healthy distance." But, if admitting to jealousy amounts to enunciating, the admission implies an enunciatee who will find himself caught up in the passional simulacrum: by enunciating his passion, the subject puts a sensitized modal arrangement into circulation, with the "contagion" effects that we have identified. This is another code, one that has to do with modesty and with a form of courtesy that requires us strongly to imply the enunciatee in the spiraling effects of sensitization.

On the other hand, a passion grasped here and now is a sentiment that expresses itself, a thymic transformation that manifests itself, an ostensible pleasure or suffering. A passion grasped as a capacity, a potential or already enacted capacity, is a passional competence, an implied disposition that characterizes the manner of being of the subject. The disposition in question regroups, in this case, the main essence of the presupposed: attachment, exclusive possession, distrust, among others. If we follow La Rochefoucauld in his ethical judgments, shame would involve a passional transformation manifested here and now, such as a suffering that calls out for revenge and that dictionaries stigmatize as "bad sentiment." On the other hand, honor would involve our presupposed, allowing the subject to take pride in something as limited as the simple fact of being capable of jealousy. He can take pride in what the thymic transformation presupposes and reactivates as modal identity.

Pressure from the Social Totality. It is above all important to note what ethical judgments have to do with and in what name they are engaged in. We should note, first, that the segmentation we are effecting here is homologous to the one that allowed us to articulate pride and underesteem: a presupposed modalization on the one hand, an implied modalization installed by the simulacrum on the other. Without our being able to know yet how the underlying axiologies are organized, the moralizations we have noted up to now allow us to advance at least three points.

In the first place, it seems that we must distinctly identify both the presupposed of jealousy and the thymic transformation strictly speaking and its specific modal environment. This relative autonomy of the two modal sequences already has appeared in connection with the distinction between the distrust brought about by the foreshadowing of the rival and the mistrust subsequently applied to the loved one. The presupposed have the status of ever-attested modalizations, even if jealousy does not break out. The modalizations that properly are of the jealousy crisis on the other hand have the status of fictive utterances that belong to a second-degree simulacrum projected from a starting point in the here and now of the jealous spectator.

In the second place, the judging spectator, even in cases in which the role is confused with that of the jealous one, is a social observer who introduces systems of value, new or foreign to him, into the passional configuration. Evaluations of merit, for example, in a way constitute a revenge of the collective subject over the exclusive individual subject, as is also the case for the universality of the object of value. For the jealous person, the problem is in not being able to resist on all fronts the pressure of social totality. Any evaluation, whether it be of the object or of subjects, is a breach in the wall that the social totality takes advantage of because evaluations are based on common and shared codes and are underpinned by the collectivity's cohesive forces. In this respect, jealousy, although it is based on tensive and quantitative phenomena of the same nature as those we proposed for avarice, is distinguished by another type of disequilibrium: in avarice, we saw the creation of an individual locus that rerouted part of the circulating flow of value and kept it back. In jealousy, with this locus already constituted, we are led to noting the effects of collective pressure on that very locus. On the one hand, the cohesive forces give way before the aggregating power of an individual locus. On the other, the cohesive force of an individual locus—which is dispersive in connection with the collectivity—is defeated in the breach by the greater attraction exercised by the collectivity.

In the last place, we should still ask ourselves why ethical judgment valorizes presupposed positions and devalorizes positions implied within the simulacrum. By way of hypothesis one might think that ameliorative judgment sanctions the attitude of a subject that defends, or is ready to defend, his attachment in the face of adversity, whereas negative judgment sanctions the attitude of one who does not play the game of competition to the end, and flees in a way from adversity, taking refuge in a passional and fiduciary crisis. It is as if, for the pragmatic resistance sequence of the rival, which we might expect because we know the jealous one's polemic precedents, jealousy were to substitute a thymic sequence that unfolds within the simulacrum. It is this substitution that would thus be condemned. But one does not prevent the other, because there is no shortage of jealous people who can take on both the "honorable" and the "shameful" attitudes.

Morality and Attitude. All of these observations would tend to prove that several ethical codes bring their effects together in the configuration. The fact that, on the one hand, the presupposed, including exclusivity and mistrust, are valorized, or at least tolerated, and that, on the other, an ethics of merit becomes involved in amorous affairs, seems to prove that a collective system of value regulates conflictual relations in the collectivity and provides a kind of *code of good usage of polemics*. It is a kind of conception of honor according to which rivalries should be resolved "once and for all" and with reference to a Sender that legislates on the respective value of the adversaries without getting caught up in the tortuous interactions of the passional simulacrum.

Another ethical code, of an individual kind this time, moralizes attachment as well as the joys and sorrows that accompany it. Many jealous people believe that the exclusivity of attachment answers a moral requirement and that this is effected, not from the point of view of the loved one, which would amount to moralizing the faithfulness of others, but from the point of view of the jealous one, which means moralizing one's own faithfulness, that is, the permanence of a passional constitution. In another sense, the jealous one positively moralizes exclusive possession because it represents what he owes himself, namely, a drastic selection of those junctions that are worthy of him. It seems that in this case what we are grasping intuitively as being "worthy of . . . " covers a criterion of value—that is, a valency. By moralizing exclusive attachment, we recognize that the property of "exclusivity" is the criterion itself for any form of value in the configuration, from the individual point of view of the jealous one, of course.

Finally, we should note an intervention of a third type of ethical code that is in no way specific to jealousy, because we have already met it in connection with avarice. What causes shame is the thymic transformation itself, engaged into an incident of passional discourse that, because it is an admission, cannot fail to manifest it directly and ostensibly. It is one of the last avatars of classical ethics for which the affective life must remain secret. In this sense, the moralization of jealousy has to do with observable behaviors or attitudes—indeed, ostensible ones, because that is the very thing that is considered to be shameful.

Lack of reserve, indiscretion in passion, seems to refer us to a *not-knowing-how-not-to-be*. "Reserve" is an observable attitude, and it is considered in dictionaries to be a "quality" (and its opposite a "fault") that consists in "not opening up indiscreetly, not committing oneself imprudently." As Stendhal points out, "Proud women hide their jealousy because of pride." The *knowing-how-to-be* system might be interpreted in this case as the system of knowledge that organizes the being of the subject. In the same way as various forms of *knowing-how-to-do* can appear as knowledge that organizes doing, in the form of a syntagmatic intelligence, there is an organization of being that indicates the existence of an "intelligence of the heart." In fact, intermodal syntax can be the object of a regulation and of an optimization in the same way as is the case for narrative syntax. This regulation and this optimization can sometimes be the object of aesthetic judgments—as is true of the classical age's *honnête homme*, or the postromantic "dandy"—but they more often will be judged according to an ethical dimension, defining thus a *morality of attitude or behavior*. We can propose, in order to account for "attitude or behavior," the model shown in Figure 22.

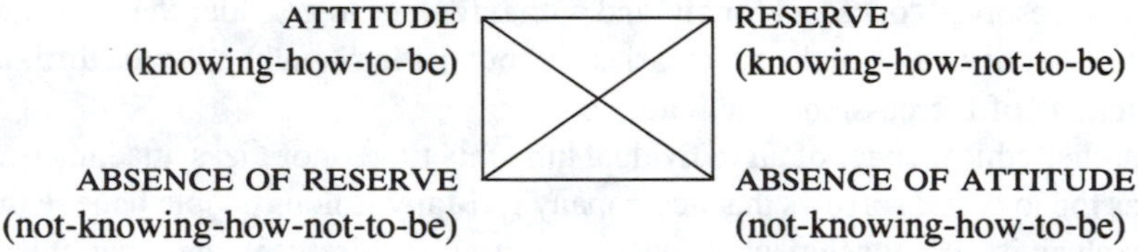

Figure 22

The moralized impassioned subject is a subject who knows how to bear himself, or who does not know how to bear himself—and then he becomes "discountenanced," unless he "comes out of his reserve." Our jealous person tends usually to come out of his reserve. We should note that the moralization of the same system can be obtained starting with a code that cancels out the effects of the first and that indicates another pathemic culture (Figure 23).

Figure 23

The difference between the two types of moralization can be explained by change in perception concerning manifestations of the affective life. In one case, keeping and selectively communicating information are appreciated most. In another case, affective "transparency" (free access to the inner life of others) is what is appreciated. It is all a matter of the way in which each culture represents to itself the regulation of interindividual relations. *Knowing-how-to-be* is in effect accompanied by a *causing-to-know* that itself presupposes, both on the part of the informer (the impassioned subject) and on the part of the social observer, a complete competence and in particular the *wanting* that controls the emission and reception of information.

The *wanting* of the preceding two cases comes into confrontation and thus determines a whole group of intersubjective relations, which we cannot develop here, but about which it can be said that they can be moralized as a function both of the "attitude" adopted by the impassioned subject and of the expectation that is normal to the social observer. That is why a "lack of reserve," even if it is involuntary (not wanting not to inform), even if it is irrepressible (not being able not to inform), can come against an observer who can either *want* or *not want* to witness passional manifestations. In one case, it is believed that lack of reserve is a factor of interindividual regulation because the manifestation of passion allows it to be recognized, allows its future development to be predicted and lets us adopt an adequate attitude in response. It is then called "spontaneity." In another case, one might conversely believe that lack of reserve is a factor of deregulation within the collectivity. For example, if S_1 reaffirms the presence of an object of value, through his passional manifestations that express his desire for attachment, that can have as an effect, if each one's desire is mediated by the other, of reactivating or mediating the desire of S_2, of intensifying competition, and so on.

Negative moralization would be the echo, here, of a social necessity: if the circulation of pathemic roles within the collectivity is to remain controllable, each one must prove that he can withhold information, or reveal it discreetly. Those are two possible versions of a social ethics based on *knowing-how-to-be*. One valorizes spontaneity and the other reserve. If now we remind ourselves of the results obtained in connection with avarice, we see two main types of moralization at work here, each more or less brought into play in one or other of the configurations: on the one hand, an *ethics of the circulation of objects of value*, and on the other, an *ethics of the exchange of modal simulacra* in communication. One concerns, in the main, descriptive values, the other, sensitized modal values. To the extent that the universe of passions is based entirely, at the semionarrative level, on sensitized modal arrangements, we can say that the codes that regulate the circulation of these arrangements in interaction are specifically and by definition *codes of passional ethics*.

The Actantial and Modal Schemata of Jealousy

Actantial Arrangement. The S_1, S_2, O, S_3 actants, when engaged in the passional simulacrum of S_1, are in a way "demultiplied" into a group of roles that are necessary for the staging of jealousy. Three types of roles have been seen up to now: actantial roles, pathemic roles, and thematic roles. The basic actants most often correspond to three actors: the jealous person, the rival, and the loved one. But this stereotyped arrangement is in a way a "street" version of the system. In more sophisticated theatrical versions, other actors intervene and play certain isolated roles. Iago, for example, who is both seeker and director in *Othello*, in Shakespeare, or Oenone who contributes in such a way as to awaken mistrust and suspicion on the part of Phèdre, in Racine. This means that passion is not limited to the actor's inner world, but that it can instead also be socialized and distributed among several actors, in particular as concerns cognitive roles and the operators of thymic transformation.

In any case, we meet three types of actantial roles: first, two competing *subjects of state* (S_1/S_2), between whom the object of value circulates; next, *manipulating subjects* (S_2 and S_3 in connection with S_1, and S_1 in connection with S_2 and S_3); and finally, *cognitive subjects* that judge, seek, and travel over the various fiduciary positions.

We should also identify two types of pathemic roles: that of S_1, which successively appear as possessive, taking umbrage, proud, jealous, and the like, and that of S_2 and S_3, which, while being accessory here, shows no less interaction with the first. The cruelty, coquetry, and lack of delicacy of S_1's two partners participate, as we have seen, in the evolution of jealousy.

Pathemic roles, finally, can overdetermine a given passional role, or be substituted for it, without our being able to say that they exist in the configuration for jealousy. This is the way it is with the "husband" who in the place of attachment sets up an institutional and stereotyped *having-to-be*. The appearance of thematic roles depends thus on particular semantic investments – in the *Marriage of Figaro* we have a "marriage" – that the object of value can take on, investments about which jealousy itself is quite indifferent. However that might be, for them to be inserted into the general arrangement for passion, these stereotyped modal blocks have to be the same, sensitization considered, as those they replace.

Modal Syntax. In intersubjectivity, in the course of the various phases of interaction, all these roles constitute variable arrangements that are formed and then dissolve, constantly. The analysis of the discourse of the "moralistes" allowed us to perceive some of these. Many others can be conceived of. Now we should establish, being all the while ready to temporarily sacrifice the discursive variety of their evolutions, the main principles of their manner of being linked together and of the modal transformations that underlie them.

To characterize the totality of the modal trajectory of the jealous person, if we wish to remain within the isotopy of love, we can begin by observing the transformation under way: love changes in nature and becomes aggressive, exclusive, suspicious. It is true that this modification is disputable. In connection with Swann and Odette in *Un amour de Swann* (Proust), Merleau-Ponty (*Phénoménologie de la perception*) rejects the idea of such a transformation. In a first reading, as Swann himself points out at the end of the story, it might seem that the concern to keep Odette from any others deprives Swann of the leisure that he would need in order to contemplate her and love her as he does at the beginning. The philosopher proposes on the contrary that we should believe that Swann's love was that way from the beginning. Swann has a penchant for Odette, indeed, but, Merleau-Ponty continues, what do we mean by "having a penchant for someone"? Proust answers elsewhere: it means feeling oneself to be excluded from the life in question, wanting to enter it and totally occupy it. Swann's love does not provoke jealousy. It is, from the very beginning, pure jealousy. The pleasure of contemplating Odette was the pleasure of being the only one to do so. And Merleau-Ponty adds that this is like a "structure of existence" that might be said to characterize the very person of Swann.

The sensitized modal arrangement is, coming back to our philosopher's expression, a "global personality project," that is temporal as such. We agree readily with Merleau-Ponty in saying that jealousy as such escapes from all duration and from any laws that might regulate events of a narrative nature. But that does not mean that it has no syntax or that it does not undergo any transformations, even if those transformations are *temporal*.

Following a sound method, let us begin with the end. The jealous one is in a way "reactivated" in his love, but much less to contemplate (Proust) – which at this period provokes more suffering than pleasure (Stendhal) – than to defend his interest. This reactivation is manifested in two directions: on the one hand, the desire becomes greater, to the point that one might sometimes have the impression that jealousy gives rise to love (Proust in connection with Albertine), when in fact it is just the revealing force. On the other hand, we see an ostensible possessive behavior. At this stage, then, *wanting-to-be* and *wanting-to-do* are linked.

Wanting here is an end point for the modal sequence. It modalizes the relation between the subject of state S_1 and his object, and it also modalizes S_1 as the subject of "possessive" or "exclusive" doing. This wanting presupposes jealousy in a restricted sense, that is, as passional crisis and thymic transformation. More precisely, it paradoxically presupposes a *believing-not-to-be*, the certainty of infidelity or failure that itself is based on a *not-being-able-to-be* that defines the exclusion of the jealous one from the "scene."

The modalizations that belong to the jealousy crisis themselves presuppose distrust and umbrage, born both of a hostile environment and of an exclusive attitude. Distrust is based on a *not-believing-to-be*. Finally, as we have seen, distrust and umbrage can be understood only if we presuppose a trusting attachment—one that is both a *having-to-be* and a *believing-to-be*.

The simulacrum of the rival is constructed in a similar way and it also changes as a function of the modalizations of the S_2/S_3 relation and in correspondence to the four main stages of the modal sequence for jealousy. Of course since jealousy supposes a setting into perspective of the whole configuration starting from the point of view of S_1, these modalizations are the ones the jealous one projects onto the rival (*wanting-not-to-be*). This presupposes that he believes in his success vis-à-vis S_3 (*believing-to-be*). In effect, in the "scene," S_2 and S_3 are brought together. Believing in the success of the rival amounts to postulating the possibility of his intervention (*being-able-to-be*) and thus to creating the "foreshadowing" of that rival. We must finally go back to the decision to opt for exclusivity to relocate a *having-not-to-be* that prevents S_2, in theory, from having any access to the object.

We thus get *two* associated modal sequences that reciprocally presuppose each other:

(S_1)	(S_2)
having-to-be believing-to-be	having-not-to-be
↓	↓
not-believing-to-be	being-able-to-be
↓	↓
not-being-able-to-be believing-not-to-be	believing-to-be
↓	↓
wanting-to-be wanting-to-do	wanting-not-to-be

The *not-believing-to-be* of S_1 and the *being-able-to-be* of S_2 presuppose each other to the extent that the rival's bursting onto the jealous one's turf causes the latter to lose confidence, unless the foreshadowing of the rival had initially already been caused by a lack of confidence. It is the same thing in the case of the two beliefs associated with jealousy: S_1's belief in his eviction and S_1's belief in the success of S_2. To the extent that an examination of modal sequences is limited to those that have to do with just the jealous one's point of view, the presuppositions that link them are the direct result of the principle of exclusivity: taking into account a few nuances, each modalization of S_1 presupposes the opposite modalization of S_2, and vice versa.

Although we have chosen to limit ourselves to S_1's point of view, because our intention is to construct jealousy alone and not the various passional efflorescences that can graft themselves onto it, we must not forget that the modal arrangements that circulate in interaction can come apart or "decompose" there and end up reconstituting themselves according to whether the adopted point of view is S_2's, S_3's, or S_1's. If it is true that there are no solitary passions, there can be no isolated passions, neither from a taxonomic point of view (avarice) nor, as is the case here, from a syntactic point of view.

The modal sequence here is thus like a *regulated and interactive reworking of several modal sequences*. In these reworking of the subjects' modal makeup through interaction, a canonical and isotopic syntax emerges, that of *believing-to-be*. It articulates confidence, distrust, and mistrust, and in it we can see the modalization that regulates the whole of the arrangement. But we cannot extract this trajectory from the whole without risking destruction of the passional meaning effect that is specific to jealousy. Each of the successive arrangements of the modalization corresponds to a pathemic role that, here, occupies a defined position in our passional sequence:

(S_1)	(S_2)	Pathemic Roles
having-to-be believing-to-be	having-not-to-be	Exclusive attachment
↓	↓	↓
being-able-not-to-be not-believing-to-be	being-able-to-be	Distrust with umbrage
↓	↓	↓
not-being-able-to-be believing-not-to-be	believing-to-be	Jealousy crisis
↓	↓	↓
wanting-to-be wanting-to-do	wanting-not-to-be	Love/hate

The whole is linked on two dimensions. Each role includes its own modal arrangement, confrontations, and internal transformations. The arrangements themselves are transformed, the one into the other, in particular under the influence of the trajectories of believing or being able that modify the specific equilibrium of each arrangement and that thereby convert each pathemic role into another. This twofold reading allows us to identify, for jealousy, two sequences that are embedded within each other: a micro- and a macrosequence.

Macrosequence and Microsequence. We can envisage the syntax for jealousy in two complementary ways: first, through a passional macrosequence characteristic of the whole configuration, which will then encompass the presupposed (or *precedents*) and the implied (or *subsequent*) of passion and subsume transformations between arrangements; or second, through a passional microsequence that takes on just one of the arrangements, the one in which the passional transformation that is specific to jealousy takes place.

But we have to note that the microsequence has to do with jealousy only to the extent that it is inserted into the macrosequence, just as the macrosequence is represented as being of jealousy only to the extent that it includes the microsequence. In summary, macro- and microsequences define each other because all *pathemic arrangements* are arrangements of pathemic roles; that is, they are arrangements of arrangements in which we find the role that is characteristic of the configuration concerned. This proposition can be represented as a syntax that has two levels, with the organization shown in Figure 24.[6]

$$P \longrightarrow P_1, P_2, P_3, \ldots Pi \left\{ \begin{array}{c} Pi_1 \\ Pi_2 \\ Pi_3 \\ Pi_4 \\ \ldots \\ \mathrm{Pi}^n \end{array} \right\}, \ldots Pn$$

Figure 24

The study of the *macrosequence* still has to do with the semionarrative level: we have to now examine the conditions under which the modal categories involved are organized within an arrangement. The whole thing can be read retrospectively, through presupposition, as we did when we were constructing it, or it can just as easily be read prospectively, following its intermodal transformations. In the second case, attachment is transformed into attachment with umbrage, one that is in turn transformed into jealousy. This jealousy finally reactivates attachment in the form of a desire to possess exclusively – indeed, to destroy out of hatred.

This reading imposes, in detail, some constraints: the breaking of the fiduciary contract can be understood here only in relation to attachment, or to a stereotyped and thematized substitute such as the role, of the "husband," because there has to be an initial trust and not just a desire. Further, the breaking of the fiduciary contract can be understood only if the foreshadowing of the rival (his *being-able-to-be*) has been noted: without rivalry, this accident of love can end only in "anguish" and "chagrin," not in jealousy. Umbrage, which in a way is a kind of conscious awareness of rivalry, has meaning here only if it is logically preceded by attachment; if not we come out of the framework of jealousy strictly speaking and find ourselves again dealing with a kind of "competition" or "emulation." Finally, the fact that jealousy can be provoked by the loved one in order to obtain an "admission of dependence," or a more dramatic love, shows that the passion of "love" is, in this strategy, both an antecedent of jealousy, in the form of attachment, and a phenomenon that is subsequent to it, in the form of a "reactivated desire." Amorous attachment can remain below the surface, secret or hidden because of modesty, and its intrinsically possessive and exclusive character is then the modal "lever" S_3 uses to oblige S_1 to manifest the totality of the underlying arrangement. It is as if, among the many possible variations of "exclusive attachment," one was more sensitive and brought on the suffering and admission of S_1: S_3's strategy then consists in looking for that particular variant. He then brings it into the interaction. Globally, the manipulation presents itself as a "causing to appear" that consists, within the passional sequence, in having attachment move from the status of implied presupposed to that of observable behavior (a subsequent phenomenon).

All of these constraints then can be approached on the level of passional meaning effects, and on the level of modalizations they guarantee the homogeneity of jealousy as a macrosequence, since each modalization produces a particular meaning effect that depends at the same time on its own modal content and its insertion into a predetermined place in the global arrangement. In fact, the specificity of these meaning effects can be explained in all cases, as a last resort, in terms of the presence of regulating modalizations, those of attachment and of rivalry. The principle according to which "it all hangs together" that subtends this syntactic analysis of the passional arrangement can be formulated in two ways. On the one hand, the meaning effect of the arrangement results from the association of its components, and on the other, the meaning effect of each component results from its place within the arrangement of the whole. This reciprocal constraint is applicable particularly to relations between the micro- and the macrosequences.

Each component of the macrosequence is itself a modal arrangement. We will study, from among the four components we have noted for the macrosequence, only jealousy in the restricted sense, located at the moment of passional crisis. The *microsequence*, which is both a presupposing uniting connection with its antecedents and a presupposed in connection with its subsequent, will be called "constitutive" of the passion under study, to the extent that it contains the thymic transformation that up to now has been identified as "passional crisis."

Reactivation, a complex of love and hate that can be translated, for example, as unconditional adoration or as sequestration or vengeance (Proust's *La prisonnière*), in general presupposes all of jealousy, but, more particularly and immediately, an observable behavior or attitude, ones by which the jealous person manifests himself ostensibly as such. The *wanting* (being and doing) that appears at this final stage of the macrosequence presupposes a global mobilization of the impassioned subject: all the roles the actor can cover—thymic, cognitive, pragmatic—are affected as a block, which means among other things that there will be a mixed character to the "attitude" or "comportment" in question, both somatic and psychic. We have already noted the "startled, instinctive reflex" of avarice on the part of Mme de Bargeton. Alexandre Dumas gives us, in *Le comte de Monte Cristo*, a sample of passional mobilization that is worrisome in another way. We see it in a jealous Italian:

> For his part, Luigi felt a new sentiment and unknown sentiment: it was a soundless pain that ate at his heart and was running now through his veins, taking over his whole body. His eyes followed Teresa's smallest movements and those of her horseman-suitor. When their hands met he felt light exploding within him, his arteries beat violently and you would have said that the sound of a bell vibrated in his ears. When they spoke to each other, whatever it was that Teresa was listening to, shy and eyes lowered, and with Luigi seeing by the ardent eyes of the young suitor that he was singing her praises, it seemed to him that the earth was turning topsy-turvy beneath his feet and that all of the voices of hell breathed suggestions to him of murder and assassination. Then fearing being carried away by his madness, he clung fiercely to the arbor he was leaning against, and with his other hand he convulsively grasped the handle of the knife that was at his belt and that, without knowing it, he sometimes had withdrawn completely from its scabbard.
>
> Luigi was jealous! He felt that, being carried away by the prideful and coquettish nature, Teresa could escape him. (Alexandre Dumas, *Le comte de Monte Cristo*, pp. 386–87)

In this cliché of "Italian" jealousy we find all the elements of the arrangement and, in particular, those of the passional microsequence: the spectacle offered up to S_1, the suffering, the *being-able-not-to-be* ("Teresa could escape him") and the exclusion of the spectator. Teresa has just finished a quadrille in which there was no room for another boy, and the text, figuratively playing on an uneven number, superficially translates the position of the integral unit in relation to the partitive totality. But we should especially note here that through all the figures that describe the manifestation of jealousy, a bringing together of the somatic, cognitive, fiduciary, and passional imposes itself on us at first reading: brutally, the pain brings about a connection, then a break, in isotopy, that benefits the somatic, and this refers us to the image of the body itself as a possible archetype of the subject of state. Further, in this fragment the movement toward the act, imminent but kept back, and above all the *wanting-to-do* that it presupposes, are explicitly presented as an immediate effect of the global mobilization of the roles the actor covers: person in love, taking umbrage, violent, bandit, impulsive, cruel. Luigi is all of these, successively and as a function of the narrative situations that arise, but he is these things all at once at this precise stage of jealousy that follows suffering and precedes movement to the act. Thus he is not just a subject of *wanting-to-do*, because the mobilization of his roles here brings in other dispositions than that of jealousy. This is the way it is, for example, with the irresistible inchoative tension toward doing that has so vigorously to be resisted and that comes from "impulsivity."

In our chain of presuppositions, by following in reverse order the modal itinerary of the jealous person, we will thus meet, before an ultimate movement to the act itself, moralization (which holds back or encourages the hand that is armed with the knife . . .). This moralization has to do with observable behavior that is nothing else, as we see in Dumas's text, than the figurative trajectory associated with the last modalization of the chain. Here the observable behavior is an emotion that is defined both as a mobilization of all of the roles and as being based on a *not-being-able-not-to-do*. This modalization accounts as much for the irrepressible agitation, both exterior and interior, that affects the jealous one, as it does for the thymic manipulation (also, in part, reflexive) by which the subject is completely mobilized. On the cognitive dimension, it characterizes the uncontrollable *causing-to-know* by which the subject betrays himself in the eyes of an observer and that might be, at the end of the trajectory, the object of an ethical judgment.

The emotion here is dysphoric because it is a suffering that results from a thymic transformation. In the modal sequence, the suffering corresponds to the acquisition of a *believing-not-to-be* that gives the jealous one the certainty of his eviction or failure. Once he has reached that point, he has reached the ultimate phase of the fiduciary trajectory.

Let us sum up: at one and the same stage, we meet a thymic state that results from a transformation (at the semionarrative level), an emotion (at the discursive level), and a behavior (the figurative trajectory). Within this stage we see superimposed on each other two modalizations: a modalization of being (*believing-not-to-be*) and a modalization of doing (*not-being-able-to-do*). But this last seems to be specific to the example under examination and results from the insertion, within the trajectory that is proper to jealousy, of a modal block specific to the actor Luigi, namely, "impulsivity." As for jealousy itself, its suffering, emotion, and comportment are all based on just this one *believing-not-to-be*.

The suffering and the emotion themselves presuppose the operation that brings them about, the "causing to suffer." Now, in the case of jealousy, the thymic transformation is of an essentially cognitive nature. It is in effect mediated by a "spectacle," that of the "image," according to Barthes, that figuratively translates a *not-being-able-to-be* that results from exclusion. Literally, exclusion is staged figuratively in the form of a spectacle offered up to the jealous one, and this spectacle, which is both an object of knowing and a subject of causing to believe, persuades S_1 of the fact of his misfortune and brings on dysphoric transformation. With

Dumas we have seen that the exclusive character of the scene was translated by the closed figure of a quadrille. The "staging," the "spectacle," the "image" therefore cover a cognitive strategy whose consequence is thymic.

If we represent this thymic transformation as a doing, it includes a resultative state (suffering), an operation (the exclusive spectacle), operators (the actors in the scene), and a subject of state (the suffering jealous person). The jealous one can play several roles and be both on the side of the operator in the role of stage director and on the side of the subject of state in the role of suffering subject.

The spectacle itself crystallizes the expected "test" and thus requires cognitive competence. Since the thymic transformation essentially adopts a cognitive usage program, we have to provide a stage of acquisition of cognitive competences for it. Given the close links between the cognitive and the thymic, the *knowing-how-to-make-suffer* will most frequently consist in a *wanting-to-observe* and a *knowing-how-to-seek-out*. The whole package of the jealous one's cognitive competence is sometimes reduced to a feeling that "there is something to know," that metaknowledge that we noted in "suspicion." The breaking of the fiduciary contract, which can undergo many other developments in the phase that precedes the jealousy crisis, prepares for the appearance on the scene of a new type of subject, a cognitive "suspicious" subject, a veritable, unhappy Sherlock Holmes. This means that passional syntax includes a "memory" and that, despite the modal transformations that we see here, each position found in the trajectory continuously produces its effects even when the movement has gone beyond it.

It remains true that suspicion, and the cognitive competence it condenses, are not fully explained just in terms of an earlier distrust and that the breaking of the fiduciary contract only partially explains the setting into motion of the cognitive quest. It is of course necessary to know whether or not there is "something to know," but it is also necessary that this "something" not be "just about nothing." *Suspicion ends up in a quest only if this "something to know" coincides with a valency*, that is, with a shadow of a value that, by definition, cannot be known by a cognitive subject, but only captured by a tensive subject. Our jealous Sherlock Holmes is driven not by curiosity but rather by a feeling that the exclusion arrangement he has installed is threatened. We must then suppose, in order to explain why jealous suspicion selects a potential category of objects, that it presupposes itself, in the microsequence, an undetermined modal position that indicates shifting back in on the tensive subject. This position will be identified here as a "worry."

Worry is to thymic doing what emotion is to somatic doing: a mobilization of the thymic subject, obtained by reengagement. We have already had the opportunity to note that the jealous one was "agitated," "worried," "concerned"; that is entirely absorbed by the phoric oscillation brought on by the insoluble tension that underlies the whole of the configuration, a tension between attachment and rivalry. For the whole of the configuration to be able to be set into discourse as a simulacrum, a shifting out must ensure disjunction vis-à-vis welcoming discourse, and an engagement back in on the tensive subject must trigger the passional crisis itself. That is why worry, which has already appeared as one of the presupposed of the jealousy crisis, seems to us to be just right for occupying this position that is presupposed by suspicion. Thus "thymic mobilization" here is tensive: the presupposed of jealousy, attachment, and rivalry are condensed and converted into worry by the reengagement. Distrust is converted into suspicion, and in a way, the metaknowledge by which suspicion proceeds works as a "summons" on a cognitive valency within the oscillations of phoria, a summons that will then allow for knowing and not just feeling.

What we have intuitively called a "passional crisis" covers two decisive operations that allow us to define our constitutive microsequence and to distinguish it from the other components of the macrosequence. They are a *reengagement on the tensive subject* and a *thymic transformation*. At the end of the "crisis," a disengagement intervenes, thanks to emotion, that authorizes an eventual movement toward the act but can also end up in a new passion.

Existential Simulacra. The initial hypothesis was that within the passional simulacrum, an existential trajectory was eventually superimposed on the intermodal syntax and gave it a predictable syntactic mechanism. The hypothesis is confirmed here because we can easily demonstrate that the modal microsequence develops against the backdrop of a canonical existential trajectory.

Worry, this concern of the subject who is absorbed by a threatened attachment, comes out of one position, at least imaginary, of conjunction–this kind of simulated conjunction that resists all aleas of effective junctions. The worried subject is thus a subject who has something to lose, a realized subject.

The suspicion and *wanting-to-know* that result from this dissociate subject from object: conjunction is no longer in the background, to the extent that, through suspicion, the jealous person is turned away from the object and sets out instead on a quest for knowledge about his partners, starting from a simple summons of a valency: he has thus become a virtualized subject.

Exclusion, staged in the spectacle given by S_1/S_2, brings the jealous one face to face with his object, but in the mode of disjunction. Before the spectacle that offers itself up to him, S_1 measures the distance between himself and S_3, thereby becoming an actualized subject.

Finally, emotion, insofar as it produces an observable behavior, at least within the jealous one himself, once again causes the jealous person to leave the area of junction: the relation with the object of value becomes less important at this stage than the relation of self with self or of self with others. The eventual figures for mastery of self, of the moralization of passional manifestations, testify to this change. Moreover, through the mobilization of all of the roles that make him up, the jealous person reaffirms his identity as discursive subject, and also prepares an eventual reaffirmation of his rights and desires. Emotion thus completes the trajectory by setting up the jealous one in the position of potentialized subject.

The two trajectories are thus in phase, with, as a commonly held "goal image" that of the jealous one whose possessive and exclusive attachment is reactivated as a *wanting*, in the form of desires for vengeance, possession or sequestration. The whole thing can be summed up in Figure 25.

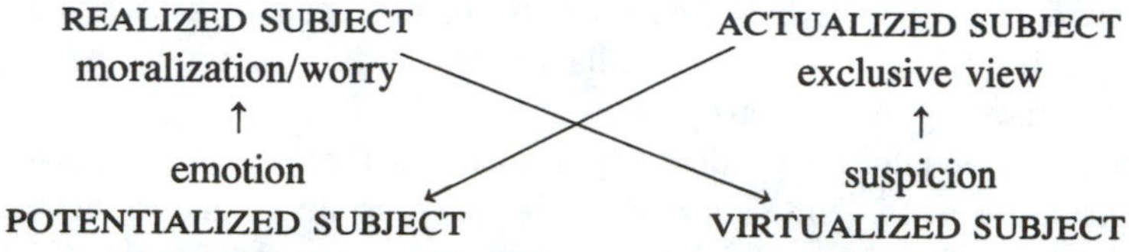

Figure 25

Despite its apparent complexity, the general organization of the disposition and the existential trajectory are based on a very simple global transformation: a modal arrangement based on "havings-to-do" engenders a modal arrangement based on "wanting." Almost all of the changes observed in the macrosequence and in the microsequence come together to bring about this progressive modification of the modal arrangement of the jealous person. This is in a way the story of a worried subject, "fixed" and oriented by adversity—indeed, converted into a monomaniac. He is also, however, a subject who, in his relations to objects of value, learns no longer to count passively on certain "states of things," on a world order in which he has his place. Instead he begins to want this intensely, and eventually he learns how to do what he must do to obtain it.

Setting into Discourse: Jealousy in the Text

Because the setting into discourse of avarice was mainly observed in a lexicographical corpus, it brought to light two basic operations of the collective or individual convocation of semionarrative structures, sensitization and moralization, and to a lesser degree, the aspectualization of passion. The setting into discourse of jealousy will be observed in literary texts, and this choice will allow us to explore aspectualization further in all its forms. In fact, when setting into discourse occurs in texts, the process of expansion forces us to implement on a large scale, as well as to infringe on, the rules of the syntactic unfolding of passion. In this way, for example, the five components of the microsequence—worry, suspicion, observation of the envied one, suffering, and moralized emotion—are atemporal, as presupposition has made them. They can just as easily be inverted, appear simultaneously, or follow one other in the canonical order. We still have to examine, among other things, the conditions under which these dispositions can be spatialized, actorialized, temporalized, and, to begin with, deployed in a *canonical pathemic schema*.

Furthermore, the constructed model is put to the test through the examination of texts. If the model is adequate, its implementation must correspond to the intuition of a cultivated reader. If it is heuristic, it must bring out in the text articulations of content that an intuitive reading would not have picked out. If it is explanatory, it must allow us to account for deviant and incomplete manifestations. As far as this is concerned, the text appears as a laboratory where borderline cases are explored experimentally, where pertinence is pursued to the *n*th degree. If the model allows us to answer the question why is so-and-so jealous, it should also allow us to say why someone else is not. By studying jealousy in Shakespeare's *Othello*, Proust's *Un amour de Swann* and *La prisonnière*, and Robbe-Grillet's *La jalousie*, as well as some scenes from Racine's plays, we go on to practical exercises, so to speak.

We will distinguish two components of expression in discourse: first, *the syntactic component*, which includes aspectualization of the process and its different spatial, temporal, and actorial figures and, second, *the semantic component*, which includes semantic investments and figurative manifestations of the different modalizations.

Aspectualization: The Syntactic Component

The convocation of transformations into discourse that converts them into a process implies capitalizing on change. What can be grasped at the semionarrative level, as a transformation between two utterances of state assured by doing, will appear at the level of discourse as a series of stages, tests, and acts. The "capitalization" on change, at the moment of manifestation, consists of deploying the discursive constituents of what in immanence could be thought of as a unique narrative operation, conjunction, or disjunction. From that moment on, we are led to postulate, analogously to discursive calling on, an engagement that pluralizes the transformation and turns it into a process.

But the semionarrative transformation is not the only thing convoked in discourse to make up process. Modulations of becoming and continuous tensive change are also convoked. This is why the aspectualization of the process produces continuous and discontinuous effects at the same time. Thus, depending on whether the point of view we take will give precedence to continuous or discontinuous effects, it will hesitate, between demarcation and segmentation. The coexistence of these two types of properties in discourse is undoubtedly the price we have to pay so that, beyond the fragmentation produced by engagement, the process can cover a homogeneity that still shows the uniqueness of the transformation. We could then say that, as a response to pluralizing disengagement, the intervention of tensivity in the process is accompanied by a homogenizing reengagement.

Aspectualization can be understood as the discursive management of plurality obtained from the founding disengagement. We can distinguish two major forms of this occurring before the figurative manifestation that only come in as a last resort. The first form, which produces canonical discursive schemata, consists of projecting the logical organization that transforms plurality into an ordered series. The canonical narrative schema, reconstructed by presupposition, is the most familiar example of this type of aspectualization, defining the logical stages of the process.[7] The one responsible for this projection is traditionally known as the "narrator," who, as it were, has "in trust" all narrative savoir faire developed by the culture within which the discourse is realized.

Yet the other kind of aspectualization causes the intervention of an "observer" endowed with a variable cognitive competence, and likely to be disengaged in the utterance. This observer puts the different stages of the process into perspective, sets demarcations, and produces, for example, the "inchoative, durative, terminative" series as well as different types of durativity: "punctuality," "iterativity," and so on, about which we have already pointed out that they implied a variation of the competence of observation, particularly where the ability to predict and identify the different occurrences is concerned.

Passional Schemata of Discourse: Canonical Forms

The Macrosequence. Beginning with intuitively recognized segments, and continuing with the chains of presupposition that link the different manifestations of the modal arrangement of jealousy, we were able to establish a huge modal syntagma that combines an all-embracing macrosequence with a constitutive microsequence. The macrosequence is a sort of pathemic arrangement, whereas the microsequence more particularly accounts for the modal series belonging to the passional crisis. The interlocking of these series produces the result depicted here:

EXCLUSIVE → ATTACHMENT	EASILY EXCITED → DISTRUST	worry suspicion exclusive vision emotion moralization	→	LOVE HATE

Here the macrosequence assumes totally the development of a polemical sequence, showing the directing role of rivalry in the configuration. *Confrontation* is implied both by exclusive attachment and by touchiness, understood as a growing awareness of rivalry and threat. By sparking the fiduciary crisis, distrust appears as a form of *domination*. In fact, it is at this stage that the jealous person possibly recognizes the qualities of his rival and the rival's "right to the object" and even devalues himself, which is another way of imagining that the rival will come out on top. The crisis of jealousy itself, in the mode of simulacrum, occupies the place of *appropriation* and *dispossession*, since it offers S_1 the spectacle of conjunction between S_2 and O, S_3. In conclusion, we can identify in the test both an equivalent of the previous contract, in the initial attachment, and a countertest, which when reactivated allows the jealous person to take up the initiative once again.

In the way of a hypothesis, we could suggest here by generalization that the macrosequence of a pathemic arrangement follows the aspectual logic of the canonical narrative schema. At the moment of setting into discourse, presuppositions between modal arrangements, specific to each basic pathemic role, are reinterpreted from the perspective of syntactic discursive logic, in such a way that the modal sequence is then seen as a series of general steps that govern the discursive competence of a narrator.

The Microsequence. Furthermore, the microsequence seems to follow a strictly pathemic logic. The aspectualization of the constitutive modal sequence in fact produces a schema whose successive steps we progressively recognized, first when we discussed avarice, then when we discussed jealousy. Worry *constitutes* the impassioned subject because it includes reengagement onto the tensive subject. Independently of attachment itself, it determines a certain "tendency" to passional crisis, no matter the crisis. Worry sets modal dynamics in motion and emerges as a crisis of jealousy if reengagement operates as an exclusive attachment. The question we ask is, where does the actual passional process begin? From this we get the second question: where in the chain of discourse does the specific pathemic tension of the passion under study begin? We will call *constitution* the step corresponding to reengagement, where the tensive style of the impassioned subject is first defined. In the case of jealousy, this takes the form of a thymic oscillation that does not manage to polarize itself. According to the times, cultures, and authors, constitution is interpreted as a "temperament" (in Stendhal or Proust), as a "fate" (in Racine), or even as the springing up of vital chaos (in Shakespeare). Thus, the constitution of the impassioned subject is the phase that gives the whole of the process its semiotic style.

NB: Starting from the modulations of tension, the study of semiotic styles must still be undertaken. For future semioticians, there is an important field of research that has a theory of aspectualization as its objective and, at the same time, an investigation of passional manifestations. The prevarications of vague desire, the languidness of boredom, besides the agitation of worry, would be some of the forms to be elucidated.

The suspicion and the ensuing investigation then provide the jealous person with the qualifications required for exclusive vision, as in a search for the modalizations necessary for thymic performance. The one who undertakes the investigation, however, does not have to be the jealous person. Swann shares the difficulties of this investigation with his friends or even with professionals. The social stereotypes of jealousy, from this perspective, have almost become institutionalized, since a large part of the activity of a private detective is traditionally devoted to this type of investigation. As for Othello, he does not lower himself to hiring an investigator, but just the same, he asks Iago to "help him see" the thing. Insofar as they work together to set up a sensitized modal arrangement within the jealous person, suspicion and investigation correspond to a *disposition*. We can see, as far as this is concerned, that even if cognitive action is delegated to other actors, the jealous person remains the *subject of state* (suspicious, distrustful) who receives the sensitive modalizations.

The exclusive vision and gaining of certainty that cover the main thymic transformation could be generalized and named *pathemization*. Pathemization will result in an *emotion*, defined as a pathemic state that affects and mobilizes all the impassioned subject's roles. Finally, emotion reveals itself through an observable behavior—that is, the main object of ethical and aesthetic evaluations, which we have agreed to call *moralization*.

If the crisis of jealousy can be narrated, it is because it obeys a logic projected by aspectualization on the modal presuppositions and because it is organized in a canonical pathemic schema having the structure shown in Figure 26.

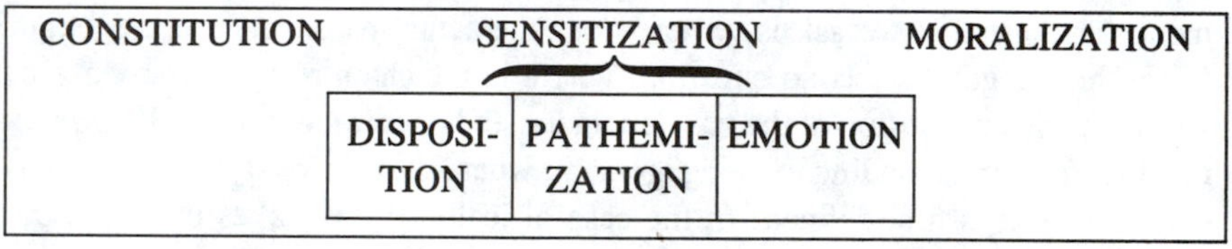

Figure 26

Moreover, constitution, sensitization, and moralization have been recognized as being the three great modes of construction of the connotative passional universes that individual and collective cultures control.[8] This is why, in the canonical pathemic schema, these three segments include references to passional axiologies, and more specifically to those axiologies that ensure the regulation of social and interpersonal relations. For this purpose they convoke idiolectic and sociolectic codes of the representation of passion, its causes, effects, and results, as well as criteria for its identification and evaluation. Furthermore, disposition, pathemization, and emotion are the successive stages of the actual passional process by which the subject is conjoined with the thymic object.

Passional Outlines: Concrete Realizations

Roxane's Fiduciary Loves. The general syntax of jealousy provides discursive and not textual units. Thus, the setting up of an aspectual form of the process does not enable us to predict the linear order of appearance of the stages of passion at the time of its manifestation. By examining some concrete realizations, we should be able to sketch a principle of textual variation.

We can look for confirmation and verification in Racine, for example. The character of Roxane in *Bajazet* gives us an almost complete and particularly detailed realization of the macrosequence. To begin with, attachment is carefully justified, in the mode of *having-to-be*:

> . . . the same boldness, dangers, and common fear
> *joined forever* their hearts and their fortunes. (act 1, scene 1; our emphasis)

Trust itself is sought, but already as the negation of distrust:

> I desire that, in my presence, his lips and face
> Uncover to me his heart *without leaving any distrust*. (act 1, scene 3; our emphasis)

One can even get trust as a first "gift of trust" that corresponds to an "avowal of dependence":

> Justify the trust that I have given you. (act 2, scene 1)

Act 2 is entirely devoted to the proposition and acceptance of the fiduciary contract; the acceptance of the agreement occurs between acts 2 and 3 and is only alluded to by presupposition at the beginning of act 3; distrust and fiduciary disturbance make their presence felt very quickly. For Roxane, acts 3 and 4 bring an attack of jealousy; the first thing we see is worry:

> This day gives me cause for worry. (act 3, scene 6)

Then comes distrust, followed by exclusive vision, called up by Roxane herself (S_1), in the form of the trap she sets for Bajazet and Atalide, that is, for S_3 and S_2, respectively. The "spectacular" aspect of exclusive vision stems not only from the requirements of dramatic representation, but also from the pathemic schema of jealousy. In fact, besides the epistemic and veridictory transformations that reveal Bajazet's indifference to Roxane and his love for Atalide (these transformations would suffice in a strictly cognitive logic), there is also a thymic transformation to be brought about, and this can be done only through the staging of the figurative simulacrum of the conjunction of S_2 and S_3. At this stage of the passional sequence, S_1 (Roxane) and S_3 (Bajazet) have nothing to exchange but signs of cruelty and indifference as well as thymic manipulations.

Furthermore, the canonical realization of the macrosequence is carefully articulated on the trajectory of fiduciary transformations. Each position in this trajectory gives a particular form to Roxane's attachment: first trustful attachment, then suspicious and touchy attachment, then distrustful attachment. But *Bajazet* also gives us a fourth position, even before trustful attachment, in the previously encountered form of the "gift of trust" that seems to correspond to an attachment formed by "abandoning distrust." The gift of trust is more particularly described as a renunciation (negation) by which S_1 gives herself to S_2, and the woman in love puts herself at the mercy of the man she loves. In retrospect, this enables us to understand why in Stendhal women like and arouse jealousy so that their power may be recognized.

The series of different forms of attachment is thus based on a complicated strategy of love in which trust and distrust presuppose reciprocity between S_1 and S_3, in the one case an exchange of thymic kindness, and in the other an exchange of wrongs. In this strategy, distrust or the lack thereof presupposes a lack of reciprocity, a unilateral attitude of love, with S_1 committing or extricating herself according to the circumstances but always without any return. All in all, the trajectory of fiduciary transformations shows that in love there is a figurative trajectory (Figure 27).

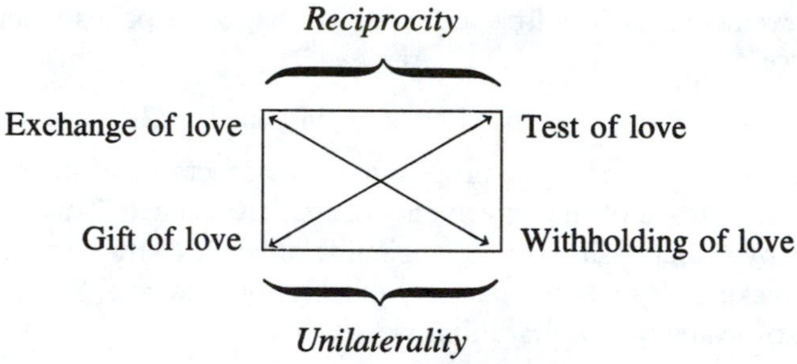

Figure 27

This type of trajectory partially explains the recurrence of the passional sequence. Although jealousy is entirely organized around the principle of the discursive schema, it can repeat the sequence several times while keeping the "memory" of previous betrayals, defections, and renunciations.

The Traces of the Narrative Schema in *La jalousie*. If we turn now to the noncanonical realizations, such as Robbe-Grillet's novel *La jalousie*, we discover a totally different option. The syntax of jealousy is entirely respected, but, paradoxically, the thymic dimension is missing from the novel. Thus, trust, distrust, suffering, and their equivalents are excluded from the level of manifestation. However, in all the stages of the passional sequence everything that concerns the pragmatic and the cognitive is carefully reported. Attachment shows through, but only as contemplation of the sensual beauty of the character called A—(i.e., S_3), and without enabling us to tell the difference between this contemplation and the contemplation of a centipede or of some banana trees that occurs just as often if not more. Umbrage is also there, but in such a way as not to show any distrust. At most we note some comments on the indiscretion of S_2 and a series of practical observations that indicate the invading presence of a masculine third party with the couple:

> Although he does not indulge in any excessive gestures, although he holds his spoon in the proper way and swallows the liquid noiselessly, he seems, for this modest task, to use up an inordinate amount of energy and enthusiasm . . . he lacks discretion.
>
> Franck tells the story of a car breaking down; he laughs and gestures with an inordinate amount of energy and enthusiasm. (*La jalousie*, pp. 23 and 110)

The text is clear, at least on one point: the invading personality of the character is not due to objectively excessive or misplaced behavior ("although he does not indulge in any excessive gestures"); what it tries implicitly to grasp through the manifestation of foreign energy in S_1's exclusive field is the emergence of the shadow of a rival, of a hostile area that is outlined in S_1's visual territory. In this case, "discretion" would be the cognitive transposition of the respect of the exclusive unity created by S_1, and lack of discretion the transposition of any encroachment on this exclusive unity. Thus, to reproach S_3 for her lack of discretion is to presuppose the existence of exclusivity.

The breaking of the fiduciary contract and distrust are obvious, but only by presupposition and catalysis. Based on uncomfortable positions of observation, for example, the narrator discreetly puts forward conclusions that presuppose his distrust of S_2 or S_3:

> " . . . impossible to *monitor* . . . " (p. 78);
> " . . . Franck's face, almost against the light, *does not give* the slightest impression" (p. 49);
> " . . . A—'s features, seen from the side, show *nothing*" (p. 46).

The absence of knowledge, expressed incidentally during the description, is attributed not to an intrinsic inability of the observer, but to a *sidestepping of the informant*, who does not "show" and who does not "give" us anything. Of course we are dealing with a very ordinary strategy of description that consists of projecting onto the object the restrictions imposed by focalization, and attributing them to a supposed intention. However, this ordinariness covers an actantial conversion that in itself is anything but ordinary (conversion of an object into a subject). This corresponds to one of the possible fluctuations of actantial arrangements within the simulacra evoked by jealousy. Moreover, distrust arising from S_1's lack of knowledge presupposes at least a metaknowing concerning the fact that there might be something to see (in A—'s face or Franck's face). This is how suspicion is born.

Among the stages of the microsequence, we no longer find emotion, since it is purely thymic and based on suffering. Nevertheless, something is left over from worry, insofar as it can appear as a simple oscillation, without any other details about euphoria and dysphoria. It therefore takes the path of cognitive alternatives that are impossible to choose between–alternatives that arise over anything and everything: Did A— eat or not? (p. 24); will A— come home by nightfall or not? (pp. 122–30). Besides, we can easily see the jealous investigation, since it is basically cognitive. We are present when clues are gathered, when the cognitive network is put in place. But proof and certainty are still missing. When we compose this missing detail with the absence of any thymic manifestation, we are led to the conclusion that the latter explains the former. With jealousy, proof and certainty would not appear unless summoned by worried expectation, to which they would likely have a thymic and no longer cognitive soothing effect. Thus Robbe-Grillet's investigator comes and goes between clues, turning the same faces and scenes over and over in his mind, without any of them seeming to be decisive. The textual withdrawal of the thymic prevents any manifestation of belief.

In conclusion, let us take note of the all-pervasiveness of exclusive vision in this novel; S_2 and S_3 are sitting in their easy chairs, with S_1's chair a little apart; S_2 and S_3 agree with each other and S_1 has a different opinion; S_2 and S_3 have read the same novel, which S_1 has not; and so on. The representation of the S_2/S_3 couple is at the heart of the narrative motifs. Meals, aperitifs, leaving, coming back, reading description invade the text because the narrative is made up only of "scenes" offered to S_1 by S_2/S_3. In this way the technique of the *nouveau roman* is resemanticized and motivated within the configuration of jealousy.

The thymic dimension being absent, Robbe-Grillet's text bears only the trace of passional syntax. We find only, like hard rocks that resist erosion, modifications and modalizations projected onto the pragmatic and cognitive dimensions by the passional trajectory without this trajectory being directly textualized. The trace, as a textual procedure, finds its explicit metadiscursive parallel in "traces," which are figures of the natural world, described in the novel itself: the trace of the centipede smashed on the wall, or the trace of words and letters on the blotter of a writing desk. The limits imposed on the narrator's knowledge are not enough to account for this procedure, because it is not only a matter of focalization; the "trace" effect arises from a real erosion of discourse, a form of textualization that goes beyond the question of narrative modes. In this novel the passional configuration is treated as a frame of implicit discursive rules that do not appear as such, but that determine the entire text. This literary effort proves both the dependence and the autonomy of the thymic dimension with respect to the two other dimensions: dependence, because the passional meaning effect is nevertheless present in the modalizations of the two other dimensions; autonomy, because it can be made totally implicit without affecting the intelligibility of the text.

Dissemination and Agitation in *Un amour de Swann*. In Proust's work, in contrast, the body of syntactic presuppositions and chains is called into question. Their principle is reaffirmed, since the syntactic presupposition is one of the most powerful tools of explanation of Proustian psychological analysis, and it is always being shaken by the permanence and recurrence of the same crises or passional dispositions throughout the novel.

Thus we learn that love can be born without initial desire, just as a story can begin in medias res:

> When we recognize one of its [love's] symptoms, we remember, and revive the others. Since we have its song, entirely engraved in us, we don't need a woman to tell us how it starts . . . to find what comes next. (*A la recherche du temps perdu*, vol. 1, pp. 196–97)

But we should immediately note that the man in love who proves capable of such presuppositions is a man of experience, who "has been smitten by love several times," and who can therefore behave as the narrator of his own passional trajectory, since he has the necessary metaknowledge at his disposal. As far as this is concerned, passion becomes a chain of events inscribed in competence, which we can, without ill effects, grasp in the middle: all the rest is reconstructed by presupposition. Thus, Proust underlines in a way the status of the cultural stereotype of these discursive schemata. Since experience or memory has "engraved in us" the whole sequence, this sequence will always reemerge in a single block.

Here is another manifestation of the impassioned subject's discursive competence. We can suffer for a long time in the same way and with the same intensity from a simple memory:

> The old suffering made him the way he was before Odette had spoken: ignorant and trusting; so that he could be stricken by Odette's confession, his cruel jealousy put him back in the position of someone who doesn't know yet. (p. 368)

The ability to operate from presuppositions is still seen here as a property of the impassioned subject, as a component of its thymic competence. Here, suffering revives the initial trustful attachment, as if, thanks to presupposition, the jealous person was programmed in each instance to relive all the stages of his passion. This is a flagrant illustration of the preeminence of syntax in the passional mechanism, since suffering can only be jealous suffering if the subject reconstructs and relives all the former stages each time, going right back to the beginning and reexperiencing all the modal ups and downs.

However that may be, the canonical syntax is disrupted and complicated by recurring attacks of jealousy. Everything happens as if at each stage of the macrosequence–exclusive attachment, suspicion, mistrust, and so on–the impassioned subject already reenacted for himself the crucial scene of actual jealousy. For example, a sketch of the microsequence of jealousy appears as soon as exclusive attachment is put in place:

> Of all the ways to produce love, of all the agents of dissemination of the sacred ill, it is actually one of the most efficient, this great wind of agitation that sometimes blows over us. Then the one we are enjoying ourselves with at that moment, the die is cast, that is the one whom we will love. . . . What was necessary was that our feeling for him to become exclusive. (pp. 230–31)

Before he experienced this exclusive feeling for Odette, Swann had only noticed her as being an aesthetic object (a painting by Botticelli). The agitation that comes over him changes his calm certainty of finding her at the Verdurins into worry and suffering. This suffering changes *having-to-be* of his former trust into *wanting-to-be* and *wanting-to-act*, which Proust expresses as "the unreasonable and painful need to possess her" (p. 231), in the same way that the suffering of the actual attack of jealousy brings with it a reactivation of love. This is why a lot of commentators say that here love is born of jealousy.

It is true that when we read *Un amour de Swann* we could be tempted to think that jealousy is revealed in its entirety in each of its constitutive stages. Thus Proust can assert that

> What we believe is our love, our jealousy, is not one indivisible, continuous passion. They are made up of an infinity of succeeding loves, of different fleeting jealousies that, because of their unbroken numbers, give the impression of continuity, the illusion of unity. (p. 372)[9]

The dispersal of the attack of jealousy into all the stages of the macrosequence can in fact be explained in two ways. First of all, each role that belongs to the pathemic arrangement can also be treated like a particular microsequence, and exclusive attachment, for example, can be analyzed as "worry–suffering–need to possess." Moreover, since each pathemic role is totally meaningful only in terms of the whole to which it belongs, at the level of meaning effects where the novelist is, each role offers strong resemblances to a specific role–here, the role of jealousy.

Furthermore, the dispersion of attacks of jealousy is a result of temporal aspectualization and of the observer's position. For the observer synthesizing this in a retrospective way passion would be seen as unique and continuous, which could be narrated as a homogeneous process. For an analytical observer placing himself at the moment of each manifestation, passion would be no more than a string of distinct crises. This would seem to confirm the usefulness of opposing "segmentative" aspectualization, which creates discursive schemata, and "demarcative" aspectualization, which creates effects of continuity and discontinuity in discourse.

In fact, the discontinuous and apparently recurrent temporalization of the macrosequence does not stop passion from developing according to the canonical schema that we have set up. For example, suffering is always present, but suffering arising from uncertainty (suspicious distrust) is different from suffering arising from certainty (exclusive vision). When Odette, in one of her rare confessions, admits her homosexual liaisons, the narrator states:

> This suffering he felt didn't seem like anything he had believed . . . because even when he imagined this, it stayed vague, uncertain, devoid of that particular horror that had come with the words "maybe two or three times," devoid of that particular cruelty that was just as different from anything he had ever known as a sickness we get for the first time. (p. 363)

Thus, even if there is a recurrence of suffering in the story of Swann's jealousy, each instance of suffering nevertheless remains specific to the particular role from which it arises. In the previous example, Odette has just given a concrete example of a homosexual encounter of which Swann knows the circumstances. All the conditions are met that will allow this confession to be transformed for him into the exclusive vision, of a "scene" of the conjunction of S_2/S_3:

> This attack on Swann was worse than the first one. . . . Although she was not intelligent, Odette had the charm of being natural. She had told, *she had acted out this scene* with so much simplicity, that Swann, gasping, *saw it all*: Odette yawning, the little rock. *He heard her* answer–gaily, alas–"What a joke!" (p. 366; our emphasis)

All the stages of the microsequence include their share of suffering, but only this last one is characteristic of the certainty of the jealous man, and it presupposes all the others. At this stage we immediately recognize the spectator who "sees all," but who is excluded from the scene, and the beloved one who, literally, like a good actor, plays her role in the scene for the edification of the jealous man. In order to be effective and justify his belief, the cognitive action addressed to S_1 must, therefore, concretely deploy the figurative trajectories expected. From another point of view, if we looked for distinctive criteria by which superficially to identify the passional processes, insofar as they require a figurative trajectory that can solicit perceptive activity from the subject, *figurative efficiency* could be one of these criteria.

Untimely Disruptions and Exits. The macrosequence's canonicity depends for the most part on the smooth functioning of the presuppositions. As soon as a presupposition misfunctions, the passional sequence veers off course, breaks off, opens onto passions that no longer belong to the configuration of jealousy, so that a person who could be jealous—if we go strictly by the love scenario apprehended in medias res—is not jealous at all. Racine's plays, in which jealousy is an all-pervasive dramatic motivation, gives us several examples of such passional rerouting.

If Thésée's jealousy in *Phèdre* stops suddenly at distrust and switches to vengeful fury, it is because the presupposition of "rivalry," and especially the presupposition of the comparability of rivals, is missing here. Thésée is in the position of Receiver with respect to Hippolyte, and he possesses competence, particularly of the type *being-able-to-do*, which his son lacks. If Antiochus's jealousy in *Bérénice* remains at the stage of worry, and is reduced to the torture inflicted by endless wavering between the phases of hope and hopelessness, it is because he lacks from the beginning *having-to-be* and *believing* and his suffering cannot, therefore, presuppose these things. Antiochus is a bashful lover whose attachment is unilateral (in the mode of the "gift of trust") and who, since he has never acquired the right to hope, cannot be jealous.

We could consider calculating possible derivatives based on the macrosequence and the variation of the presuppositions, but we will only sketch here the outline of this calculation. First of all, as we have done from the start, we must distinguish between two main types of putting into perspective. Either the joining of S_2/S_3 occurs beforehand, and then jealousy becomes a fear (a prospective suffering) or else it is yet to come and then jealousy is a sorrow (a retrospective suffering), therefore reflecting the dichotomy between two major tendencies of the human imagination, represented on one side by passions of *expectation*, and on the other by passions of *nostalgia*. Whatever angle we take, the worry of the jealous person, as in Proust, is always concerned with an event that is present in the passional simulacrum. But the calculation of the derivatives must account for this splitting, which occurs as soon as the presumed jealous person no longer stays within the bounds of the canonical trajectory. Every time he exits, he can choose between two routes. Thus, for a "fearfully jealous person" exiting at the stage of trustful attachment will be a form of "hope," whereas for the "distressfully jealous person" it will be a kind of "security" or "relief" (i.e., the rival is no longer there). Derivation based on suspicion will cause "apprehension" for the "fearfully jealous person" and "resentment" for the "distressfully jealous one," and so on. No longer bound together by coherent syntax, derived passions become autonomous, and we can no longer consider that the pairs "hope/relief" or "apprehension/resentment" each constitutes a single passion likely to vary according to a change in the point of view. We are concerned here with different passions.

The group of passional derivations grafted onto the macrosequence make up a pathemic configuration in which the syntactic potentialities of jealousy are deployed. Because one of the presuppositions is absent or badly secured, at each stage, a way out takes shape that can be used during textualization, either by condensation or by expansion, until the development of the main branch stops short.

Realized Forms of the Microsequence

The outbreak of the passional attack requires two discursive operations: reengagement onto the tensive subject, and the inscription of the sensitized arrangement onto the axis of seeming. These two operations result in the meaning effect of "entering" into passional simulacrum.

Swann's Worry. The initial stage of the microsequence, worry and its figurative variants, appears in Proust as numerous manifestations of the tensive properties of phoria. The best example of the desemanticization of the object of value reduced to being nothing more than a valency is no doubt Odette's association with Vinteuil's little musical phrase. A syntactic framework, based entirely on aspectual arrangements, is outlined behind the figurative and sensory description of the musical phrase: lateness, delays, expectations, surprises, incidences, and decadences. These aspectual figures are explicitly associated with Odette de Crécy, the object of value. At a moment when each time the phrase is heard Odette's image is called up, Proust writes:

> The violin had risen to high notes where it stayed as if waiting, a wait that would continue without its stopping to hold the notes, in the exaltation he experienced seeing the expected object approaching, and with a desperate effort to last till she arrived, to welcome her before dying, to keep the way open, with all its last strength, so that the object could come through, just as we hold open a door that would close if we were not holding it open. (p. 345)

The musical metaphor is not accidental. It allows us to reduce the whole of the passional trajectory—expectation, exaltation, despair—to this aspectual arrangement suggested by the verbs "continue," "stopping to," "approaching," "last," "with a desperate effort," "dying," "holding open." From then on, the object in question is no longer an object of value strictly speaking, because it is only an operator of lateness or earliness, of aspectual incidence or decadence. This amounts to deinvesting it as an object of value, reducing it to tensive properties: the "object" of passion seems in fact to be a valency. Thus the pleasure (before disappointment) that Swann feels is a

> pleasure that does not correspond either to any exterior object and that, however, instead of being purely individual like the pleasure of love, imposed itself on Swann as a reality above concrete things. (pp. 236–37)

The "not . . . either" refers to a similar impression produced by associating Odette with another aesthetic form. Swann's object is a "shadow of value"; furthermore, as a valence, it is explicitly revealed in this commentary:

> So that the parts of Swann's soul where the little phrase had erased the worry of material interests, human considerations worthwhile for all left them *empty and blank*, and he was free to *inscribe Odette's name there*. (p. 237; our emphasis)

Modulations of tension, carefully expressed here in the form of variations in the continuum of the musical phrase, outline in a way the place of any object, one that will owe all its value defined afterward to the "proform" into which it is integrated. This is why any name of an object that is acceptable can be inscribed here.

Moreover, the subject here revives minimal feeling. It is nothing but perception, blended into its object, and is also external to the human community:

> Great rest, mysterious renewal for Swann, . . . to feel himself changed into a creature foreign to humanity, blind, lacking logical faculties, almost a marvellous unicorn, a dream creature that perceived the world only through hearing. (p. 237)

The properties we have given to phoric tensivity make us particularly attentive to the comments that accompany this aesthesia. For example, we notice that auditory perception is associated with feeling whereas visual perception shares in the cognitive development of signification: sight is in fact unable to operate like hearing this precognitive, preregression that enables us to

> come into contact with a world we are not made for, that seems formless because our eyes do not perceive it, without meaning because it escapes our intelligence. (p. 237)

Sight seems to include a demand—for example, of the gestalt kind—and leads to the categorization of the perceived world, whereas hearing seems to limit itself to grasping infracognitive modulations (Proust writes elsewhere of "an ultraviolet world"), which, by definition, would be "formless." We could even think that Proust imagines the identification of "shadows of value" as appearing on the ontic horizon, presented as an unknowable revealed, of which the valency would be the revealer; but he just touches on this idea:

> Perhaps it is nothingness that is real, and our whole dream does not exist, but then we feel that these musical phrases, these ideas that exist in relation to it, are also nothing. (p. 350)

Following this, the whole evolution of tensive space from the ontic screen that is only presupposed by the tensive modulations of the melody, the motif of Vinteuil's little phrase thus leads us to summon a place that is the first act needed to enter the cognitive domain where signification is developed.

The phase of worried agitation ends the tensive reengagement and the entry into the passional simulacrum by placing the jealous person on the thymic dimension where he will be able to suffer and enjoy, like a constituted impassioned subject. Worry literally makes Swann into a new being, and the narrator describes as alienation and a splitting of the personality the "schize" arising between the narrative subject and the impassioned subject, as a result of tensive reengagement:

> He was indeed forced to state that, in the same carriage that was taking him to Prévost's, he was no longer the same and no longer alone, that a new being was there with him, sticking to him and combining with him, a being he might not be able to get rid of and might be forced to treat carefully, the way one treats an authority or a sickness. (p. 228)

Let us keep in mind that the splitting of the actor, into an ordinary narrative subject, who rides around in a carriage looking for a young woman, and an impassioned subject who has "entered into simulacrum" already begins with the "unicorn," that "dream creature" conjured up by auditory perception, that form close to minimal feeling. Because worry is "agitation," it only confirms or heightens the strangeness of this new kind of subject. Thus, after this dissociation, the first Swann, who belongs to and stays in the pragmatic cognitive universe, can further the plans of the impassioned subject (for example, by bringing him to the woman he loves), but he can also play the role of an outside observer.

The entire story of Swann's love is therefore made of shifts between agitation and calmness, worry and regained serenity. Each phase of worry sketches an attack of jealousy, a microsequence whose more or less important textual development depends on the solidity of suspicion and on pathemic competence—the aptitude for suffering among others—that the jealous person has at his disposal.

Othello's Suspicions. We can distinguish three modal phases in suspicion: first, cognitive specification and intensification of worry; next, the epistemic modalization of the phases of investigation; and last, veridictory modalization and the passion of truth.

In Swann, suspicion is caused by a contradiction in Odette's behavior or speech. In this, it originates from metaknowing, because the cognitive subject must go on to a higher level in order to compare two known facts and find a contradiction.

The same is true for Othello, but with the added distinctive feature that metaknowing appears here as knowledge with passion itself as its object. For example, remembering that Desdemona has gone beyond her father's open hostility toward Othello and that she has even flouted him publicly, the Moor can recognize in her a disposition to live by and submit herself to intense passion. Knowledge about passion, and more specifically, knowledge of the pathemic roles of others, most often, though, has a regulating role, in that these pathemic roles enable us in intersubjectivity to predict behavior and strategy. But on the contrary, in the case of jealousy, all knowledge about passion – and to have this it is enough for the jealous person to examine himself or the one he loves – is deregulating and fuels passion itself.

In fact, the jealous person can decide unilaterally about the exclusivity of the object of value, but he does not have this power over passional simulacra and sensitized arrangements that continue to circulate and switch with one another. For the jealous person who is concerned about exclusivity, knowledge about passion, and particularly about the passions of the rival and the loved one, corresponds to a knowledge concerned with the largely unpredictable and uncontrollable nature of the circulation of pathemic roles. Such knowledge can only fuel worry, because the jealous person discovers through this a breach in his system of exclusivity. Hence the recurring Shakespearean metaphor of the "monster that feeds on itself," which gives expression to the property noted in the sensitized arrangements of spreading themselves in intersubjectivity.

As for the cognitive intensification of worry, it is particularly well attested to in *Othello*:

> By the world,
> I think my wife be honest, and think she is not;
> I think that thou art just, and think that thou art not.
> (p. 119, ll. 380–82)

Suffering, which here is not yet the suffering of jealousy, is provoked by fiduciary instability. As suffering, as dysphoric junction, it is a demand for stabilization, that is, in this case, an expectation of that other kind of suffering obtained through certainty and exclusive vision. Thus, worry is "inchoative" not only because it is found at the beginning of the attack, but especially because it demands future stabilization. The lack of phoric stability is therefore stronger than the fear of truth, because it keeps the subject in the meaningless world of unarticulated and unpolarized tensions. Now we cannot escape from this instability except by "opening up" a phase of becoming that is expressed both by a volitional type of modalization (*wanting-to-know*) and by an inchoative type of aspectualization (triggering the investigation). Suspicion is the cognitive figure that assumes this modulation by intensifying thymic instability to the point where it is intolerable and by instituting *wanting-to-know*.

It is possible for the future jealous person, like Othello, not to have any prior tendency toward jealousy, which means, here, no worry or suspicion. Shakespeare's hero is in fact calm, sure of himself, and only moderately attached to Desdemona. Thus, he must be manipulated in order to know jealousy and, especially, to gain necessary pathemic competence. Another actor, Iago, who is jealous himself and extremely knowledgeable about the mechanism of this passion, will concern himself with this for the sake of revenge. An intuitive semiotician, he begins by getting Othello the metaknowing of suspicion, and by setting worry in motion. He says nothing consistent; he knows nothing for sure, but he says it. He expresses vague doubts and then challenges them but leaves them in suspense.[10] Then he gives content to this metaknowing; using a veritable didactic strategy, he teaches his master the necessary minimum about the way passion works. Then, retroactively and by presupposition, worry creates the first exclusive attachment and touchiness, and sets off the passional process of the microsequence. Everything happens with Othello and Swann as if, once set in motion, worried agitation actualized an already acquired competence that enables the impassioned subject both to reconstruct all the missing presuppositions and to carry on with the rest of the process.

The possibility of considering putting a passional disposition into place by manipulation, as we are doing here, shows that passional competence does not fall within the territory of "individual psychology." Two actors are convoked here to make up an impassioned subject and break asunder the usual syncretisms.[11] The distribution of modal roles and stages of the microsequence allows us to assert that here Iago is the cognitive subject, the subject operator of thymic doing, whereas Othello is the thymic (and cognitive) subject of state, linked to the dysphoric results of Iago's doing. He will not become the subject of doing until the moment of reactivation, which takes the form of murderous hate. Here the distribution of roles sheds light on the canonical functioning of jealousy, hidden most of the time by syncretisms. A thymic and cognitive subject of doing tortures a thymic subject of state. Also, we can verify that the sensitized modal arrangements are not intrinsic properties of individual subjects but indeed simulacra interchanged in actual intersubjective syntagmas.

Swann and the Passion for Truth. The metaknowing belonging to suspicion is an element of competence from two points of view. First, as we have seen, by intensifying the oscillations of worry, it sets up the *disposition* of the jealous subject, and second, as suspicion, it sets up the *wanting-to-do* of the subject of a cognitive quest. This quest will take place on two distinct levels: the level of epistemic transformations that determine fiduciary and thymic transformations, and the level of veridictory transformations, apprehended from the perspective of the jealous subject or the outside observer.

In fact, we have to account for both systems of reference because they produce two types of different meaning effects. First of all, as a whole, veridiction is concerned with the inscription of the passional simulacrum on the axis of seeming. Next, in the very stage of investigation, it is solicited by the emergence of a real passion for truth on the part of the jealous person. This interlocking confirms the basic veridictory status of the semiotic articulations of the imaginary. As they are totally interpretable on the mode of seeming, they are purely phenomenal, and being—the "noumenal"—for semiotics would be only a conjectured supposition, but made perceptible in passional discourse by the meaning effects of reengagement onto the space of tensivity.

We have already shown that worry created two distinct roles in Swann: the birth of a new Swann, according to seeming, who commits himself to passion, and by contrast makes the former Swann a subject according to being. A whole world of discourse is set up around the new Swann, a world that includes another kind of space, another perception of time, and other systems of reference, thanks to the generalization of simulacrum and the spreading of the sensitized arrangement onto all actors, places, or moments:

> Beings are usually so indifferent to us that when we have placed in one of them possibilities of suffering and joy for us, that being seems to belong to another world; he or she is surrounded by poetry and makes our life a sort of *moving expanse in which he or she will be more or less close to us*. (vol. 1, pp. 235–36; our emphasis)

It is remarkable that the expression "he or she is surrounded by poetry" suggests the expansion of sensitization and, at the same time, the vehicle by which it is expanded: the figurative world. In fact, life only becomes "a moving expanse" where the sensitized modal arrangement is diffused insofar as the poetization of the figures of the world takes on this diffusion. A little later on, we will examine the principle of the figurative "vehicle" of sensitization.

When seen from within the simulacrum and by the new Swann, this moving expanse seems to be poetic; but when seen from without and by the old Swann, it seems totally artificial. Swann the observer notices, for example, that the new Swann changes his tone when he recalls the actors of his passional universe; he denounces

> the slightly artificial tone he had assumed until now when he described the delights of the little circle and praised the magnanimity of the Verdurins. (p. 286)

We are actually dealing here with a veridictory test, in which two points of view confront each other, the former setting up the illusion (seeming and not being), and the latter shattering it. From this we gather that artificiality is a sort of falsity first obtained by denouncing an illusion, and then moralized.

On the basis of a first illusion the veridictory transformations belonging to jealousy will develop. Although in principle they belong respectively to two different levels of modalizations, these two types of transformations appear in Proust's text as complementary manifestations of the same artificiality found in social and interpersonal relationships. Furthermore, from the perspective of Swann, who is playing an internal and an external role in relation to the simulacrum, it is always a matter of the same shadow play that accompanies the passional trajectory—so much so, that for him, to discover the truth is to fulfill the demands of his jealousy while at the same time proving himself right. Everything happens as if, the roles of the impassioned subject and the observing subject being syncretized, the only way to give free rein to truth within the passional simulacrum is, paradoxically, to leave the simulacrum.

It is nevertheless true that inside this simulacrum, veridictory positions are also affected by sensitization and treated as dispositions. When Swann tries to figure out why Odette is lying to him, for example, he tries to find out whether her lies are accidental or if they reveal a pathemic role, a permanent disposition. We would in a way be tempted to answer yes. Swann sees in her a real veridictory *knowing-how-to-do* that consists of putting a little bit of truth into each lie in order to make it authentic (p. 278). But the trick is obvious for a jealous man provided with metaknowing:

> Swann immediately recognized in what she said one of these bits of true fact that liars caught unawares use to comfort themselves by inserting them into the composition due to the fact they are making the whole thing up. (p. 278)

This veridictory competence—the art of authentifying lies—is clearly presented as a disposition, endowed with its own syntactic dynamics and producing a passional microsequence. In Odette, we observe, to start with, manifestations of the *constitution* and *disposition* of the impassioned subject:

> No sooner did she find herself with the one she wanted to lie to, than *she became embarrassed*; all her ideas *became completely confused*. (p. 278; our emphasis)

Pathemization and *emotion* then follow:

> The sorrowful look she continued to have finally surprised him. . . . He had already seen such sadness, once before . . . when Odette had lied while talking to Mme Verdurin. . . . What depressing lie was she telling Swann now to give her such a sad face, such a sad voice that seemed to tremble with the effort that she forced herself to make and to ask pardon? (pp. 280–81)

According to the canonical schema, emotion is followed here by shame and by embarrassment felt toward the victim of the lie, that is, by *moralization*.

For a clever observer like Swann, the existence of an entire microsequence indicates the effective presence of a pathemic role, of a modal dynamics that has been sensitized, stereotyped, and finally moralized. The role, however, cannot be elevated to the rank of a "character trait" because Swann realizes that for Odette it is not a matter of a general system but of a "specific type of expedient" (p. 291).[12]

For Swann, nevertheless, truth is a passion likely to have a long-term effect on his character, and it is compared to the passion a scholar can feel toward his research. In Swann's case we also see the main elements of the microsequence, and among others, *moralization*:

> And everything he might have been *ashamed* of until now, spying at a window, who knows? Tomorrow maybe, cleverly getting unconcerned people to talk, bribing servants, eavesdropping at doors, seemed to him, like deciphering texts, comparing testimonies, and interpreting monuments, to be *just methods of scientific investigation that had real intellectual value* and were appropriate in the search for truth. (p. 274; our emphasis)

Strangely, the passion for truth seems to desensitize the investigation; this can be understood only if we remember that Swann is endowed with the thematic role of the "intellectual" and that, as a result, his passion for truth can be taken charge of in a thematic isotopy of a cognitive nature, which has been independently sensitized and moralized. Furthermore, the search for truth that has been undertaken within the simulacrum to satisfy jealousy can, if it persists beyond the simple gaining of negative knowledge, end with jealousy leaving the simulacrum, which is the ultimate veridictory test. The jealous man then escapes suffering, again fusing with the old Swann, who is able to make reasonable judgments about everything. This is why we witness here an actual recategorization of jealous "mistrust and distrust," which transforms the unfortunate Sherlock Holmes into a sort of archaeologist of the life of Odette, by means of a disengagement that ends the simulacrum of jealousy in order to begin one of scientific curiosity.

Proof: Othello in the Labyrinth. In this case what seems most typical of jealousy is that our detective-archaeologist does not entirely obey the normal rules of constitution of proof. Thus, as Iago remarks in Shakespeare:

> Trifles light as air
> Are to the jealous confirmations strong
> as proofs of holy writ. (p. 116, ll. 319–21)

Cognitive action is here overdetermined by expectation, tension toward stability that we have identified in worry and suspicion. Thus proof fills a thymic, not a strictly cognitive, demand, so that phoric oscillation can stop, even if dysphoria wins out. It is undoubtedly this expectation that makes it possible to explain why the search for truth goes so far in Swann that it changes into a "passion" for truth. Our unfortunate Sherlock Holmes turns out to be a poor detective and an unscrupulous scholar, because he *knows* beforehand what he will find, and he only goes through the motions of carrying out an investigation to prove to himself that he *was* right.

Thus, it will be enough to make his suspicion consistent, to give body to scattered facts. Just as in medical diagnosis, where establishing a full chart of symptoms of the illness can under certain conditions replace firsthand knowledge of the "being" of the illness, whereas the isolated symptoms are only the "seeming," the investigation of the jealous person has to give the full chart of the betrayal:

> Make me to see't: or, at least, so prove it
> That the probation bear no hinge nor loop
> To hang a doubt on. (p. 118, ll. 361–63)

Here the metaphor expresses the closure of the expected scene. The approach taken suggests *abduction*. In a study devoted to this procedure, Pierre Boudon remarks that the cognitive activity of the investigator falls under abduction because, first of all, it consists of gathering clues that must come together to form a network.[13] But the labyrinthine logic of the network results in proof only by an operation that, metaphorically speaking, we could call a "precipitation": a "multiple echo" between the clues, a "collective hapax" from which totalization results. But, in the case of jealousy, cognitive stabilization does not account for everything. In fact, the process of cognitive totalization is overdetermined by fiduciary expectation, which makes the subject passionally competent to anticipate the proof, in the strict sense of the word, and to anticipate the fulfillment of the actual cognitive process. The figurative effect of completion, produced by "mere triffles," will be enough to precipitate the network of clues into a totalized scene. This is why abduction is not a "logical" process, and it is also why it basically obeys fiduciary restrictions; quantification, occurrence, is always based, from a semiotic perspective, on tensive phenomena.

NB: Let us define "scene" as both a hierarchized ordered inventory and as an iconic representation, since proof that makes the network consistent must be *figurative*, and must immediately suggest a *spectacle*, or at least an imaginary one, of the conjunction of S_2/S_3. Again, passional effectiveness is figurative, because only the jealous person or any other impassioned subject, would accept a concrete, isolated tiny fact as proof.

The metaphors and figures that describe the change of the clues into a convincing scene in literary discourse, as well as in an intuitive analysis, all reveal stopping, freezing, ending: "consistency," "give body," "precipitate," "hinge," "loop."

> And this may help to thicken other proofs
> Than do demonstrate thinly. (p. 120, ll. 426–27)

We can recognize two components here: an aspectual one and a figurative one. From an aspectual perspective, access to proof presupposes a very special *knowing-how-to-end* that allows the acceleration of the process to bring it to completion earlier than its purely cognitive course would have let it: a sort of aspectual accident, as it were.

From a figurative point of view, proof should produce the effect of "solidity" (cf. "congruence," P. Boudon, see note 13). To recognize the solidity and congruence of a network of clues is to be able to associate with certainty a figurative manifestation with modal positions, actantial and thematic roles, and abstract values. Also, the effect of "solidity" is based on the modality of *being able*, and more exactly, on an unfailing resistance. Now, to imagine a resistance of the cognitive object is to endow it with competence and to transform it into a subject. In brief, the jealous investigator is satisfied only when he has managed to change the object of his search into a subject that resists his doubts.

In a more general way, "precipitation" of proof authorizes an inference that, beginning from an obvious appearance, reconstructs an immanent being. When Othello sees Cassio with the handkerchief he has recently given to Desdemona, he makes an inference through the generative trajectory, an inference that could be broken down into the following steps:

reconstituting the itinerary of the handkerchief (figurative trajectory);
imagining the meeting of S_2 and S_3 (actantial arrangement);
gaining certainty, starting from *not-being-able-not-to-be;*
imagining, finally, that Desdemona has rejected all the values their love was based on, among others, purity and frankness.

All in all, precipitation is the end of the cognitive process after it has taken a catalytic course through all these levels; and proof then appears as the determining figurative element that makes evident all the immanent conversions of the generative trajectory. Nevertheless the actual cognitive aspect of this phenomenon should not overshadow the accelerating role of expectation, because through its sensitizing power, expectation encourages us to endow the object with the role of resisting subject.

A Lobotomized Investigator. Robbe-Grillet's novel offers the countertest that in a way confirms this type of proposal. The investigation is at a standstill here, so much so that it no longer seems like an investigation, because we get no further than establishing a network of clues. Yet, as we already pointed out, the thymic dimension is missing, and the novelistic bias shows only the indirect effects on the pragmatic and cognitive dimensions. What is missing from the network of clues for "precipitation" to occur? It seems that *belief* is missing. The erasure of any fiduciary or thymic trace prevents the precipitation of proof, and the cognitive process simply keeps on trotting out the inventory of clues and correlations. We can, *a contrario*, imagine what would happen if one of these figurative clues were raised to the level of proof. By presupposition we would be led to reconstruct an expectation, a demand, for stabilization and consequently a fiduciary dimension.

We now understand why the investigation cannot be *narrated*, as it has no beginning or end, no aspectual demarcation, nothing more than, say, the emblematic and monotonous chant of the plantation slave. The narrator wanders in the labyrinth of his clues, goes over each one several times, extracts new figures of distrust from them, but in this way blurs all chronological reading, since the temporalization of a process by rights presupposes its aspectualization. What is textualized here is not a case of infidelity and jealousy—a story that we have to reconstruct by catalysis and, moreover, based on what we know about the syntactic organization of passion—but the wandering of a lobotomized (i.e., an athymic) narrator.[14]

By deduction and by opposing the example and the counterexample, the conditions for the appearance of belief in the jealous person are more clearly outlined. The certainty of betrayal presupposes first of all (1) a trajectory of clues going in all directions that changes the clues into a network, understood as a partitive whole, then (2) a thymic anticipation about the result of interpretative activity, seizing on the least "iconic" pretext to stop the trajectory, and finally (3) the closure of the network that makes it an integral, congruent whole. The cognitive fiduciary object is treated like a collective actant whose transformation into an integral whole would make it a resisting subject.

Sensitive Aspectualization. From worry to gaining certainty through proof, an aspectual trajectory is deployed that accompanies the canonical segmentation of the microsequence:

inchoative	durative, *iterative*	terminative
"worry" and "suspicion"	"investigation" and "abduction"	"precipitation of proof" and "certainty"
(setting into motion)	(rise of tensions)	(release)

All along the trajectory of the jealous person, suffering is almost permanent, but it is at the same time always renewed. In fact, its source, intensity, and consequences change at each stage. When we follow Swann and Othello step-by-step, within the attack of jealousy we can even distinguish two different kinds of suffering; on the one hand, worry and fiduciary instability cause "archaic" suffering, the suffering of the original tensions of meaninglessness; on the other, negative certainty and the "scene" cause the suffering that is particular to jealousy. The second kind of suffering is the price to be paid for the calming of the first. We must suppose here that sensitization operates on two distinct levels. Besides the sensitization of the actual modal arrangements that we can see in the second case, there also seems to be *a sensitizing of aspectual forms* that makes the inchoative unbearable here, and works in such a way that the jealous person can be soothed in another way, even when the conjunction of S_2/S_3 is tormenting him.

The independence of these two levels of sensitization, as well as the two thymic trajectories produced by them, can also be seen in the fact that, even when he is reassured as to the faithfulness of S_3, the jealous person is still "shaken up" by the first suffering. Thus, after the episode of the lighted window that turns out not to be Odette's window after all, Swann continues to suffer from the incident and is ready to consider new suspicions. The existence of these two levels of sensitization, with one affecting modalities and the other affecting aspectualities, tends to confirm that sensitization also affects tensive modulations, producing, as we have suggested, semiotic styles that become fixed through common usage and, in turn, can be convoked during the setting into discourse at the same time as the stereotyped modal blocks with which they are associated.

The Lighted Window: Figurative Simulacra and Spatial Aspectualization. In the "scene" the simulacrum is subjected to a complete figurative investment: the rival takes form, if this has not already happened; the relations of conjunction and disjunction are spatialized according to the principle of exclusion; the whole is presented, whatever the actual moment of the conjunction of S_2/S_3 in the narrative.

In Proust, the independence of the exclusion scene with respect to the actors and the moment shows the crucial nature of spatial aspectualization. Thus, the exclusion of the boy when his mother receives guests at Combray is identified with the exclusion of the lover when the woman loved is at a party by herself. The actors and the moment are not really important, what matters is

> the anguish we experience when we feel that the one we love is *in a place of enjoyment where we are not present and where we cannot get to that person.* (vol. 1, p. 41; our emphasis)

In this case the constant is a modal arrangement (a *wanting-to-be* opposed by a *not-being-able-to-be*) and its spatial manifestation, which seems to typify the abstract relations of exclusion. From this respect, the dominant passional type is a variable. According to Proust, this "anguish" can be singularized both by the actors brought together and by the different periods of life. This singularization is a thematization because, depending on the circumstances, this particular anguish can become "child's jealousy" (toward the mother), "friend's jealousy" (toward the friend), "lover's jealousy" (toward the person one loves). It would seem, then, that spatialization is here responsible for revealing the passional modal constant in a purely syntactic way, whereas actorialization and temporalization are responsible for the different semanticothematic investments.

Thus all the spaces of jealous exclusion look the same: an *enclosure* determines the borders of the place off-limits to the jealous person; a *direction* indicates the possible crossing zone of this border. The only operations possible on this arrangement are (1) crossings—entries or exits—that is, directional movements toward the borders of the enclosure, and (2) movements around the enclosure, movements that are "peritopical" for the jealous person, since he cannot cross the border, and "paratopical" for the two others, since they remain confined within the enclosed space.

This spatial arrangement also defines just as clearly the *spectacular arrangement* that sets up the enunciatee delegated to a space apart from the space where the actors of enunciation are speaking and acting. For Swann, just as for the audience of a show, the enclosed and off-limits space is a stage that hides wings, and this space is exposed on the cognitive dimension, in the mode of *not-being-able-to-see*, and refused on the pragmatic dimension, in the mode of *not-being-able-to-give-access*.

The scene of the lighted window in *Un amour de Swann* is exemplary in this regard. An enclosed space, the room, that supposedly contains the scene of the conjunction S_2/S_3, includes an opening, the lighted window; Swann can only make peritopical movements around this space, movements that reveal, among other things, worry and agitation. It is only after lengthy deliberation that he takes the risk of being "seen while seeing," and he knocks (the three knocks sounded when the curtain rises) at the window. The text is clear on this point: sensitization acts on a spatial arrangement that reveals a modal arrangement. This is why the lighted window that indicates the presence of actors inside and possible visual access from the outside is the spatial and modal instrument of torture:

> . . . the light, which tortured him by telling him, "She is in there with the man she was waiting for." . . . Odette's other life . . . , there, fully lighted under the lamp, he held Odette's other life an unconscious prisoner in that room, where he could get in at any time he pleased, take her by surprise, and capture her. (p. 273)

The Stage as Trap. But, as the last sentence shows, the spatial arrangement is ambiguous: the scene of exclusion that torments S_1 turns into a trap for S_2/S_3; it can even be taken this way from the beginning by the jealous person himself.

The jealous person, especially in Racine's and Shakespeare's plays, is always more or less the producer of exclusive vision, a staging that enables him to condense in a single place and time two stages of jealousy: on the one hand, gaining negative certainty and, on the other, revenge. Whether it be Othello assigned to the wings of the stage set up by Iago, Néron hidden in the antechamber of the stage that he has himself set up (*Britannicus*), or Roxane kept to the side by the rules of the harem (*Bajazet*), each of them is in one way or another both an observer of the stage by sight, hearing, or a stand-in, and an actor excluded as such but having manipulated the others and directed the production. Roxane staged the meeting between Atalide and Bajazet; Néron told Junie what role to play for

Britannicus; Othello more or less ordered Iago to put on a convincing show for him.

The manipulation of representation confers a property already suggested on the impassioned subject. He is a second-degree enunciator, and as such he is also excluded from the stage, because he is not allowed to reengage onto his own "enunciated discourse," under penalty of casting doubt on setting into discourse itself. Thus, the jealous person cannot take part in the play without destroying it as a play. In a way, the jealous person would be an enunciator either too crude or not perverse enough to be included through partial reengagement onto the scene he has created himself.

As a delegated enunciator, he has the power to vary perspective, to change the orientation of the modalized space without altering the modal arrangements as such. Thus the *not-being-able-to-enter* becomes a *not-being-able-to-leave*, and the captivated look becomes a captivating look. Everything happens as if the gaining of certainty weakened S_3's captivating power over S_1 and, inversely, gave back S_1's capturing power over S_3.

We will easily be able to see both the power of a narrator who has become omniscient, capable of deriving and interpreting the secondary modal effects of the spatial arrangement he helped put into place, and the competence of a discursive subject who has "internalized" an actantial scene and can therefore vary their positions and polarities. He sees then that the sensitization of the closure of the place is a function of the perspective that is assumed. Exclusion and suffering from the perspective of the disjoined subject, and a trap and a threat of retaliation from the perspective of the conjoined subjects: it is enough for him as an impassioned enunciator to assume the latter perspective in order to switch the signs of sensitization and orientation of space. Homologation between passional functioning and setting into discourse (production, enunciation, variations in perspective) in a sense confirm that every passional simulacrum presents itself in discourse as another embedded discourse.

The transformation of the space of exclusion into a trap corresponds to the ambivalence of exclusivity itself. For example, Swann comes to understand that if he is the only one excluded from the places where Odette parties, it is because he is her only lover (p. 349); the others, who are not so privileged, do not suffer the consequences either. This first transformation, which can be predicted based on the analysis of exclusivity, therefore can be followed by a second transformation, changing exclusive vision into capture.

The succession of these transformations leads us to inquire about the syntactic functioning of exclusivity. First of all, in the functioning of exclusive possession, S_1 captures S_3 and excludes S_2; second, in the functioning of exclusive vision, S_2 captures S_3 and excludes S_1; third, in an actual dialectic surpassing of the first two stages, S_1 catches S_2 and S_3 red-handed (the news item!). This third step prepares for a renewal of exclusive possession that could then go as far as isolation and that would take acquired experience into account. However, one step is still missing here. To invert exclusivity, S_1's possession of S_3 must be cast into doubt; S_1's suspicion and worry reveal that this has taken place. The syntax of exclusivity is shown in Figure 28.

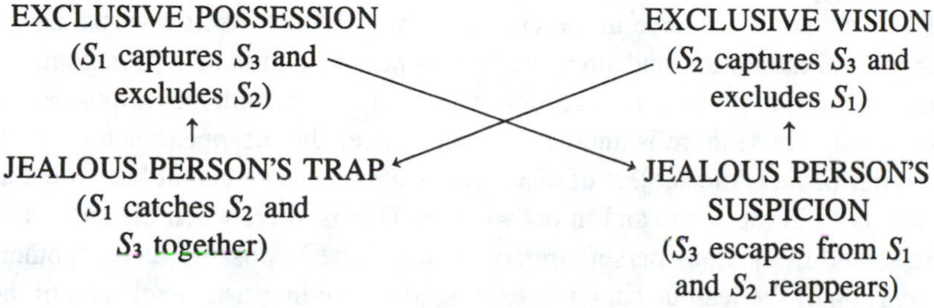

Figure 28

At each new movement on the "exclusive possession" position, the strategies get more complicated or hardened. The transformations of exclusivity preserve the memory of the previous positions, in a way dramatizing the passional trajectory.

As a passional world of transformations and ambivalence, jealousy is the perfect domain for the propagation of sensitized arrangements; the existence of a syntax of exclusivity that expresses the entire passional trajectory proves at least two things. First, whatever the respective positions of the partners, the modal arrangement typical of passion—here, the arrangement of exclusivity—is an atemporal constant that governs all passional interaction. Second, the variation of these positions is regular, ordered, and narratible. We might even be tempted to think that this syntax belongs to the passional competence of the jealous person, in the form of "pathemic intelligence." In fact, at the very moment when he programs the production of exclusive vision, he can already know that it will act as a trap for the loved one and the rival. Moreover, we have seen that by decreeing S_2's exclusion, he was setting up his own exclusion. The syntax of exclusivity acts in a certain way like a "disposition," that is, like a discursive programming that is endowed with its own dynamics and unfolds on its own if nothing stops it.

***La jalousie:* Ego Has Vanished**. As far as exclusive vision is concerned, *La jalousie* is still a laboratory for testing our hypotheses and establishing the limits of their validity. The text is wholly circumscribed by simulacrum; its enunciation is nothing other than passional enunciation, which, although certainly athymic in a paradoxical way, leaves no place for the first enunciation; the entire enunciated space is the surrounded space from which the jealous person is excluded, a space apprehended by the spectator who is present at the scenes he narrates but who does not take part in them as an actor. The welcoming enunciated discourse has vanished, the story is out of range, and only the reader's patient labor can put bits and pieces of it back together. This statement is a sufficient explanation of several particularities of the text, for example, temporal and aspectual dislocation: there is no longer any outside observer who distances himself sufficiently to order and define the scope of the processes.

Moreover, since we have in the enunciation of the text itself a verbalization of passional simulacrum, and since the jealous person cannot be a protagonist of this simulacrum, the subject of discourse who merges here with the jealous person has vanished. Thus, there is another disappearance, the disappearance of the I. As a matter of fact, the subject of discourse is present as an actant but absent as an actor, both in the scene and in his writing. This is why, when the subject of discourse and the jealous person are completely superimposable on each other, the exclusion of the jealous person is expressed by the linguistic exclusion of the I. It is impossible for EGO to call itself EGO, since this makes S_1(I) appear on the scene of writing. Thus the subject of discourse is an empty place that can be reconstructed only by deduction, based on observations like these:

> To get to the pantry, the simplest thing is to go through the house. . . . *Light shoes with rubber soles don't make any noise.*
>
> To be safer, *it is enough to ask her* if she doesn't think the cook puts too much salt in the soup. "Oh no," she says, "you have to eat salt not to perspire."
>
> Now it is Franck's turn to smile, but he doesn't answer, as if he is bothered by the tone of their conversation—*in front of a third party.* (pp. 48, 24, and 194; our emphasis)

Since we cannot count all the linguistic transformations in *La jalousie* that aim to make the agent or dative case implicit when it could be designated only by "I" or "me," let us pick out some representative types in the utterances we have quoted: impersonal transformations ("it is enough"), movement to the third person by periphrasis ("a third party"), infinitive transformations and generalizations ("to get to"), or pressure from the case of Instrument to the position of phrastic subject ("shoes") in place of the Agent. It is then up to the reader to make the connection between the indirect manifestations of a third actor and the modalizations that, even though referring back to the subjectivity of the implied narrator, must be attributed to this same third party. The same is true of the narrativized and modalized question "it is enough to ask her," which is answered in direct discourse. Modalization has to do with the indirect third party ("it is enough"), but since the answer is in direct discourse, we suppose that the speaker merges with the modalized third party.

This is an exercise in virtuosity that assumes its full meaning only when it is integrated into the syntax of jealousy. Very often, the deduction by which we can find the empty place of the subject is simply a mathematical deduction. There are four seats on the terrace: one is free, two are taken by S_2 and S_3, and the fourth is taken by a third party, who can only be S_1, the narrator-observer. In fact, to indicate that the seat is taken, it is explained at great length that it is placed awkwardly, to one side, at an angle that does not give the occupant a good view of S_2 and S_3. The empty place of the subject of discourse is thus textualized as a position and a competence in observation, with the help of limits imposed on this competence within the space described.

One of the consequences of this discourse strategy, which consists of considering the simulacrum of the jealous person to the exclusion of any other, is that it implicates the enunciatee in the simulacrum. Indeed, this enunciatee is constantly appealed to by this empty place, led to make inferences, and forced to occupy the place mentally in order to understand everyone's positions and the organization of the scenes described. This strategy is both semiotic and hermeneutic, and it transforms the reader into a jealous discursive subject: is jealousy the prototypical passion of enunciatees, or could it possibly be?

Jealousy Set into Discourse: The Semantic Component

Little Concrete Details. The jealous person is obsessed with details; he is an incurable fetishist. The suffering particular to jealousy is intrinsically linked to the "concrete," that is, both to the "effects of reality" and to figurative axiologies. So much so that, during interaction, to make S_1 suffer, it is enough just to "give details"; for example, Odette, when pressed by Swann, is not at a loss for details. But, since the abstract and the concrete can be scaled, the jealous person has partial control over the intensity of his suffering by varying the degree of abstraction or figurativity in the way he imagines the situation to himself:

> He realized that the whole period of Odette's life that had passed before she had met him, a period that he had never tried to imagine, was not the abstract stretch that he had vaguely seen, but it had been made of specific years filled with concrete incidents. But he feared that by learning them, the colorless, fluid, and acceptable past would take on a tangible, unclean body, an individual, devilish face. And he kept on not trying to imagine it, no longer because he was too lazy to think about it, but because he was afraid to suffer. (vol. 1, p. 368)

The "concrete" nature of the simulacrum does not involve only syntactic figurativization—whether it be actorial, temporal, or spatial—but the entire set of semantic isotopies called up for the representation of passion, whose power of figuration is, as we have seen, one of the keys to suffering. With regard to this, Proust's metaphors could constitute a path of exploration, since they consider the invasion of representation by the concrete as a recovery of the body by discourse, "*a tangible, unclean body, an individual, devilish face*."

Nonetheless, the invasion of the concrete is based on a competence of the jealous person, a competence in figurative utterance and working out a discursive representation of the simulacrum, or a *knowing-how-to-tell*. This shows that to be jealous, it is not enough to be exclusive; one also has to have a minimum of imagination. This competence is not necessarily the competence of the passional actor; the *knowing-how-to-present* and imagination can just as easily belong to another actor. Odette will possess these things instead of Swann, and Iago instead of Othello.

The concretization of the scene thus refers back to two components: to the actual principle of figurativization (as opposed to abstraction) and to the competence necessary for passional enunciation. This is why the concern for concrete details is the distinctive trace in the discourse of jealousy, of a type of figurative and representative writing governed by making figures isotopic and by the rules of a "genre." Iago is a playwright and producer, Odette is a narrator full of charm and naturalness, with a talent for mimicking, and Robbe-Grillet's jealous man is an obsessive describer who seems in a way to have reinvented the *nouveau roman*.

We have referred several times to the "presentification" of an utterance, an event, or a situation in passional simulacrum; another aspect of this meaning effect is seen here. A pretense, an iconized reproduction that follows the discursive rules of representation particular to each culture and each genre in each culture, takes charge of the simulacrum; to disengagement and engagement that set up a simulacrum, we should add the operation of *textualization*. It is in this way that nostalgia would seem, as figurative writing, to lend itself more to poetry, at least in a romantic culture, whereas jealousy obviously hesitates, depending on whether we approach it as classicists or modernists, between the dramatic stage and descriptive pause of the novel.

The Mineral and the Vital. Pure affect—that is, the thymic state in its unrefined and elementary state—cannot be expressed; unless we trot out the elements of a lexical field that is readily exhausted (suffering, pain, and so on), the dysphoric state can be described only laconically. Our texts, however, contain a lot on this subject, thanks to symbolic or semisymbolic procedures that take charge of the manifestation of the dysphoric state: certain figurative isotopies specialize in this. In *Othello*, we will especially remember the "poison":

IAGO: I do suspect the lusty Moor
Hath leaped into my seat, the thought whereof
Doth, like a poisonous mineral, gnaw my inwards . . . (p. 87, ll. 286–88)

> Dangerous conceits are in their natures poisons,
> Which at the first are scarce found to distaste,
> But, with a little act upon the blood,
> Burn like the mines of sulphur. (p. 116, ll. 323–26)

In these metaphors, the mineral destroys the animal, and attacks the actual life-principle. Such figures, which have the benefit of depsychologizing passion by clearly separating the subject and the antisubject, give us a timely reminder that the thymic test and its resulting suffering follow reengagement onto the tensive subject and pose a threat to life itself or at least to the simulacrum of life.

In the verbal enunciation, the dysphoric state is expressed, in *Othello*, at the time of the crisis, by the obliteration of the subject of discourse: exclamations, disruption of syntax, syncopes, and parataxes result in the abolition of speech and the disappearance of the actor.

In Proust as well, the suffering of the jealous person is "like a poison that one might take in" (p. 428), and jealous love produces only "poisoned fruit" (p. 429). Poison is again opposed to animality and more precisely to the life-principle, since the jealous person who suffers from a simple recollection is like "a dying animal that is again shaken by a convulsion that seemed to be over" (vol. 1, p. 429). This forces the jealous person (and the analyst) to ask about the ambivalence of S_3: under certain conditions an object of value and under other conditions an antiobject of value, S_3 fluctuates according to the stages of jealousy. Passional syntax even gives him an ordered trajectory, since, after having acted as a "poison," he is also called to act as a "soothing agent" or an "antidote." This is as much to say that from the perspective of the impassioned subject, S_3 is just a (nonpolarized) valency, and becomes categorized and polarized only by means of the sensitized simulacra projected in succession by S_1.

Neither does Proust free himself from the metaphor of the mineral attacking the vital, this time in the form of a wound:

> He repeated the words she had said: . . . "Two or three times," "What a joke," but they did not reappear disarmed in Swann's memory; each one of them had a knife and struck him another blow. (p. 367)

It is as though the literary expression of jealousy and the suffering that arises from it followed a stereotyped semantic investment that would seem to refer back to the status of the impassioned subject as a feeling body, and to the status of the passional crisis as a setting into discourse of minimal feeling. The instrument of suffering (the thymic antisubject) must be presented as a nonliving thing, and the crisis as *a conflict between the living and the nonliving*. The body of the jealous person that, on the syntactic level, was kept off the stage now claims its right to the semantics of suffering.

Insofar as S_3 does not appear to be polarized, in itself and outside of the simulacra projected by S_1, and since, being a poison or an antidote, it must be "taken" by S_1, we are led to believe that the entire figurative network built around the conflict between living and nonliving is a direct revelation of the prehistory of the protoactant: a return to fusion, but a destructive return that ends up being insignificant through annihilation.

The Isotopizing Power of Suffering: Idiolects and Sociolects. It is not surprising that we encounter nothing of this sort in Robbe-Grillet's *Jalousie*, since in this work the thymic dimension is suspended. The body of the jealous person is forced to keep silent and to use means other than the conflict between living and nonliving to reveal his suffering quietly. In fact, insofar as writing itself has here become the passional instance, the descriptive figures are going to assume the task of indirectly displaying the semantics of jealousy, on the level of expression as well as the level of content.

As far as this is concerned, the isotopy of quantification is a good example. First of all, as such it overwhelms description: we find the multiple and the fragmented in several images that reappear constantly: the balustrades, the jalousies (i.e., the venetian blinds), A—'s hair, the rustling and crackling, the banana trees on the plantations, and especially the centipede smashed on the wall. The description of the centipede clearly shows the extent and the function of this overwhelming isotopy: "The image of the smashed centipede is drawn not *in its entirety*, but in *fragments* that are clear enough *not to leave any doubt*" (p. 56; our emphasis). Instead of the image of the natural world, we see its written trace, the style of a form about which we are told, by the way, that it no longer has any thickness, that it is like ink: a simulacrum frozen in time. Yet, although we can identify the centipede, it resists totalization and integration. The only certainty comes from recognizing several typical fragments, that is, units in which we can distinguish certain characteristic features, and thus partitive units to the detriment of the complete totality.

The question of the integral and the partitive has come up on two different occasions in our study of jealousy: in the definition of exclusivity and in the description of abduction. Recurrence of the motif refers back to the all-pervasiveness of quantification and the constitution of the collective actant in the configuration of jealousy. In one way, the isotopy of the fragmented, understood as "nonintegrable multiple," figuratively reveals the aborted abduction, the impossible rejects of the proof in this novel. However, as a group of partitive units—a fascinating, obsessive, and therefore sensitized group—the fragmented reveals the conflict of the participative and the exclusive, of the partitive and the integral at the heart of jealous attachment. Much to the detriment of the jealous person, who is the champion of integral units, here conflict favors the partitive.

Furthermore, in the same generic isotopy of quantification, jealous attachment appears a second time. In this novel, exclusivity is expressed in the form of an actual mathematics of jealousy. The "even versus odd" category gives us the main argument for this. To begin with, we observe a set of mathematical manipulations, in utterance, that are most often arranged by A— herself, and that aim to establish the recurrence of the number three, either by addition (2 + 1) or by subtraction (4 − 1): for example, three chairs, one of which is to one side, four place settings, one of which is taken away.

But the "even versus odd" category is used much more generally in the text: for example, the banana trees are arranged in staggered rows (4 + 1), and the irregular number of rows that are described in great detail also follow the rule of addition or subtraction of one unit. Therefore, this category reveals both exclusivity and exclusion. There is exclusivity, because counting up the number of rows in this mathematics of jealousy forces us to grasp the partitive units to the detriment of the whole. There is exclusion, because, in this game of additions and subtractions, as in proxemic arrangements, there is always one excluded individual in the number.

Thus, the semantic contamination of the figures in the text by the arrangement of jealousy does not result from a single metaphor. There would be such a metaphor only if this arrangement were explicit in the text. This is not the case, all the more so because the arrangement is not a textual given but rather results from reconstruction by catalysis. We must agree here that the proliferation of the two categories of quantification:

even versus odd and
fragmented versus integrated

functions like a feature of enunciative competence, like a form of *not-being-able-to-say*, and in a text where the syntax of passion takes refuge in writing, this is equivalent to *being-able-not-to-make-known* which is usually typical of the outward behavior of the jealous person.

In relation to the microsequence of jealousy, this feature of competence seems, therefore, to correspond to behavior that can be observed and moralized. It is not by accident that many commentators have interpreted the constant recurrence of the same images and the invasion of the text by quantification as an obsession that is an expression of the suffering of the jealous person. The recurrence of the same semantic categories in discourse seems to find an explanation in the isotopizing power of suffering. As a result, emotional intensity can be measured by the expansion of the figurative isotopies that assume the task of revealing the emotion. This expansion makes an enunciative subject according to ability (*not-being-able-to-say*), whereas the little concrete detail, the basis of the pretense of the presentation, constituted an enunciative subject according to knowledge (*knowing-how-to-say*). In a certain way, following a model that is widespread in modern and contemporary literature, from Marivaux to Proust, among others, *La jalousie* relates the circumstances under which an observer has acquired the competence to describe things as they are in fact presented to us in discourse.

The fact that there is in Robbe-Grillet an isotopy of the fragmented and an isotopy of the odd, as well as the absence of any isotopy that would take direct charge of the revelation of suffering, leads us to ask about the nature of figurative semantic investments of passion. We have discovered the existence of sociolectal investments that can be recognized by their stereotypical aspect and are responsible for a manifestation of suffering that seems direct and obvious only because of its stereotyped nature in a given culture: the motivation of figures is in this case linked with the fact that they belong to a connotative taxonomy. Moreover, *La jalousie* gives us an example of an idiolectal investment that only seems indirect and implied because of its nonstereotyped nature.

All passional discourse can therefore link these two types of semantic investment. Hence we are led to suppose that in Proust or Shakespeare, passion also has idiolectal figurative investments that can be hidden by the stereotypes of poison, the wound, the living, and the nonliving.

In Proust, for example, we encounter a figurative isotopy that corresponds to the definition of the puff of breath. The "great puff of agitation" that appeared along with worry has as its echo the image of Swann "panting" in his moment of suffering when Odette has just confessed her homosexual affairs to him. Predictably, to calm down, to get back confidence, for the jealous person is the same as to "catch one's breath again" (p. 429). This isotopy is well attested to elsewhere throughout the entire novel, through the opposite figures of the "well spaced" and the "confined," brought to the fore recently by Jean-Pierre Richard,[15] and which, in every instance, reveal the sensitization of modal arrangements even accompanied by notations that are clearly euphoric or dysphoric.

Shakespeare, on the other hand, is satisfied with reviving the stereotype by developing it, making it his own, and especially combining animality and abnormality: we see this in the images of the "monster" and the maniac:

> . . . some monster in his thought
> Too hideous to be shown. (*Othello* p. 108, ll. 106–7)
>
> It is the green-eyed monster, which doth mock
> The meat it feeds on. (p. 110, ll. 164–65)
>
> Marry, patience!
> Or I shall say you're all in all in spleen
> And nothing of a man. (p. 135, ll. 87–88)

"Frenzied" and "monstrous," the jealous person in Othello loses part of his humanity. "Humanity," in this case, is characterized by sociability and control, that is, basically through the regulation of passional manifestations. What shocks the

Venetians most in the Moor are his deviations of public behavior, the loss of his social *savoir être* (*knowing-how-to-be*), and the surging forth of instincts.

Moreover, Othello had spoken prophetically of Desdemona:

> Excellent wretch! Perdition catch my soul
> But I do love thee! And when I love thee not,
> Chaos is come again. (p. 107, ll. 90–92)

For Othello there was really a sort of attachment governed by *having-to-be*, but this *having-to-be* has nothing subjective about it; here, the attachment of love inspires trust in human order and the weakening of this trust can only bring us back to animal chaos and contingency, before being destroyed in the conflict with the nonliving. In Shakespeare, the orders of nature – human (*knowing* and *having-to-be*), animal (*not-knowing* or *not-having-to-be*), and mineral (*not-being*) – are thus hierarchized and ordered modal instances in a vast epistemological and passional trajectory, which the jealous person follows in regression until he reaches insignificance.

In the three texts under examination the figurative investment of suffering offers us an extraordinary semantic coherence that encourages us to look for its syntactic organization. The idiolectal investment first of all gives us the isotopy for the constitution of the impassioned subject. Agitation is a puff of breath that in Proust consumes the breath of the subject; it is a rising up out of the chaos that existed before the *having-to-be* of Shakespeare; in Robbe-Grillet, this role is played by the fragmentation of the figures of the natural world.

We find the same figurative investment revealing thymic consequence, that is, suffering and *emotion*, by which the life-principle, previously put in motion, is worn away, either by being stopped (the puff of breath is blocked) or by spending too much of its energy (chaos leads to self-destruction).

At the moment when *moralization* takes place, it can also serve as a referent to evaluate passional behavior and especially the degree of control (of breath, of instincts, and of its excesses) that it reveals.

Finally, in the case where the impassioned subject becomes the subject of doing, the figurative investment sets in place the isotopy on which activity will occur. Othello thinks that by murdering Desdemona he will wipe out the bestial stain he accuses her of having, but at the same time he will act like a maniac and behave chaotically, which is even more destructive than passion. Swann takes hardly any action, except as a cognitive subject, but, later on in *La prisonnière*, the narrator will take action and, in a way, will "confine" Albertine in the narrow, stifling field of his jealousy.

The figurative isotopy of the breath is, in fact, maintained to show the thymic risks run by young Marcel. To begin with, using a sort of reasoning by analogy, these risks are compared to the risks of asthma:

> Jealousy is one of these intermittent illnesses that has a capricious cause. (. . .) There are asthmatics who can only calm their attacks by opening windows and breathing the fresh, clean air from the hills, and others who do it by hiding in the center of the city, in a smoke-filled room. There is hardly any jealous man who does not admit certain departures from this. This one agrees . . . another . . . (vol. 3, *La prisonnière*, p. 29).

Thus worry is a confinement, and reassurance is a breath of fresh air. At the least reassuring sign

> the atmosphere of the house became breathable. I felt that instead of being filled with rarefied air, it was filled with happiness. (p. 57)

An actual *semisymbolic system* anchors the isotopy onto the thymic dimension:

ventilation : confinement :: happiness : hardship

in such a way that, through metaphor, happiness can replace rarefied air in the space of the house.

As a result, everything is in place so that, at the end, the movement of action takes its expression from the isotopy of breath. As a matter of fact, the possession by the lover of the captive Albertine happens like an intake of breath. After a long daydream about the breath of the sleeping woman, the narrator says:

> Her life was in subjection to me, and exuded its light breath out toward me. I listened to this mysterious murmuring emanation, sweet as a sea-breeze, fairylike as moonlight, that was her sleep. . . . her breath was close to my cheek, in my mouth which I opened a little over hers, where her life passed against my tongue. (pp. 70–74)

If the association of breath and jealousy was a simple analogy, we would not have left the domain of comparison between asthma and passion, asthma being for the narrator the prototype of all suffering; but the association is extended into the action of love, outside of suffering. It is true that the metaphor is extended, but there is a good reason for this. The figurative investment must appear at every stage of the passional microsequence that gets its modal and syntactic structure from the isotopy requested.

In the impassioned subject in general, and in the jealous person in particular, besides the *modal competence* made up of sensitized modal arrangements and gathered together into a disposition, we must therefore distinguish a *semantic competence* made up of sensitized figurative isotopies that he selects, either as a social or an individual subject, specifically to represent passional trajectories. All in all, figurativity serves passion, deploying motifs (the poison, the centipede, the wound) and isotopies in the actual passional syntax. Excluded from passional objects of value because of the preeminence of modal syntax, figurative semantic contents make a quiet comeback by means of semisymbolic systems that link the different steps of the sequence to *pathemic figures*.

A Note on Quantification

It should be noted that during our analysis of pathemic configurations, we were led to have recourse to this or that aspect of the quantification of the phenomena considered. On taking up a semisymbolic relationship with passional categories, the pathemized figurative isotopies themselves make use of quantifiable figures. In one writer the fragment and the centipede, in another mortices and tenons, which refer back in one way or another to the dialectic of the whole and its parts, of the one and the multiple.

Thus, the miser appeared to be morally reprehensible because he seemed to disturb a certain order of things by seeking to accumulate or by refusing to share, that is, by asserting the *exclusivity* of his relationship with objects of value. However, this disturbance could be understood only if we admitted by presupposition a "nonexclusivity" in the circulation of values. If we consider each axiological universe as a whole that is closed and fragmented into parts that belong to everyone, objects of value achieve the status of nonexclusive partitive units belonging to subjects. The miser's intrusion consists in the transformation of a partitive unit into a complete unit, or, better yet, in this unit's achieving a double status as part of a whole, and at the same time as a whole, that is, as an independent entity. What was for the subject a way of participating in the wholeness of values now becomes a form of gaining independence. In a way this transformation covers the transformation of a subject immersed in his culture's value system into an impassioned subject.

Hence we come back again to the well-known model suggested by Claude Lévi-Strauss, in which the circulation (or communication) of objects is basic to social structures, and in which the circulation of goods, women, and speech gives rise to the three basic dimensions of every society. But we must consider distinguishing two distinct levels of generalized exchange: first, discrete objects that we can gather, divide, distribute and exchange on the basis of discontinuous equivalences; and, second, pathemic objects, which also participate in exchange, but in a continuous mode by assuming forms of dissemination, fluctuation, and contagion.

And just as in passional microcosms the flow of circulation can get out of control or be blocked, in societal evolution, we can just as easily imagine a destructive process that, by an uncontrolled acceleration of exchange (potlatch or dumping), puts the collectivity in danger, as that of an excessive slowing process, in which individual appropriation (hoarding or stocking) takes place to the detriment of social cohesions. It is not surprising, therefore, that socioeconomic mutations or accidents, such as the birth of private property, speculative monopolizing, collectivization, and stock-market crashes, are also pathemic events.

With the help of jealousy, we then see how easy it is to slip into the domain of the declared exclusivity of women, guaranteed by kinship. Such exclusivity, however, allows for a certain liberty of circulation as well as individual appropriation. In this respect, the choice of avarice is an example. We noted that avarice is not interpreted solely within the frame of generalized exchange where it becomes a profitable substitute for the hardships of marriage that have become unbearable. We also noted that it brings in *exclusion* twice, as a cognitive and imaginary process that aims either to preserve the exclusivity of the object when it is at risk, or to exclude itself from the trio recognizing as a fact, if not as a right, the exclusivity the rival takes advantage of. In this last case it is most noteworthy that avarice operates by circumscribing, to the benefit of the subject whose loved one is an object of value. But at the same time the veil of exclusivity covers all of intersubjectivity—the couple or the double, it does not matter which—by setting a line of demarcation between the whole and a new "partitive unit." This raises once more the problem of which came first, the single or the double.

The last example of exclusion in motion, as it were, reveals itself in the way cognitive operations are carried out during the search for proof. While the jealous subject passionately desires knowledge, he nevertheless refuses all partial knowledge. Within the manipulation of epistemic modalities through the refusal of doubt or probability, exclusivity is seen here as the suppression of median terms between certainty and exclusion. The search for certainty at any cost can then be interpreted as a craving for totality in danger of being lost, as the precipitousness of the partitive unit anxious to find its completeness.

The forms of quantification encountered are found in the traditional—and the less traditional—grammar books under the title "indefinite," which a short while ago we suggested should be considered as "indefinite quantitatives." This curious group of strange entities—pronouns, adjectives, adverbs and articles—that has long puzzled the most learned linguists (Viggo Brøndal and Gustave Guillaume, to name just two), has become over the years a burning question in philosophy. Thus, in order to prevent a prior confusion, when Paul Ricoeur, raising the problem of identity of the subject and, more precisely, the "narrative subject," invites us to distinguish between *sameness* and *ipseity*, we find striking similarities between this and the definition of the *one*, a complex term with a variable dominance, composed of a *discrete* element (that is, "sameness") and an *integral* element (that is, "ipseity"), the former allowing us to distinguish the "one" from the "other" and the latter ensuring its consistency (since the whole is opposed to the concept of *totality*).

From another point of view, if we examine *becoming*, especially that of communities, we are presented with a continuous variation of balances and imbalances between cohesive and dispersive forces, the conflict of which has as its stakes the emergence of meaning itself and more particularly the emergence of interactantiality as well.

On the one hand, in the description of passional configurations, the pathemic subjects, be they collective or individual, seemed to be haunted by a whole troop of modal subjects whose setting into place poses a problem. In fact, this plurimodalized subject, just like an athlete in the stadium, can fall apart or pull himself together; he can concentrate or disperse the modal charges that define him. This is why, in order to bring within the reach of the tensive subject relatively stable forms that will last a long time in spite of modal oscillations, it was necessary to call on "semiotic styles" and aspectual styles that reveal them in discourse, and that are considered as balances/imbalances between opposing forces.

On the other hand, the different quantifiable aspects of objects seem to be grouped into three main strata. Iconized object-figures are grouped first of all into categories based on the modal and syntactic properties that enable us to talk about *objects of value*. Second, these *classes of iconized figures* are endowed with the grammatical determinations of quantification (indefinite, partitive, complete, definite, etc.). Third, by simultaneously encompassing the quantification of subjects *and* objects, we could consider that junction itself is quantified: a single subject for *n* objects, a single object for *n* subjects, a single subject for a single object, and so on. These distinctions enable us to establish and differentiate between, for example, hoarding, consuming, distributing, and sharing.

The question then arises of the criterion of value: why can this or that class quantitatively defined represent a value for this or that subject? The criterion is provided by *valencies* that allow us to build *classes of objects of value*, based on their participative or exclusive properties, among other things. Finally, outside of the valencies "shadows of value" are outlined for the tensive subject within the oscillations of interactantiality in the process of becoming, grappling with cohesive and dispersive forces.

In the configuration of jealousy the case of the "object" is in this respect an example. It appears first of all as a *pocket of resistance* in generalized circulation, as a zone of slowdown and even blockage of the communal flux: this is the "shadow of value." The discretization of flux, and its reformulation in terms of exchange, makes this "shadow" a valency, in the form of *exclusivity*. As an object of value, the object of the miser will subsume all the iconized figures that conform to the definition of an *integral unit*.

Whatever interpretation and solution are decided on, they justify our concern with how to situate the problems of quantification and the first formulations of the undefined concept of entity, at the very heart of an epistemology attempting to enunciate the preconditions for the appearance of meaning. Our allusion to pre-Socratic thought, obsessed as it is by the problem of the one and of its bursting asunder, tensions whose goal is reconstituting totality might have seemed a little out of place. Our reference to a forced cohabitation, if not a reconciliation of the dual concept of a universe sometimes thought of as discontinuous and sometimes as continuous, seems to be justified. All the more so, at several levels of the generative trajectory, we see it is necessary to have recourse, intermittently or simultaneously, to definite and discrete quantitatives and to indefinite quantitatives that, after the breaking up of the whole, are likely to attain the status of integrals. This enables us to understand, among other things, how *exclusion* can be a logical concept and a passional attitude.

In Conclusion

It is curious to state that the problem of quantification that we have just taken up could be posed in such an insistent way just at the time when we were concerned with introducing a passional component into semiotic theory. This can be understood partly if we take into account that the question of the status of entities—subjects or objects of value—could of necessity reappear only when tensivity with vague fluctuations and contours was postulated at the horizon of things. The concept of the universe as twofold and complementary, continuous and discontinuous, had to be receptive to the understanding of totality as carrying a twofold becoming, becoming of partition and of scattering.

This could not fail to affect the level of the instance of enunciation, accounting for existence as well as structures involving articulated discrete units, integrated communities and sociocultural institutions, cultures and sociolects. It then becomes possible to understand the constant play associating both partitive and complete units, which give rise to individuals who are participative and yet integral, and whole and discrete subjects equipped with "ipseity" and "sameness." From this perspective history appears as a perpetual becoming, in which people and cultures are deformed and reformed.

Thus, commercial societies can be constituted like living totalities, composed of discretely articulated individuals, just as so-called archaic societies can produce integral persons who are even equipped with a sense of property. It even seems possible to us that this type of quantitative material could serve as a framework for defining the "global project of personality" that would not be watered down to a simple "identification," but also for starting on a typology of moods and constitution of persons.

For—and we are only too likely to forget this—semiotics is and must remain, in order not to lose its soul, a scientific project located on the "human scale": if the world of odors is accessible for us as a set of meaning effects, there is a molecular, nuclear, etc., dimension beyond that refers to a form no longer semiotic, but scientific in the strict sense of the word. In a way, even from within the semiotic frame, by varying the epistemological distance to accommodate our vision we can obtain different images of the same phenomena: distant modulations and fluctuations and close-up categorization and modalization. But for semiotic vision there remains a horizon beyond which it cannot reach, the horizon that separates the "world of meaning" from the "world of being."

Undoubtedly it is sometimes difficult to avoid getting into some confusion; it is nevertheless true that it is our perception *and* our interaction with the environment that serve as the touchstone in our efforts to understand the world of common sense, and that it is the body itself that gives this world access to the universe of meaning—a feeling, perceiving, reacting body; a body that mobilizes all the different roles of the subject into a stiffening, a start, an enthrallment; the body as barrier, stopping, leading to the painful or happy somatization of the subject but also as a place of transition and pathemization that brings about an opening onto the modes of semiotic existence.

If we can still believe the old saying that the solidly maintained point of view turns any field into a "discipline" and confers on it the status of object of research, it is indeed this semiotic space, inhabited by pathemized cognitive forms where the rational and the irrational have fused into different rationalities and multiple pathemic configurations that is the homogeneous place being explored.

Homogeneity of the place and pertinence of the vision: coherence in things and minds is the only basis of our activity left to us when the other criteria of truth have become obsolete. To "com-prehend," that is, to grasp phenomena together, is the expected extension of Saussure's "everything holds together" where the search for meaning for the world meets the intent of the subject questioning himself about his own trajectory. To understand the world is to refuse to break it up into local models by positing its coherence; that is the only way to tackle "complicated things" that are frightening or seem to demand too much effort. We have tried, in our works on passions, to satisfy this condition by integrating them into the whole of semiotic theory, with a success that will be judged in the future.

Having been led to examine the manner of being and organization of values, we would like to note the value that has guided us throughout this work. Whether the question of the object proper to semiotic activity is posited at the level of preconditions, the level of discourse, or the intermediate levels, the different solutions must fulfill the demand for coherence: cohesive forces in the tensive universe; narrative model, constitutional model, and syntactic dialectic at the semionarrative level; isotopy and aspectualization at the discursive level. Coherence seems to us to be the "shadow of value" reflecting the universe's aspiration to unity, but also the valency that covers values all the way along the epistemological trajectory: the hope of the lost I of the Subject, the support of the researcher searching for effectiveness.

Notes

1. The Epistemology of Passions

1. This notion of the advent of signification mirrors to a certain degree the one developed by René Girard in *Des choses cachées depuis la fondation du monde* (Paris: Bernard Grasset, 1978). Thanks to the election of an emissary victim cultural signification emerges from the undifferentiated natural and the propagation of social violence. What we are dealing with here is a summation-negation, which, according to Girard, founds the first cultural signifier.

2. Claude Zilberberg attempts to reconcile tensivity and categorization by establishing in a semiotic square four tensive forms that greatly resemble the modulations of becoming:

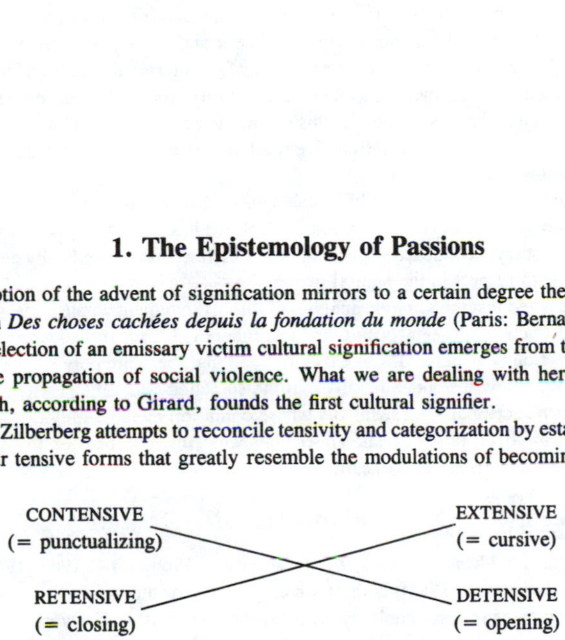

This option, which is somewhat tantalizing, is nevertheless not compatible with our description of the deep level. If tensive forms can be categorized it is because they are stable, and consequently, they are no longer tensive. Perhaps this is only a question of formulation.

3. Cf. Jean Petitot, "Les deux indicibles, ou la sémiotique face à l'imaginaire comme chair," in H. Parret and H. Ruprecht, eds., *Exigences et perspectives de la sémiotique* (Amsterdam: Benjamins, 1985). If, as Petitot does, we only consider the two definitions of "value," we are then dealing with an aporia. But this means we are not considering valency, the "value of values" that regulates *both* the generation of value within the category and the value of the object intended by the subject.

4. Member of the Groupe de recherches sémiolinguistique at l'Ecole Pratique des Hautes Etudes in Paris.

5. We could envision here calling on possible-world theory so that for the stubborn person, con-

junction can be envisioned even if it is not possible in the actual world. But this tells us little about a possible world that would be specifically passional. Such a duality also evokes the *self*, this relation of self to self that metapsychology considers fundamental in passional phenomena. But this relation of self to self has not yet been theorized in semiotic terms. The importing of concepts is fruitful, in fact, only if it is no longer an import.

6. Member of the Groupe de recherches sémiolinguistique at l'Ecole Pratique des Hautes Etudes in Paris.

7. "Instructional Semantics for Presuppositions," *Semiotica*, 64, 1/2 (1987).

8. Member of the Groupe de recherches sémiolinguistique at l'Ecole Pratique des Hautes Etudes in Paris.

9. Member of the Groupe de recherches sémiolinguistique at l'Ecole Pratique des Hautes Etudes in Paris.

10. These few examples clearly show that a modal series that is not convoked as a "disposition" at the time of setting into discourse, in fact, does not appear as an "arrangement." It is has been proved here that as an intersection of modal categories, the arrangement remains virtual and that only the retroactive effect of the praxis of utterance can actualize it and make it expressible and perceptible for the enunciator. More concretely, it is the existence of an internal dynamics of the arrangement, in the form of intermodal syntax, that brings it to the attention of the analyst as being an arrangement. This would seem to lead to the conclusion (but this still has to be proved) that the presence of an intermodal syntax in modal series is also the retroactive result of the praxis of utterance and of the application of passional taxonomies.

11. NB: In order not to interfere with the metalanguage that we have little by little developed for ourselves, we will leave aside the term "passion," which we have arbitrarily kept as a generic term of the universe under study, and the term "disposition," which we have specifically defined and which is just as arbitrary with respect to the natural lexicon.

12. It should be noted that the semiotic analysis of this arrangement would underscore the principle on which the distinction between "primitives" and others is based. In Descartes (*The Passion of the Soul*), the distinction is evident: "It can easily be seen that there are only six such passions," he says of the primitives. Now we notice readily that the so-called primitive passions are the ones in which we encounter no actantial syncretism and whose definition includes only two actants, the subject and its object. Moreover, this suggestion does not seem sufficient, because this criterion applies only partially to the list provided by Descartes.

2. On Avarice

1. See Lévi-Strauss's *Mythologiques I, II, III, IV* (Paris: Plon, 1964, 1967, 1968, 1971), and, *La potière jalouse* (Paris: Plon, 1985), both of which provide examples of cultures in which excrement and vomit participate in semisymbolic systems expressed in myths. The works of Helkin on Australian totemism also show, under certain conditions, a valorization of human bodily waste.

2.

"The Dairymaid and the Pot of Milk"

Perrette, a pot of milk upon her head
Firm on its little cushion set,
With step assured to market sped.
Light and short-gown'd, she strode through dry
and wet;
For since she had no time to lose,
She had selected for the morning's wear
Plain petticoat and flat-heel'd shoes.

Our Milkmaid, thus accoutred, thought
What price her milk would fetch, and laid it out.
First in her busy brain she bought
A hundred eggs, and hatched them deedily.
All must go well, with her devoted care!
'I'll rear the chickens in the yard,' said she.
'However sharp the fox may be,
He'll leave enough to buy a pig.
The bran to fatten him won't ruin me—
(Of course I bought him reasonably big).
Then, pigs are such a price to-day,
I'll sell him for a good round sum, and pray
What should prevent me setting up a cow?
A cow and calf—why, I can see them now,
Jumping about among the flocks!'
Suiting the action to the rapturous thought,
Perrette jumps too—and brings her hopes to
naught.
Down goes the milk; adieu, cow, calf, pig, hens
and cocks!
Their mistress, ruefully retreating
From the grim scene of the disaster,
Goes home t'explain it to her lord and master,
And face the prospect of a beating.
The Pot of Milk—you know the play
Founded on the events of this unlucky day.
(trans. Edward Marsh. London: William
Heinemann, 1933).

3. A careful examination of the interior discourse of Perrette reveals other signs of the passionate and "dissipating" character of her daydreaming. We see that the milk loses its status of descriptive object of value and becomes a simple modal object, a kind of *being-able-to-do* that authorizes a series of speculations, each new acquisition (eggs, chickens, pigs, etc.) undergoing the same mutation. Further, the linking of predicates (sell, earn, buy, cede, etc.) seems to obey a law of circulation of goods that is *cursive and accelerated*. This explains why in the passional simulacrum projected by Perrette objects of value as such have disappeared, because the blocking of circulation, resulting always from dissipation, suspends even valencies. Finally, the somatic manifestation that interrupts the daydream, coming here as a shifting back in upon the sentient body of the tensive subject, underlines in another way the "sensitive" and passionate character of the process of dissipation.

4. Cf. J. Fontanille, "Les passions de l'asthme," *Nouveaux Actes Semiotiques*, vol. 6 (Limoges: Trames-Pulim, 1989).

5. *Esquisse d'une théorie de la pratique* (Geneva: Droz, 1972).

6. William Labov, *Sociolinguistique*, introduction by Pierre Encrevé (Paris: Editions de Minuit, 1976).

7. It would in this way transcend the innate/acquired opposition as well as the body/mind one.

8. We must be careful to distinguish a *knowing-how-to-be* that might be explained in terms of a "knowing that has to do with the content of being" from a *knowing-how-to-be* that would be seen as a "knowing how to organize and present being." This would be the difference between knowledge and behavior. Compared to the modalizations of doing, the first version of *knowing-how-to-be* corresponds to a "knowing pertaining to the content of doing," and the second pertains to a *knowing-how-*

to-do defined as ability. The *knowing-how-to-be* that interests us here, that of the second meaning, is a form of syntagmatic intelligence, in the same way as is the case for *knowing-how-to-do* in its most current usage.

9. It is quite remarkable, for example, that a role such as that of "mother" can appear as a passion when the iteration of "maternal" doing is disseminated "out of context." Mme Bridau, in Balzac's *La rabouilleuse*, is the perfect prototype of impassioned mother. On the one hand, in connection with Joseph, her youngest son, she is simply thematized mother. She helps, cares for him, prepares his meals, etc. On the other hand, with her eldest son Philippe, the bad subject, she is impassioned mother, especially when the narrative situations in which she finds herself do not lend themselves to that role: embezzlements, debts, despoilments, of which Philippe is guilty. Unable to recognize in the behavior of her son those kinds of behavior that would implicate the "maternal-filial" theme, she forgives all, forgets all, allows herself to be ruined and then rejected. This is all the more significant for the fact that this pathemic role, noticeable in the main because of its apparently anarchical recurrence, is the object of a moral judgment for which there is no appeal, enacted during a confession that shortly precedes the death of the culprit.

10. Théodule Ribot uses these categories, with other terminology, to identify sentiments (unemphasized), passions (frequentative), and emotions (punctual). The same distinctions are found in the discourse of general physicians who, when faced with a given symptom, in particular in the area of immune disorders, are obliged to fall back on aspectual categories in order to make a diagnosis. For example, faced with a disorder that keeps recurring but in which they cannot recognize any regularity or factor of predictability, they conclude with reference to punctuality (individual instance), and treat accordingly. The analogy is not without foundation since in cases of immune disorders just as in the semiotics of passions, the analytical procedure must identify the extent to which the *being-of-the-subject* is implied in the concrete manifestations observed.

3. Jealousy

1. René Girard uses the notion of mediation to describe the functioning of mimetic desire in its various forms. Mimetism, in this case, like its psychoanalytical version, identification, refers us to an archaic stage of culture and of the psyche.

2. Jean Petitot has shown, starting with the catastrophe that is called "butterfly," that what is initially found here is a stratum of *pure conflict*, then strata that are *mediated* by the object, thus attaching value, according to the author's suggestion, to two different forms of *intentionality* comparable to the two forms of envy and jealousy, *S-O* and S_1-S_2 (*Morphogénèse du sens* [Paris:, PUF, 1986]).

3. We should neither over- nor underestimate discursive structures. If, for example, we consider the idea of point of view, it is useful to distinguish between point of view as a discursive configuration and point of view as a methodological tool for description. The first characterizes the treatment of knowing at the moment of setting into discourse. The second concentrates on, among the virtualities of semiotic structures, the particular schemata they can present. We know, for example, that complex utterances with two subjects and one object virtually include the point of view of renunciation and that of attribution, among others. But that does not make this a discursive structure. The actantial structure allows us to see to actantial schemata, combinations that are comparable to combinations we obtain when modal structures intersect and that we have called "modal schemata." Enunciation has to choose, because of the linearization of programs, some of these schemata. Then, with selection having been made from among the possible combinations, a discursive setting up of point of view is envisageable, starting with an observer and his cognitive doings. It is thus not surprising if the mechanisms of sensitization are manifested, as sorting and selecting mechanisms, as discursive points of view, but they are still not independent as such from the discursive structures that manifest them.

4. In *L'homme qui rit* (book 1, chapter 1), Victor Hugo gives a particularly detailed portrait of fidelity and its narrative consequences. Lord Clancharlie, a contemporary of Cromwell's, is an Eng-

lish noble, seduced by republican principles and who remained committed to them under the Restoration, when Charles II, then James II ruled. In ten pages that in a masterful way demonstrate the independence of attachment vis-à-vis narrative transformations, Hugo in a parallel and simultaneous way shows the historical evolution of England and the successive adaptations that those who comply with the successive transformations of the context must undergo. He also shows the immobility of the faithful republican. Lord Clancharlie, bound by his "attachment" to a historically "outmoded" idea, appears, in the eyes of those who have adapted to the new political reality, as a *subject who is caught in a passional simulacrum, a subject who has chosen to live in his imagination instead of within political reality*. Thus, it is not surprising that pathemic roles are assigned to him that appear as passional efflorescences of "attachment," folly, pride, "puerile obstinacy," "senile stubbornness," etc. Further, passional shifting out and shifting back in receive a thematic and spatial representation: Lord Clancharlie has *exiled* himself, far from where political changes are taking place, on the shores of Lake Geneva, and the passional engagement lets us see right into his attitude: "You could see this old man, dressed in the manner of the common fold, pale, absent minded. (. . .) *scarcely paying any attention* to storm or winter, walking *haphazardly*" (*L'homme qui rit* [Paris: Garnier-Flammarion, 1982], vol. 1, p. 247).

5. Umberto Eco and Patricia Violi, "Instructional Semantics for Presuppositions," *Semiotica*, 64, 1/2 (1987), pp. 11–14.

6. This general model has already empirically been tried and illustrated in various monographs: in connection with anger, in particular (A. J. Greimas, "De la colère," *Actes Sémiotiques*, Documents, III, 27 [Paris: CNRS, 1981]) and despair (J. Fontanille, "Le désespoir," *Actes Sémiotiques*, Documents, 16 [Paris: CNRS, 1980]). Its construction has been sketched out and has undergone preliminary theoretical formulation in "Le tumulte modal" (J. Fontanille, *Actes Sémiotiques*, Bulletin, XI, 39 [Paris: CNRS, 1987]).

7. The canonical narrative schema is too often wrongly considered as belonging by rights to the semionarrative level. In fact, there is nothing universal about it, both because it is an ideological construction useful in accounting for the way in which the narrative subject superficially organizes its trajectory in order to give meaning to its life's work, and because it functions as a grid for cultural reading – Paul Ricoeur would say that our *understanding* of the story goes through a first apprehension whose tools emanate from the culture to which we belong. In this sense, the traditional narrative schema would be, at the most, a *primitive* setup on the semionarrative level by the retroactive process we have imagined for the passional dispositions: collective usage gives rise to a cultural stereotype, which then has a place in the reservoir available for a new calling up into discourse.

8. See chapter 2, "On Avarice," "Sensitization" (under the heading "Two Cultural Phenomena").

9. There is much that could be said about this dialectic of the continuous and the discontinuous. Proust would decide to consider the discontinuous as being first and the continuous as being second, as a result, in a way, of the infinitization of the discontinuous: when the segmentation of a process is pushed to the limit it appears to be continuous. We have to see that everything depends on the observer's capacity for accommodation, or the distance he takes in his observation. This presentation is typical of the theory of knowledge that underlies all of *A la recherche*, according to which knowledge is formed only in the dialectic between the pluralization and homogenization of figures thanks to movement between the positions of observation.

10. Just one of several examples:

IAGO: Ha! I like not that.
OTHELLO: What dost thou say?
IAGO: Nothing, my lord; or if – I know not what." (p. 104, ll. 35–37)

11. We must also note here that many contemporary psychological and metapsychological theories are interactive and are based on a system with several actors. It is rather the philosophical theories of the passions that are based, even today, on a unique, egopathic subject who is the only possible seat of passion.

12. This Proustian nuance would perhaps allow us to refine the difference between a "pathemic role" and a "thematic role." The pathemic role can be recognized on the level of discursive manifestation by the canonicity of the microsequence it produces; on the other hand, the thematic role can be recognized by the systematic recurrence of the same competence and the same behavior in a given circumstance. The particularity of Odette's lies is due to the fact that they are not systematic, because if she has to choose between truth and lying, she always prefers the truth. Thus, she is not a "liar" (a thematic role); she is simply carried away passionally into lying (a pathemic role) when the sensitization of interaction lends itself to this, because of her own intensity.

13. Pierre Boudon, "L'abduction et le champ sémiotique," *Actes Sémiotiques*, Documents, VIII, 36 (Paris: CNRS, 1985).

14. The "disappearance of the thymic" in Robbe-Grillet's *La jalousie* could be linked to the "disappearance of the e" in Georges Pérec's *La disparition*. In either case, it seems that readers and critics have taken a certain amount of time to become aware of the process put into motion by the author; it is clear enough what the results and the limits of such an operation can be on the signifier, but things are different when it affects the signified: then we are dealing with experimentation having to do with expression in discourse and with textualization.

15. *Proust et le monde sensible* (Paris: Le Seuil, 1974), pp. 44ff.

Bibliography

Aragon, Louis. *La semaine sainte.* Paris: Gallimard, 1958.

Balzac, Honoré de. *Le contrat de mariage. Comédie humaine*, vol. 3. Paris: Gallimard, Bibliothèque de la Pléiade, 1976.

——. *Les illusions perdues. Comédie humaine*, vol. 5. Paris: Gallimard, Bibliothèque de la Pléiade, 1977.

——. *La rabouilleuse. Comédie humaine.* Paris: Gallimard, Bibliothèque de la Pléiade, 1972.

Barthes, Roland. *Fragments d'un discours amoureux.* Paris: Seuil, 1977.

Barthes, Roland. "Introduction to the Structural Analysis of Narrative," in *The Semiotic Challenge.* New York: Hill & Wang, 1988.

Beaumarchais, Pierre-Augustin de. *Le mariage de Figaro*. Paris: Société d'Edition d'Enseignement Supérieur, 1966.

Boudon, Pierre. *L'abduction et le champ sémiotique. Actes Sémiotiques*, Documents, VIII, 36. Paris: CNRS, 1985.

Bourdieu, Pierre. *Esquisse d'une théorie de la pratique.* Geneva: Droz, 1972.

Camus, Albert. *La chute.* Paris: Gallimard, Bibliothèque de la Pléiade, 1962.

——. *L'étranger.* Paris: Gallimard, 1982.

Claudel, Paul. *La ville.* Paris: Gallimard, 1982.

Descartes, René. *The Passion of the Soul.* Indianapolis, Ind.: Hackett, 1989.

Doležel, Lubomir. *Occidental Poetics.* Lincoln and London: University of Nebraska Press, 1990.

Dumas, Alexandre. *Le comte de Monte Cristo.* Paris: Bandits Romains, 1981.

Dupuy, Jean-Pierre, and Paul Dumouchel. *L'enfer des choses: René Girard et la logique de l'économie.* Paris: Seuil, 1979.

Eco, Umberto, and Patricia Violi. "Instructional Semantics for Presuppositions," *Semiotica* 64, no. 1/2 (1987).

Eluard, Paul. *Capitale de la douleur.* Paris: Gallimard, 1970.

Fabbri, Paolo, and Paul Perron. Foreword to *The Social Sciences: A Semiotic View.* Minneapolis: University of Minnesota Press, 1990.

Fontanille, Jacques. *Les passions de l'asthme.* Limoges: University of Limoges, 1989.

Freud, Sigmund. *Introductory Lectures on Psychoanalysis.* Harmondsworth: Penguin, 1987.

Greimas, Algirdas Julien. *Semiotics and Language: An Analytical Dictionary.* Bloomington: Indiana University Press, 1982.

——. *On Meaning: Selected Writings in Semiotic Theory.* Minneapolis: University of Minnesota Press, 1987.

——. "On Meaning" in *Greimassian Semiotics, New Literary History,* 20, no. 3 (1989): 539–50.

——. *The Social Sciences: A Semiotic View.* Minneapolis: University of Minnesota Press, 1990.

Girard, René. *Des choses cachées depuis la fondation du monde.* Paris: Bernard Grasset, 1978.

Hugo, Victor. *L'homme qui rit.* Paris: Garnier-Flammarion, 1982.

Kierkegaard, Søren. "On Despair" (treatise 749), *Søren Kierkegaard's Journals and Papers*, vol. 1. Ed. and trans. Howard V. Hong and Edna H. Hong. Bloomington: Indiana University Press, 1967.

Labov, W. *Sociolinguistique.* Trans. and intro. Pierre Encrevé. Paris: Minuit, 1976.

La Bruyère, Jean de. *Caractères.* Paris: Gallimard, Bibliothèque de la Pléiade, 1951.

La Chaussée, Pierre Claude de. *Retour imprévu.* In *Oeuvres de Nivelle de La Chaussée*. Paris: Le Jay, 1777.

Lafayette, Mme de. *La Princesse de Clèves.* Paris: Carrère, 1989.

La Fontaine, Jean de. *La laitière et le pot au lait.* London: Heinemann, 1933.

La Rochefoucault, François de. *Maximes.* Paris: Gallimard, Bibliothèque de la Pléiade, 1950.

Lévi-Strauss, Claude. *Mythologiques.* 3 vols. Paris: Plon, 1967–68.

——. *La potière jalouse.* Paris: Plon, 1985.

Maupassant, Guy de. *La ficelle.* In *Contes et nouvelles*, vol. 2. Paris: Gallimard, Bibliothèque de la Pléiade, 1974.

Merleau-Ponty, Maurice. *Phénoménologie de la perception.* Paris: Gallimard, 1976.

Parret, H., and H. Ruprecht, eds., *Exigences et perspectives de la sémiotique.* Amsterdam: Benjamins, 1985.

Pérec, Georges. *La disparition.* Paris: Gallimard, 1989.

Perron, Paul. Introduction, *On Meaning: Selected Writings in Semiotic Theory.* Minneapolis: University of Minnesota Press, 1987.

——. Introduction, *Greimassian Semiotics, New Literary History,* 20, no. 3 (1989): 523–38.

Petitot-Cocorda, Jean. *Morphogénèse du sens.* Paris: PUF, 1986.

Proust, Marcel. *A la recherche du temps perdu.* Paris: Gallimard, Bibliothèque de la Pléiade, 1987.

——. *Un amour de Swann.*

——. *La prisonnière.* Paris: Gallimard, 1989.

Racine, Jean. *Bajazet.* In *Oeuvres complètes de Racine*, vol. 1. Paris: Gallimard, Bibliothèque de la Pléiade, 1951.

——. *Bérénice,* Preface. Paris: Société d'Edition d'Enseignement Supérieur, 1974.

——. *Britannicus.* In *Oeuvres complètes de Racine*, vol. 1. Paris: Gallimard, Bibliothèque de la Pléiade, 1951.

——. *Phèdre.* In *Oeuvres complètes de Racine*, vol. 1. Paris: Gallimard, Bibliothèque de la Pléiade, 1951.

Richard, Jean-Pierre. *Proust et le monde sensible.* Paris: Seuil, 1974.

Ricoeur, Paul. "On Narrativity" and Greimas's Narrative Grammar," in *Greimassian Semiotics, New Literary History,* 20, no. 3 (1989): 551–62, 581–608.

Robbe-Grillet, Alain. *La jalousie.* Paris: Minuit, 1957.

Schleifer, Ronald. *A. J. Greimas and the Nature of Meaning.* Lincoln: University of Nebraska Press, 1987.

Shakespeare, William. *Othello.* Ed: Kenneth Muir. Harmondsworth: Penguin, 1968.

Shelley, Mary. *Frankenstein.* London: Dent, 1963.

Spinoza, Benedictus de. *On the Origin and Nature of Feelings.* In *L'éthique.* Paris: Gallimard, Coll. *Idées,* 1954.

Stendhal [Henri Beyle]. *De l'amour.* Paris: Le Divan, 1957.

Zilberberg, Claude. *Raison et poétique du sens.* Paris: PUF, 1988.

Subject Index

Author Index

Passions Index

Algirdas Julien Greimas (1917–92) was professor of general semantics at the Ecole des Hautes Etudes en Sciences Sociales in Paris. His theoretical work on structures of discourse has been seminal for numerous semiotic research projects around the world. The University of Minnesota Press also published his *On Meaning: Selected Writings in Semiotic Theory* (1987) and *The Social Sciences: A Semiotic View* (1990). Greimas's other titles available in English are *Semiotics and Language: An Analytical Dictionary* (1982); *Structural Semantics* (1983); *Maupassant: The Semiotics of Text* (1990); and *On Gods and Men* (1992). **Jacques Fontanille** is professor of linguistics and semiotics at the University of Limoges in France, and also cochaired a seminar in general semantics at the Ecole des Hautes Etudes en Sciences Sociales with Greimas.

Paul Perron is professor of French and chair of the Department of French at the University of Toronto. **Frank Collins** is professor of French at Victoria College, University of Toronto. They also translated Professor Greimas's other two books published by the University of Minnesota Press.

Paolo Fabbri is professor of philosophy at the University of Bologna and the Collège International de Philosophie, in Paris.